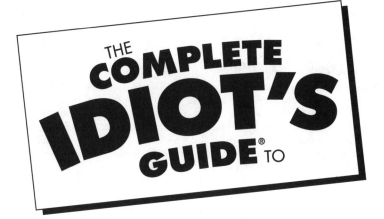

THE COMPLETE **IDIOT'S** GUIDE® TO

Filmmaking

by Joanne Parrent

ALPHA

A Pearson Education Company

To my partner, Brenda Feigen

Copyright © 2002 by Joanne Parrent

International Standard Book Number: 0-02-864340-2
Library of Congress Catalog Card Number: 2002101642

04   03   02   8   7   6   5   4   3   2   1

Interpretation of the printing code: The rightmost number of the first series of numbers is the year of the book's printing; the rightmost number of the second series of numbers is the number of the book's printing. For example, a printing code of 02-1 shows that the first printing occurred in 2002.

Printed in the United States of America

Note: This publication contains the opinions and ideas of its author. It is intended to provide helpful and informative material on the subject matter covered. It is sold with the understanding that the author and publisher are not engaged in rendering professional services in the book. If the reader requires personal assistance or advice, a competent professional should be consulted.

The author and publisher specifically disclaim any responsibility for any liability, loss, or risk, personal or otherwise, which is incurred as a consequence, directly or indirectly, of the use and application of any of the contents of this book.

Publisher: *Marie Butler-Knight*
Product Manager: *Phil Kitchel*
Managing Editor: *Jennifer Chisholm*
Acquisitions Editor: *Mike Sanders*
Development Editor: *Michael Koch*
Production Editor: *Katherin Bidwell*
Copy Editor: *Drew Patty*
Illustrator: *Chris Eliopoulos*
Cover/Book Designer: *Trina Wurst*
Indexer: *Tonya Heard*
Layout/Proofreading: *John Etchison, Gloria Schurick*

Contents at a Glance

Contents at a Glance

Contents

Foreword

Filmmaking (both studio and independent) is a far more complex topic than most people realize. It involves not only what the producer and the director do—those we usually call the "filmmakers"—but the efforts of many others, including the writer, cinematographer, production manager, editor, production designer, sound mixer, gaffer, grips, costume designer, script supervisor, transportation captain, make-up and hair artists, special-effects artists, stunt coordinators, animal wranglers, tutors, chaperones, craft services, assistant directors, production assistants, and other crew members. Without the expert and efficient contributions of each of the collaborators, a film either will not get made at all, or it will not get made as well or on time and within the agreed-upon budget.

When I began as a first-time producer working on a big-budget Hollywood studio movie (*Navy SEALs*, Orion, 1990), I needed a crash course not only in the actual physical production of a movie but in music, publicity and marketing, and all the aspects of distribution. If I had had this book at that time, the process would have been so much easier. For example, I would have known that I should have spent my time trying to persuade the studio to spend more money publicizing early who the Navy SEALs are, rather than counting on a blitz of television trailers three weeks before the movie opened in the middle of summer when every studio was releasing big movies. I would have asked that buttons be made for the shirts worn by theater ticket sellers (subliminal advertising), and thus would have spared myself the chore of delivering *Navy SEALs* water bottles to ticket sellers at all the theaters where my movie was playing in Los Angeles. I certainly would have clarified my own role as "creative" producer before agreeing to hire a line producer who failed to understand the concept of collaboration.

Reading this book today, I was surprised at how much I learned about filmmaking that I didn't know before, despite my own 24 years in the industry. Joanne Parrent has done a remarkable job distilling information about the entire filmmaking process, including feature films, movies for television, and documentaries. She has synthesized what every aspiring producer and director must know—about the process of screenwriting, the production of a movie, the editing of a movie, and the marketing and distribution that follow. In addition, she has collected priceless leads for aspiring filmmakers, including lists of studios, networks, filmmaking organizations, unions, guilds, books on specific aspects of filmmaking, and online resources that alone are worth the price of this book. And the information she collected will not become dated, because the industry changes very little—even over long time spans.

If you are an aspiring filmmaker, I recommend you read this book—you will stand a much greater chance of getting your film made, and it will be a far better film for it.

Brenda Feigen
Producer and Entertainment Attorney
Los Angeles, California
January, 2002

Introduction

This book is for everyone who wants to make a movie and anyone interested in how movies are made. Whether you want to make a slick Hollywood film, a quirky independent feature, a controversial documentary, an infomercial promoting your business or a home movie of your trip to Italy, the basic steps of the process are the same.

I've worked as a screenwriter in Hollywood and have also written, produced, and directed dozens of documentary and short films. In this book, I've drawn on my own experience as well as that of many friends and colleagues to distill for you the basic process of filmmaking in a simple, clear fashion.

What You'll Find Inside

This book is divided into five parts that take you from the conception of your film project through the distribution of the final film. Here's how the book is organized:

Part 1, "Establishing Shots," begins by establishing the background you need to be a filmmaker. It covers film and video history and the different genres of movies, as well as the different types of non-fiction films. Then I provide a chapter on the basic elements of all films, followed by two chapters—one introducing independent filmmaking and one on making films through the Hollywood studio system.

Part 2, "Opening Sequence: Script and Pre-Production," begins the actual process of making a film. It covers script development, preparing a schedule and budget, hiring your cast and crew, and all the other tasks you must accomplish to be ready to shoot your film or video.

Part 3, "Roll Camera: Production," takes you through the process of production, focusing on everything the director is responsible for, such as planning a shot list, directing the crew, and working with actors. This part also covers tips for a smooth production and includes a chapter on producing and directing non-fiction films.

Part 4, "It's a Wrap: Post-Production," describes the process of editing your project, either on film or on video with non-linear editing equipment. This part also covers other aspects of post-production such as post-production scheduling, sound editing, the sound mix, music, opticals, titles, and more.

Part 5, "Now Playing at ...? Distribution," takes you through the various ways of getting an audience for your film, from the Hollywood distribution system, television sales, independent film distribution, non-theatrical distribution, and new forms of distribution on the Internet.

A Few More Things About the Book

This book also features extra tidbits called *sidebars*. These asides are designed to supply you with extra information, tips, and cautions. Here's what you'll find:

Verbal Action _____
These sidebars give definitions of common film and video terms.

Script Notes _____
These notes provide bits of information that might help you make your film.

Counterpoint _____
These boxes give you warnings about what not to do or of potential trouble to watch out for.

Cutaway
These anecdotes give you more in-depth or extra information about the topic of the chapter.

Acknowledgments

Many people have been helpful in the making of this book. First and foremost, I'd like to thank producer and entertainment attorney Brenda Feigen, who both read the book for its accuracy, bringing to it her decades of experience in the film industry, and also enthusiastically wrote the foreword for the book. As my partner and agent, Brenda also deserves extra special thanks for her incredible support and patience in helping me meet a very tight deadline for this book.

More generally, I'd like to thank all the filmmakers—writers, directors, producers, editors, art directors, production managers, sound mixers, gaffers, and other crew members—that I have worked with and learned from, giving me the background to be able to write this book. For me, there is no better way to learn than from watching other people who do what they do well, and I have had the privilege of working with many people who are very skilled at their jobs. Some very kind and talented people stand out. Perhaps no one can be more important than the person who gives you your first break. Woody Clark did that by giving me my first job writing a documentary film and later giving me my first directing job. Some great cinematographers taught me much, including Emiko Omari, the late John Alonzo, John Toll, and Nancy Schneider, all of whom I had the honor to work with on various documentary projects. Erwin Dumbrille, an incredible editor, showed me his skills on many projects. In television, Beth Sullivan, the successful writer-producer and creator of *Dr. Quinn, Medicine Woman*, taught me many things and believed in my work, for which I am very grateful. In studio feature development, I was given my first opportunity by

Bette Midler and Bonnie Bruckheimer; it was a great privilege to work with their company on a project. Benjamin Fitzgerald asked me to produce an independent film that he was executive producing and, despite the fact that it went the way of many independent films—nowhere—it was still a great learning experience. The late, great actress Joan Hackett taught me much about the acting process, as did my acting teacher, David Lehman. Murielle Hamilton, a wonderful composer, worked with me on many projects, and I learned something new from her on each one. I also had the enormous privilege of working on one project with two extraordinary musicians, Van Dyke Parks and Thomas Newman.

There are many people I haven't named here, but that is because of my faulty memory, not because their contribution to the knowledge I had to have to write this book wasn't critical and important. Nor should I forget to thank all the filmmakers I admire—those from decades past whose talent first drew me to the movies and those working today, both in film and in television, who are able to craft films that give me (and millions of others) hours of enjoyment each week.

Specifically in the making of this book, I must also thank the "two Michaels" who worked on the book. Mike Sanders, the acquisitions editor, championed the project from the beginning, and Michael Koch, the development editor, prodded and pushed me to complete the book. Drew Patty, the copy editor, went beyond the call of copy editing with a number of interesting suggestions for improving the book. Not the least of all, I was grateful for Kathy Bidwell in the final stages of the book, a cheerful, helpful, and detail-oriented production editor.

Finally, I must not leave out the two people who introduced me to the movies as a kid— my mother, who brought me to dramas and love stories with her when my dad wouldn't go to them, and my late father, who dragged me to see the westerns and action films that my mother refused to see. From them both I learned to love all kinds of movies, so they, too, most certainly deserve my thanks.

Special Thanks to the Technical Reviewer

The Complete Idiot's Guide to Filmmaking was reviewed by an expert who double-checked the accuracy of what you'll learn here, to help us ensure that this book gives you everything you need to know about filmmaking. Special thanks are extended to Brenda Feigen, producer of *Navy SEALs* and entertainment attorney.

Trademarks

All terms mentioned in this book that are known to be or are suspected of being trademarks or service marks have been appropriately capitalized. Alpha Books and Pearson Education, Inc., cannot attest to the accuracy of this information. Use of a term in this book should not be regarded as affecting the validity of any trademark or service mark.

Part 1

Establishing Shots

The desire to create a work of art, to tell a story, or to entertain others has been a fundamental part of human nature for many thousands of years. As an art form and a type of entertainment, however, films are relatively new on the scene—the technology for making films is only about a century old. But films have captured the imaginations of people around the globe and particularly here in the United States. Films, in theaters and on television, are the most popular form of entertainment of our time.

If you want to become a filmmaker, where do you start? This part of the book will cover the basics: film history, film genres, and the elements of making a film. It will then compare the two routes available for making a theatrical film today: the independent route and the Hollywood studio system.

Flashbacks: A Short History of Filmmaking

In This Chapter

- ◆ The inventions that created motion pictures
- ◆ Highlights of American film history
- ◆ Changes in film technology
- ◆ The invention of television and video recording

Most of us rarely spend a day without viewing some form of motion picture—the news, a television show, a rented video or DVD, a film at a movie theater, home videos, video games, or perhaps moving digital images on our computer. In the world in which we live today, where moving images are so pervasive, it is hard to imagine a time when there were no films, no videos, no television. Yet, it wasn't that long ago when people had only books and live theater for entertainment, only newspapers and magazines for news of the world. Motion pictures have only been with us for a little over a hundred years—yet they have revolutionized our lives. The American movie business is a highly successful global enterprise that spreads American images, values, and stories to countries around the world. And television has shrunk the globe so that within minutes after the terrorist attacks on the World Trade Center in New York on

September 11, 2001, not only most Americans but people around the world watched as the events of that day of infamy unfolded.

This book is for those who want a quick course on filmmaking, who want to know how to make their own films and videos—whether independent films, Hollywood blockbusters, television documentaries, or simply home videos. The techniques are similar for all; only the scale and the purposes are different. Before I get into the art and craft of making a film, however, I'll take you back to the time when the very first moving images were captured on film and we will go on a quick journey through the history of film and television to see how it has changed and where it stands today.

The First Machines

In 1877, Thomas Edison, inventor extraordinaire, entrepreneur, and entertainer, who had already brought the world the electric light, invented the *phonograph*. For those of you who have only heard of CDs and CD players, the phonograph was the earliest way to listen to music and other recorded sounds before CDs were invented. By 1878, this device became the hottest item on the shelves—everybody wanted one. But it wasn't enough for Edison. Like a nineteenth-century Bill Gates, he envisioned another machine, which he called a *Kinetograph* and described as a "home entertainment machine." That machine would display images to accompany the sounds from the phonograph.

Edison studied the work of French scientist Etienne Marey and American photographer Eadweard Muybridge, who had both been experimenting with motion picture photography. He then commissioned a laboratory assistant, William Dickson, to come up with a Kinetograph machine. Dickson, who would later break with Edison and form his own movie company, was no slouch. In 1889, at Edison's laboratory, he invented the first motion picture camera that would be used commercially and also a device called the *Kinetoscope* to view the moving images. The Kinetoscope allowed an individual viewer to watch a continuous film loop through the magnified lens of a box-like peep-show machine.

 Verbal Action _____

> **phonograph**   A machine invented by Thomas Edison that reproduces sound by means of a stylus in contact with a grooved rotating disk.
>
> **Kinetograph**   The first viable motion picture camera, invented by William Dickson in 1889.
>
> **Kinetoscope**   A projection machine invented by William Dickson to display images filmed on the Edison Kinetograph. It was essentially a peepshow device used by individual viewers to view short, unsophisticated film strips.

A man named Andrew Holland took the initiative to open the first Kinetoscope parlor or "theater." He converted a shoe store in Manhattan into The Kinetoscope Exhibition Company. Holland charged 25 cents per person for a chance to sit at one of five Kinetoscopes and view the film that had been shot on the Kinetograph. The price soon went down to a nickel as the novelty wore off.

The early film strips viewed on Kinetoscopes featured common sideshow and fairground entertainment such as a wrestling match, a trapeze act, ballerinas dancing, boxing cats, vaudeville performers doing short slapstick comedy routines, a trained-bear act, or a celebrity like Buffalo Bill doing an act. There was no story, only people or animals in motion, but audiences were still fascinated by the moving pictures. In the beginning, it was the novelty of the new technology that drew audiences rather than the content of the films.

Soon, other inventors began to improve on both the cameras and the projection devices. The Lumière brothers in France invented a machine that they called the Cinématographe. This portable machine was both a camera and a projector. On March 22, 1895, the Lumières projected their first film to a private audience in Paris. The film, titled *Workers Leaving the Lumière Factory*, is considered by many to be the first motion picture. It was certainly the first film to be displayed to an audience of more than one, since the Kinetoscopes could only accommodate one viewer at a time.

About six months later, the Lumières rented a room in Paris to show films to a paying audience. Action movies got their start with one of the films shown then, *The Arrival of a Train at a Station*. Audience members were so frightened by the realistic sight of a train barreling toward them that many jumped up and rushed out the door.

By 1896, Thomas Edison, wanting to keep up with the French, had purchased U.S. inventor Thomas Armat's perfected projection machine called the Vitascope. April 23, 1896, was the date of the first Vitascope projection for an audience of paying customers in the United States. The Edison Company's Vitascope projected a ballet sequence to a Manhattan audience.

Cutaway

How do motion pictures actually work? The illusion of motion in film is caused by the way in which our brains perceive the images that are projected—a cognitive process known as the *"persistence of vision."* Motion picture film cameras capture a series of individual still photographs, a single frame at a time. These frames, when projected at certain speeds, create the illusion of continuous motion. Our brains retain images cast upon the retina of the eye for approximately one-twentieth to one-fifth of a second beyond their actual removal from our field of vision. The illusion of continuous motion can be induced in our brains at rates as low as 12 frames per second, but most films' speeds are faster—24 frames per second.

As the nineteenth century was ending, it was clear that films were not just a novelty but were going to be a good "entertainment" business for the future. The first real cinema building—solely for the purpose of showing films—was built in Paris in 1897. In the United States, the first theater to exclusively show movies was Thomas L. Talley's storefront 200-seat Electric Theater in downtown Los Angeles. It opened in 1902 and charged patrons a dime.

The First Stories

People often talk about the "magic of film" and, interestingly enough, it was a magician named Georges Méliès who was the first to bring a certain kind of magic to film—the magic of storytelling. He was the first to use film as a device for showing dramatic *scenes*. Méliès was also probably the world's first independent producer-director-writer, because he did not work for any of the companies that owned the camera and projection equipment, as did most filmmakers at that time, but produced his own films. At a film studio he built outside Paris, Méliès made over five hundred films between 1897 and 1913. Most of his movies were filmed stage plays, with the additional use of magic tricks and illusion.

An American named Edwin S. Porter would take the narrative film even further than Méliès. In 1903, Porter wrote, directed, photographed, and edited *The Great Train Robbery*, a film that was about fourteen minutes long and consisted of approximately twenty separate shots filmed at a dozen different locations. No movie before it had such a variety of scenes. This first Western—about a train robbery taking place in the old West— was also the first film to be shot out of chronological sequence and to use cross-cutting or parallel action, cutting between scenes before they ended, without dissolving or fading. It established the *shot* as the basic unit of filmmaking, rather than the scene, as in Méliès's films.

Verbal Action _____

persistence of vision   The physiological reason for the illusion of motion in films: the fact that an image remains on the retina of the eye for a short period of time after it disappears from the field of vision.

shot   The basic unit of film; a continuously exposed, unedited piece of film of any length or a single cinematic view or take.

scene   A series of shots in a movie constituting a unit of continuous related action in the story or narration.

The Great Train Robbery was an enormous success—the first blockbuster. It was shown in vaudeville houses throughout the United States in 1904 and continued to be used for years on the opening programs of the new "nickelodeon" theaters, which were opening up everywhere in the first decade of the new century. Nickelodeons were the first permanent movie houses and, like the first one in Los Angeles, were usually converted storefronts.

The Silent Era

By 1907, there were more than seven or eight thousand nickelodeons in operation. Movies had become a lucrative form of mass entertainment, and were particularly popular with working-class Americans. The programs were much shorter than the films of today, usually only one- or two-reel films, lasting no longer than fifteen to thirty minutes. And, of course, no one had yet figured out how to synchronize sound with the picture, so the films were silent and accompanied by either piano-playing, sound organs, gramophone discs, musicians, sound-effects specialists, live actors who delivered dialogue, or sometimes even full-scale orchestras.

The Rise of the Studio System

In 1908, a group of East Coast-based companies that produced films (the Edison Company, Biograph, and others) formed a partnership to attempt to control and monopolize this burgeoning film industry. Named the Motion Picture Patents Company (MPPC), this partnership or trust pooled everyone's patents in an attempt to protect profits and film copyrights, fight movie piracy, and reduce the power of film distributors. The partnership also insisted that its members limit the length of films to one or two reels, charge royalties to exhibitors using their films and equipment, refuse to give screen credits to players, and prevent exhibitors from showing films not made by producers who belonged to the MPPC.

The exhibitors—those who owned nickelodeons or distributed films—were understandably upset about the MPPC and so were many early filmmakers, who felt the trust was limiting their artistic freedom. Independent filmmakers began to move to Southern California to produce films that would compete with those of the mostly eastern-based companies that formed the MPPC. In 1907, the first film was made in Los Angeles. By 1911, Hollywood's first motion picture studio, the Nestor Film Company, at the corner of Sunset Boulevard and Gower Street, was established. By 1912, 15 film companies were operating in Hollywood.

Some of the future moguls of the movie industry—Adolph Zukor, Marcus Loew, Jesse Lasky, Sam Goldwyn, the Warner brothers, Carl Laemmle, William Fox, and Louis B. Mayer—had gotten their start in nickelodeons, as proprietors, investors, or distributors, and were now in California competing with the MPPC. These men would be instrumental in establishing the "Hollywood" movie studios and making Southern California the film capital of the world. They were assisted when the U.S. government filed a successful anti-trust suit on behalf of the independent Hollywood-based film companies (including Paramount, Fox, and Universal) against the MPPC in 1912. The government won the case and the MPPC was disbanded.

After 1912, more modern movie theaters or "picture houses" that charged from 10 to 15 cents admission began to appear, replacing nickelodeons. Some of the best artists from European filmmaking circles were brought to Hollywood and films continued to improve in quality. By 1918, the cinema was one of America's leading industries and Hollywood films were even beginning to dominate the European market.

In the 1920s, the basic economic organization of the film industry—the studio system—was established as the firms that were to rule Hollywood filmmaking were born. Warner Bros. Pictures incorporated in 1923. In 1924, MGM formed from the merger of Metro Pictures, Samuel Goldwyn Pictures, and the Louis B. Mayer Pictures Company. Columbia Pictures, Paramount, and MCA (later Universal) were all founded soon thereafter.

The Birth of the Feature Film

In the first decade of the movie business, most producers and exhibitors felt that audiences wouldn't sit through films longer than a single reel (about 15 minutes). But in 1912, Adolph Zukor, the founder of Paramount Pictures, proved that there was an audience for a four-reel, "feature-length" French film, *Queen Elizabeth*, starring famous French stage actress Sarah Bernhardt. Her appearance in the film also increased respect for motion picture acting. Soon, it was clear that audiences wanted feature-length films, and many filmmakers wanted to make these longer pictures.

One filmmaker who wanted to make longer films was D. W. Griffith, perhaps the greatest of the early American filmmakers, who established many of the filmmaking conventions people take for granted today. Griffith had been working for the Biograph company making one- and two-reel films. When the MPPC was formed, he left to work with an independent Hollywood company so he could make feature-length films. In many of his early short films, Griffith had already experimented with techniques such as close-ups, establishing shots, and medium shots that he would later perfect in his longer feature films. He used the camera and film in new, innovative ways, including such then-revolutionary techniques as camera movement, changing camera angles, split-screens, cross-cutting, intercutting, dissolves, fades, parallel editing, soft-focus, lens filters, experimental/artificial lighting, and shading/tinting. He also created and trained his own company of actors including such future stars as Lillian Gish, Mary Pickford, and Lionel Barrymore.

In 1915, Griffith created the first American epic feature film, a 12-reeler set during the American Civil War, titled *The Birth of a Nation*. The film was very controversial because of its stereotyped racial caricatures—white actors in black-face and sympathetic portrayal of the Ku Klux Klan. The film was denounced by the NAACP and caused racial disturbances in several cities across the country. Technically, however, Griffith's film was a masterpiece. It had imaginative and beautifully structured battle scenes, realistic costumes, and a compelling story, as well as innovative editing and photographic techniques such as dollying, masking, use of irises, flashbacks, cross-cuts, and fades. And, despite—or maybe because of—the controversy surrounding it, *The Birth of a Nation* was a smash hit.

The following year, Griffith responded to the criticisms that he incited racial prejudice with a new film, this one over three hours long, titled *Intolerance*. It premiered in New York to mixed reviews and limited box-office success, but was a remarkable historical pageant that interwove four stories chronicling intolerance and inhumanity throughout history.

Cutaway

Although the American film industry soon became dominant, foreign filmmakers were also producing innovative films. French filmmaker Abel Gance, in his film *Napoleon* (1927), achieved a technological advancement when he created a panoramic "trip-tych" with three screens side by side to create a widescreen effect at its climax. In the early 1920s, three German films that experimented with dark shadows and angled shots were to have a strong influence on the coming development of U.S. films: Robert Wiene's surrealistic fantasy/horror film *The Cabinet of Dr. Caligari* (1920), F. W. Murnau's classic vampire film *Nosferatu, A Symphony of Horrors* (1922), and Fritz Lang's last major silent film, *Metropolis* (1926), which had innovative techniques and futuristic sets. Also, Russian director Sergei Eisenstein's landmark film *Battleship Potemkin* (1925), released in the United States in 1926, advanced the art of cinematic story-telling with its riveting scene on the Odessa steps in which civilians and rioters are ruthlessly massacred.

The Silent Comedies

As the film industry grew, various genres or types of films (see Chapter 2, "Loglines: An Overview of Film Genres"), such as westerns and melodramas, became popular. Also immensely popular were slapstick comedies. Mack Sennett, a Canadian vaudevillian who was famous for this brand of comedy, was originally a writer, director, and actor for D. W. Griffith at Biograph. After three years there, he left to co-found the Keystone Pictures Studio in 1912, with Cecil B. DeMille and D. W. Griffith. Sennett became well known for his "Keystone Comedies," and, in 1914, he made the first American feature-length comedy, *Tillie's Punctured Romance*. Many comedians such as Fatty Arbuckle, Charlie Chaplin, Gloria Swanson, the Keystone Kops, Mabel Normand, Ben Turpin, Harry Langdon, and Chester Conklin trace their roots to Sennett and the Keystone Studio. Most of these early action-based, zany films were filled with improvised action, manic slapstick, madcap chases, pie-throwing, pranks, near-misses, mishaps, and other physical comedy.

Script Notes _____

A wildly successful comedian who worked with Sennett was Charlie Chaplin. In 1913, he played small parts as a Keystone Kop. He then originated his trademark mustached, baggy-pants "Tramp" character in several short Sennett comedies and by 1915 had perfected the character. In 1916, he moved to the Mutual Film Corporation for $10,000 a week, making such films as *The Immigrant* (1917). Soon afterward, Chaplin signed the first million-dollar film contract with First National and made *The Kid* (1921).

The "Talkies"

In 1926, Warner Bros. launched the first sound and talking pictures with the development of a synchronized sound system called the *Vitaphone*. This technology, developed by Bell Telephone Laboratories, was a sound-on-disk process that allowed sound to be recorded on a phonograph record that was electronically linked and synchronized with a film projector. Although it would become obsolete by 1931, the method produced the first feature-length film with synchronized sound effects and a musical soundtrack, but without dialogue. It was Warner Bros.' romantic adventure *Don Juan*. Starring John Barrymore as the hand-kissing womanizer, Don Juan, the film premiered in New York in August 1926, but failed to generate the sensation that Harry, Sam, and Jack Warner had expected.

Meanwhile, Fox Film Corporation developed a competing version of sound pictures with its *Movietone* system. This new technology added a "soundtrack" directly onto the strip of film and would become the predominant model for sound technology in the future. The first films that used Fox's Movietone system were the comedy *What Price Glory?* and a newsreel about the Lindbergh flight across the Atlantic, both of which premiered in early 1927.

But it was another Warner Bros. film that was released in 1927 that would really usher in the sound era and revolutionize motion pictures forever. *The Jazz Singer*, starring Russian-born American vaudeville star Al Jolson, was the first feature-length talkie and first musical. The film had a partially synchronized soundtrack and featured six songs and about 350 "spontaneously spoken" words. The film was based on the 1925–26 Broadway musical about an aspiring cantor's son who wanted to become a jazz singer. Audiences loved *The Jazz Singer*, and its success marked the beginning of the era of the "talkies."

The major film studios realized that the new sound technology was going to bring about a big change in their business. They signed an agreement to analyze the competing sound systems and jointly choose a single system. Most of the studios started to convert from silent to sound film production immediately and many films that began production as silents were quickly transformed into sound films.

The studios were also confronted with many problems related to the coming of sound that had to be solved. Some of the issues included actors or actresses who lacked good voices, stationary microphones that impeded the movement of actors, the need for expensive new equipment and sound-proofed stages, restricted markets for English-language talkies, installation of sound systems in movie theatres, and noisy movie cameras that had to be housed in huge sound-insulated booths.

The early talkies were successful at the box office, but many of them were of poor quality. A number were dialogue-dominated play adaptations, with stilted acting and an unmoving camera or microphone. At the same time, however, there were many superb and innovative sound films. One example is the first film of the Ben Hecht-Charles MacArthur play *The Front Page* (Lewis Milestone, 1931). The film combined a mobile camera with inventive, rapid-fire dialogue and quick-editing. After 1932, the development of sound-mixing freed films from the limitations of recording on sets and locations. The studios also brought many talented playwrights and novelists to Hollywood, and scripts gradually got better with witty dialogue, realistic characters, and plots.

More New Technologies: Color and the Widescreen

The next significant technical innovation to impact filmmaking was the introduction of color film. One of the first "color" films was Thomas Edison's short *Annabell's Butterfly Dance*, in which the frames were individually hand-tinted. It would take the development of a new three-color camera, however, in 1932, to usher in true full-color Technicolor. The first film in three-color Technicolor was Walt Disney's animated *Flowers and Trees* (1932). The next year, Disney, which was becoming known for pioneering sophisticated animation, released another color animation film, *The Three Little Pigs*. In 1934, the first full-color, live-action short was released, titled *La Cucaracha*. Hollywood's first full-length feature film photographed entirely in three-strip Technicolor was Rouben Mamoulian's *Becky Sharp* (1935), an adaptation of English novelist William Makepeace Thackeray's novel *Vanity Fair*.

In the late 1930s, color was beginning to be used in more films. Two beloved movies, *The Wizard of Oz* (1939) and *Gone with the Wind* (1939), were expensively produced in Technicolor, and the trend would continue into the next decade in classic MGM musicals such as *Meet Me in St. Louis* (1944) and *Easter Parade* (1948).

There were also advances in special-effects processes by the late 1930s, making it possible for many more films to be shot on sets rather than on location.

The age of widescreen movies began in 1952 with the release of the popular *This is Cinerama*, a film using three cameras and three projectors to cover a huge, curved screen. In 1953, 20th Century Fox released *The Robe*, the first CinemaScope film, made by another widescreen process, often termed "true widescreen" because it was made by a single camera process and not by several cameras or by masking off part of the lens to make the image appear wide.

CinemaScope used lenses invented in the late 1920s by Henri Chrétien. His lenses were based on an optical "trick" in which an image contains a distortion that is removed with a complementary viewer. A horizontal squeeze of 100 percent was imparted into the image on film, resulting in a picture twice as wide as an image taken and projected through conventional lenses. CinemaScope quickly became the standard widescreen process of the 1950s.

In 1957, Panavision Inc. introduced a new high-quality widescreen lens to compete with CinemaScope. By the 1970s, Panavision lenses became the "standard" for widescreen and are still used by most major studio productions today. In 1963, Otto Preminger's *The Cardinal* was the first film to use Panavision 70, a film process in which a 35mm film was enlarged to 70mm for widescreen projection.

While the major studios began to adopt Panavision for their widescreen films, the old CinemaScope lenses didn't disappear. They gradually made their way into the hands of independent filmmakers and continue to be used today.

The Golden Age of Hollywood

The 1930s and 1940s have often been called "The Golden Age of Hollywood." During this period the film industry was dominated by five major studios that exerted their influence over actors, writers, directors, and producers. The majors were then 20th Century Fox, Metro-Goldwyn-Mayer, Paramount, Warner Bros., and RKO. Two other studios, Columbia and Universal, were close behind.

Cutaway

One of the biggest movies of the Golden Age was David Selznick's *Gone with the Wind* (1939). Selznick purchased the film rights from first-time author Margaret Mitchell for $50,000 (an astronomical sum at the time), cast the stars for the film (gambling on Vivien Leigh as the fiery Scarlett O'Hara), bullied director George Cukor and finally dismissed him, and insisted on using the audacious words of Rhett Butler's farewell ("Frankly, my dear, I don't give a damn") in defiance of the Hays Censorship Office and was fined $5,000 for using the word "damn." Although he had originally intended to make the film his own independent production, the fact that highly paid contract superstar Clark Gable was borrowed from MGM and the subsequent high price of the film forced Selznick to agree to let MGM release the film (and receive half the profits).

The 1930s was the age of lavish glamour, and MGM was the predominant, biggest, and most star-studded studio of all. MGM had the largest "stable" of stars, including Joan Crawford, Clark Gable, Myrna Loy, William Powell, Greta Garbo, Norma Shearer, Jean Harlow, Robert Montgomery, and Spencer Tracy. It claimed to have "more stars than are in heaven." It also had great filmmakers such as King Vidor, Victor Fleming, and George Cukor. Paramount Studios, on the other hand, had a more European, continental sophistication and flavor, with husky-throated Marlene Dietrich and director Josef von Sternberg, Gary Cooper, Cary Grant, Fredric March, Maurice Chevalier, Claudette Colbert, and director Ernst Lubitsch, who made sophisticated comedies like *Trouble in Paradise* (1932), *Angel* (1937), and *Ninotchka* (1939). Universal was known for its archetypal *Dracula* and *Frankenstein* horror films, and RKO had a blockbuster with its monster film *King Kong* (1933). Fox Studios capitalized on its association with Shirley Temple after the mid-30s, and Warner Bros. was noted for cutting-edge, realistic films or biopics, socially-conscious films, and the inauguration of the crime-gangster film.

Non-Fiction Films

Of course, filmmakers did not use the motion picture camera only to tell fictional stories. From the beginning, motion pictures were used to document true stories and world events. The term "documentary" came into being to describe non-fiction films that documented real life. In 1920, documentary filmmaker Robert Flaherty made the landmark ethnographic study of the Inuit Eskimos—the low-budget film *Nanook of the North* (1920). This landmark film brought more life and realism to the screen than other early film documentaries that merely recorded historical events, such as films of the San Francisco Earthquake in 1906. *Nanook of the North* set a standard for documentary films and earned the form new respect.

Today, most documentaries and other non-fiction films are shown on television, although some documentaries such as those made by popular filmmakers like Barbara Koppel (*Harlan County, U.S.A.*) and D. A. Pennebaker (*The War Room*) are released in theaters.

A New Medium: Television

In the 1940s, another new technology was introduced that would have an incredible impact on the film industry and on the world: broadcast television. Television would compete with movie theaters for viewers but would also provide an outlet for the films of many more filmmakers. Television would also bring something new to the world that motion pictures hadn't been able to—instant broadcasting of news and information, a capability that would change the world in profound ways.

The modern-day television set can be traced back to the discovery of light-sensitive selenium in 1817. Then, the second major technical innovation that would lead to television was the cathode ray oscilloscope, developed by German physicist Karl Braun in 1897. This invention would later be applied to the scanning system for television.

Finally, in 1928, inventor Philo Taylor Farnsworth, in what is usually considered the first television broadcast, put together a device that sent the image of a dollar sign across his San Francisco apartment. In 1929, Vladimir Zworykin, a Russian scientist who worked in the United States for Westinghouse, applied for an electronic TV patent after inventing the iconoscope, the electronic camera pickup tube.

Then Farnsworth, who had already invented an electronic television, devised the television camera, which converted the captured image into an electronic signal. This camera, called a *Kinescope*, dominated TV recording for time delay in the early 1950s. It was basically a special 16mm or 35mm film camera mounted in a large box aimed at a high-quality monochrome video monitor (a Kinescope). The Kinescope made respectable and reliable TV recordings.

In 1939, the National Broadcasting Company (NBC) began regularly scheduled television broadcasts to 400 sets in the New York area. In 1941, the Federal Communications Commission first adopted recommendations for 525-line, 30-frames-per-second black-and-white TV. By the early 1950s, most middle-class Americans had television sets. Today, it is estimated that there are 605 million television sets worldwide.

In the early days, film, used by the Kinescope, was the only medium available for recording television programs. Magnetic tape was already being used for sound, but the greater quantity of information carried by the television signal demanded something new. During the 1950s, a number of American companies began investigating the problem.

Charles Ginsburg led a research team at Ampex Corporation that developed the first practical videotape recorder (VTR). The system used a rapidly rotating recording head to apply high-frequency signals onto a reel of magnetic tape. The VTR revolutionized television broadcasting because it was so much less expensive than film and did not require developing.

In 1956, CBS became the first network to employ VTR technology. The historic first broadcast via videotape was the CBS airing of the program *Douglas Edwards with the News* on November 30, 1956, from New York. CBS Television City in Hollywood replayed the broadcast three hours after it was received on the West Coast. Confidence at CBS in the new machines was not all that high, and for a month the network ran a backup Kinescope just in case.

By 1958, networks and stations were still using VTRs primarily for time-delay broadcasts. True editing of videotape was not yet a reality. Simple mechanical edits could be performed, but the process was complex and difficult. Even so, CBS aired the first totally

VTR-produced program, "Playhouse 90," in 1958. Physical splicing of tape continued through the early 1960s, until timecode editing appeared in 1967. Computerized editing was introduced to the industry in 1971.

The Least You Need to Know

- The first films were short film strips that had no story, only people, animals, or objects in motion.
- Edwin Porter's *The Great Train Robbery* established the shot as the basic unit of film.
- Hollywood became the film capital of the world in the 1920s when filmmakers and distributors moved there to escape the attempt by several East Coast companies to monopolize the industry.
- Sound technology in the early 1930s ushered in the "talkies" and the "Golden Age of Hollywood."
- NBC began television broadcasting to 400 homes in New York City in 1939, and by the late 1950s, most Americans had television.

Loglines: An Overview of Film Genres

In This Chapter

♦ The major fiction film genres
♦ The types of non-fiction films
♦ Short films as calling cards

You've just learned a little about the history of film, your interest is piqued and you may want to make a film, but what kind of film do you want to make? What are the types of films that have been popular throughout the history of film? In this chapter, you'll get a chance to familiarize yourself with the categories of films or *film genres* that are made by filmmakers in Hollywood and around the world. There are certain general patterns of content and form that define a film genre, and some genres, like the drama or comedy, are pretty timeless. Others, like the western or musical, were more popular in the past than they are now.

Although genres are pretty self-evident, there are particular characteristics of each genre that have evolved that I'll cover in this chapter. The more you know about what has been done well in the past, the better your film will be. If you want to make a thriller, for example, don't just sit down and start to write your script. Get to know the genre by watching the great ones, as well as the thrillers in current release. With videotapes and especially DVDs, which often have information about the making of the film, everyone can study the films of the past and learn from them.

In addition to the genres of fiction films, I'll also describe the kinds of non-fiction films or videos that you may be interested in creating.

Exploring Fiction Film Genres

Most of the movies we see at theaters or rent at the video store are fiction films. Even if they are based on a true story or an actual event, such as the sinking of the *Titanic* or the attack on Pearl Harbor, the films themselves are stories that are imagined or invented by the screenwriters. Within the broad category of fiction films, there are many different genres, which I'll cover in the following sections.

Dramas

All fiction films are essentially dramas because, as you'll see in Chapter 6, "Act 1: Developing the Script," scripts are written using dramatic structure. But when someone says "it's a drama," it usually means that the film is a serious one with realistic characters, settings, life situations, and stories. Drama is probably the largest film genre, containing within it a variety of sub-genres. Although many dramas don't, some dramatic films deal frankly and realistically with social problems such as racial prejudice, intolerance, drug addiction, poverty, political unrest, the corruption of power, alcoholism, gender inequality, mental illness, corrupt societal institutions, or violence toward women. Many dramas are *adaptations* of novels or plays or are drawn from dramatic historical events. There are literally hundreds of great dramatic films. Two of my personal favorites are *Sophie's Choice* (Alan J. Pakula, 1982) and *Ordinary People* (Robert Redford, 1980).

 Verbal Action

film genres   Categories, classifications, or groups of films that have similar, familiar, or instantly recognizable patterns, techniques, or conventions. In a film genre, one or more of the following—setting, content, themes, purpose, motifs, styles, structure, or situations—are consistently the same.

adaptation   A film that is based on a novel or a play and is transformed into the medium of film by the film's screenwriter.

Love Stories

Love stories or romance films are a special sub-genre of dramatic films that focuses on passion, emotions, and the romantic involvement of the main characters (usually a leading man and woman). These films make the love story the main plot and not simply a sub-plot, as in other genres. Often, lovers in screen romances face obstacles and hardships—financial trouble or differences in social class, status, occupation, or a family that threatens to break their union—which is why, in the old-fashioned sexist Hollywood shorthand, the plot of a love story is often described as "boy meets girl, boy gets girl, boy loses girl, and boy gets girl again." As in all romantic relationships, the tensions of day-to-day life, various temptations, and differences in compatibility enter into the plots of romantic films.

Love stories explore such themes as love at first sight, young (and older) love, unrequited love, obsessive love, sentimental love, spiritual love, forbidden love, sexual and passionate love, sacrificial love, explosive and destructive love, or tragic love. Romantic films serve as great escapes and fantasies for viewers, especially if the two people finally overcome their difficulties and experience life "happily ever after."

Comedies

Comedies are essentially lighthearted dramas, whose main purpose is to amuse, provoke laughter, and provide an escape from the troubles of life. Comedies are about human foibles and life's frustrations. Many comedies have happy endings, although some have a serious or dark side. Throughout the history of film, there have been a variety of popular sub-genres of comedy:

- **Slapstick comedy:** Slapstick films are filled with broad physical action, including harmless fights, horseplay, and sight gags like a pie in the face, a loss of trousers or skirts, runaway crashing cars, and so on. The term slapstick was originally taken from the circus, where clowns slapped together wooden sticks to encourage the audience to applaud.

  Slapstick was typical of early comics like Laurel and Hardy, Abbott and Costello, W. C. Fields, The Three Stooges, Harold Lloyd, and the Keystone Kops. More recent examples include the *Pink Panther* films with Peter Sellers as Inspector Clouseau and Jim Carrey's *Ace Ventura, Pet Detective* (1993) and *The Mask* (1994). Animated cartoons such as the Roadrunner and Wile E. Coyote are also good examples of slapstick comedies.

- **Screwball and romantic comedies:** Screwball comedies were a very popular film genre in the 1930s and 1940s. They are lighthearted, romantic stories, usually focusing on sexual tensions and conflicts. Like slapstick, they often include visual gags, but also typically have eccentric characters, a fast-paced plot, and rapid-fire, wise-cracking dialogue. The characters might have contradictory desires for individual freedom and for a relationship, or they might be seeking romance under unorthodox or implausible circumstances. In the end, in screwball comedies, good old-fashioned romantic love usually triumphs.

Today, the screwball comedy has evolved into what is commonly known as the romantic comedy. These films are essentially love stories that are filled with comedic situations, often based on misunderstandings and misinformation.

♦ **Verbal comedy:** Films that depend on dialogue for most of their comedy are often termed verbal comedies. Some typical examples include the sarcastic wit of W. C. Fields, Mae West's sexual innuendo, the absurd dialogue in Marx Brothers' films, or, more recently, the self-effacing humor of Woody Allen.

♦ **Black or dark comedies:** Black or dark comedies usually examine subjects and themes not often dealt with in comedies, such as war, death, or illness. One of the greatest black comedies ever made was Stanley Kubrick's classic Cold War satire, *Dr. Strangelove or: How I Learned to Stop Worrying and Love the Bomb* (1964). Other examples include Danny DeVito's *The War of the Roses* (1989) and John Huston's *Prizzi's Honor* (1985).

♦ **Parody or spoof:** A parody or spoof is a humorous take-off of a more serious film or genre, ridiculing the style, conventions, formulas, or motifs of a serious work. Many of Mel Brooks's films are spoofs. Rob Reiner's take-off on a rock-and-roll documentary, *This is Spinal Tap* (1984), is another example of a spoof. The Marx Brothers' satiric masterpiece *Duck Soup* (1933) is often considered one of the best of this sub-genre.

Cutaway

All fiction films have at least one major genre, but many films are considered cross-breeds or hybrids because they contain aspects of several genre types. There are also many sub-genres of films. Some sub-genres include: aviation films, biographical films, buddy films, caper films, chase films, disaster films, espionage films, experimental films, legal dramas, martial arts films, medical films, military films, police dramas, political dramas, prison films, religious films, road films, slasher films, sports films, swashbucklers, and more. In addition to genres, films are also classified by the different forms or types of films, such as animation, feature, serial, documentary, or short.

Thrillers

Thrillers or suspense films have been popular throughout the history of film and continue to be very popular today. Thrillers cause excitement, anticipation, uncertainty, anxiety, adrenaline rushes, and nerve-wracking tension in audiences. A genuine thriller is a film that relentlessly provides thrills and keeps folks in the audience on the "edge of their seats" as the plot builds towards its *climax*. The tension usually arises when the main character is placed in a dangerous situation from which escape seems impossible. Life itself is threatened, usually because the principal character is unsuspecting or unknowingly involved in a dangerous or potentially deadly situation.

Thrillers are often hybrids—suspense thrillers, action thrillers, crime thrillers, western thrillers, *film noir* thrillers, even romantic comedy thrillers. Suspense thrillers come in all shapes and forms: There are murder mysteries, private eye tales, chase thrillers, courtroom and legal thrillers, erotic thrillers, and atmospheric, plot-twisting psychodramas. The themes of thrillers can range from political conspiracies to romantic triangles that lead to murder.

Script Notes

Alfred Hitchcock was the acknowledged master of the thriller genre. His films often placed his main characters—usually average, responsible persons who become innocent victims—into strange or life-threatening situations. He then would usually let the audience know before the characters that some horrible event will happen, creating unbearable suspense while waiting for the inevitable. Hitchcock's films often explored the darker side of human nature, including themes of voyeurism, guilt and punishment, or paranoia and obsession.

Action and Adventure Films

Action films are characterized by non-stop motion, lots of stunts, chase scenes, rescues, battles, fights, and escapes. Action films come in a variety of forms or genre hybrids: sci-fi, thrillers, crime-drama, war, horror, and so on. Always, however, they have a resourceful hero—or more recently, heroine—struggling against incredible odds or an evil villain, with victory finally attained at the end.

A quintessential action hero is the James Bond 007 character, who was loosely based on the same character in Ian Fleming's novels. Beginning in the 1960s, the slick Bond pictures appealed to large audiences with their exotic locales, tongue-in-cheek dialogue, nifty gadgets, fast-action suspense, and audacious stunts.

The action film first became popular with weekly Saturday serials, running in installments that often had "cliff-hanging" endings to entice viewers to return for the next show. Heroine Pearl White in *The Perils of Pauline* (1914) was the first major superstar of the serials. Hollywood has always enjoyed lucrative returns from the action-film genre, although the genre has been worn thin with re-treaded stories, excessive macho-posturing of the hero, and a heavy reliance on special effects and stunts rather than original stories.

Adventure films are similar to action films in that they are designed to provide an action-filled experience for the viewer, who can live vicariously through the travels, conquests, explorations, and situations that confront the main characters. Some adventure films are set in harsh, uncivilized locales—a desert, an island, a jungle, or a cold polar area, where an individual (or a group) must struggle against the forces of nature to keep alive. The threats of death, the selfishness of other individuals in the group, and other forces test the spirit and ingenuity of the survivors under these grueling circumstances. Under the category of adventure films are traditional swashbucklers and historical spectacles, treasure hunts, disaster films, or searches for the unknown.

Counterpoint

Action/adventure films have traditionally been aimed at male audiences and have created major male stars who usually portray courageous, patriotic, or altruistic heroes fighting for their beliefs, struggling for freedom, or overcoming injustice. As people tired of the same types of male heroes, the box-office returns for action films began to diminish. Losing money because they were out of sync with the times, the studios have only recently begun to feature strong female characters in some films of this genre.

War Films

Another special genre of dramatic action films are war and anti-war films, which explore the horror and heartbreak of war, with scenes of combat providing the primary background for the film's action. Typical elements in war films include POW camp experiences and escapes, submarine warfare, espionage, heroism, "war is hell" brutalities, air dogfights, tough trench/infantry experiences, and male-bonding buddy adventures in wartime. War films frequently include elements of other genres, such as romance and suspense.

Themes explored in war films include the futility and inhumanity of war, heroic sacrifice and struggle, and other moral and human issues raised by and during wartime. Some so-called war films are actually historical epics that attempt to recreate the wartime experience on screen.

War films as a major film genre emerged after the outbreak of World War I. A number of films were produced then to inspire anti-German feeling in the United States. War films have often been used as "flag-waving" propaganda to inspire national pride and to display the nobility of one's own forces while harshly criticizing the villainy of the enemy.

Crime, Gangster, and Detective Films

Crime and gangster films are stories about criminals or gangsters, particularly bank robbers or mob and underworld figures. They are related to detective films—because of underlying similarities between these cinematic forms—but in detective films the main character is the detective rather than the criminal.

Crime stories often recount the rise and fall of a particular criminal, gang, bank robber, murderer, or lawbreaker in conflict with law-and-order figures, a competitive colleague, or a rival gang. Headline-grabbing situations, real-life gangsters, or crime reports are often the subject matter in crime films. Crime plots also revolve around questions of how the criminal will be apprehended by police or authorities, or mysteries such as who stole the valued object. Crime and gangster films are essentially morality tales, in which criminals are doomed to failure and inevitable death but are portrayed as the victims of circumstances to whom all other "normal" avenues to the top are unavailable.

Criminal/gangster films date back to the early days of film during the silent era. Sound increased the popularity of these films because sound brought to life the world of crime—machine-gun fire, screeching brakes, screams, chases through city streets, and squealing car tires.

Film Noir

Film noir is a style of American film that evolved in the 1940s, during and after World War II, and lasted until about 1960. The term "film noir," meaning "black film" in French, came from French film critics who noticed how dark and black the looks and themes were of many American crime and detective films. Film noir is similar to crime/gangster sagas from the 1930s such as *Public Enemy* (1931) and *Scarface* (1932), but different in tone and characterization. Film noir is less a genre and more a description of the mood or tone of a film.

Classic films noir are melancholy and bleak. They use low-key lighting, disorienting visual schemes, circling cigarette smoke, and unbalanced compositions. Interiors are often dimly lit apartments and hotel rooms in big cities. Exteriors are night scenes with deep shadows, wet asphalt, and flashing neon lights. Narratives are frequently complex and convoluted, typically with flashbacks (or a series of flashbacks) and voice-over narration. Heroes (or anti-heroes) are often low-lifes or down-and-out detectives or private eyes who are cynical loners, struggling to survive and ultimately losing. Revelations regarding the hero are made to explain his cynical perspective on life.

The women in film noir are often one of two types: dutiful, reliable, trustworthy, and loving women; or *femme fatales*—double-crossing, gorgeous, predatory, tough, manipulative, and desperate women. Usually, the male lead character in film noir has to choose between the women—and invariably he picks the femme fatale.

The earliest films noir were detective thrillers, with plots and themes often taken from adaptations of crime fiction by authors like Raymond Chandler, James M. Cain, or Dashiell Hammett.

Modern films noir include the dark detective thriller *Chinatown* (1974), the twisted, sexy *Body Heat* (1981), about a lawyer enticed to murder a woman's husband, the sci-fi thriller *Blade Runner* (1982), the 1950s Hollywood crime drama *L.A. Confidential* (1997), or the dark *The Last Seduction* (1993), starring Linda Florentino as an amoral, evil femme fatale.

 Verbal Action

climax   A moment of great or culminating intensity in a narrative film or play, especially the conclusion of a crisis, when the tension created by the problem set up in act one is resolved.

femme fatale   In film or in literature, a mysterious woman of great seductive charm who leads men into compromising or dangerous situations.

Westerns

Western films, one of the most characteristically American genres, focus on the early days of the American frontier, usually during the latter part of the nineteenth century (1865–1900). The settings are romantic, sweeping frontier landscapes or rugged rural terrain. Western themes often include the conquest of the wilderness and the subordination of nature in the name of civilization. Settings are frequently lonely isolated forts, ranches, homesteads, saloons, jails, and small frontier towns that are forming at the edges of civilization. Over time, westerns have been redefined, reinvented and expanded, dismissed, rediscovered, and spoofed.

Western plots are rooted in conflict, such as good vs. evil, white hat vs. black hat, new arrivals vs. Native Americans, humans vs. nature, civilization vs. wilderness, schoolteacher vs. saloon dancehall girl, lawman vs. gunslinger, law and order vs. anarchy, the rugged individualist vs. the community, East vs. West, settler vs. nomad, and farmer vs. industrialist.

Typical elements in westerns are gunfights, horses, trains, robberies, stagecoaches, shootouts and showdowns, outlaws and sheriffs, cattle drives and cattle rustling, posses, breathtaking settings, and distinctive western clothing. Western heroes are often local sheriffs, marshals, or skilled fast-draw gunfighters. They are normally persons of integrity and principle—courageous, moral, tough, self-sufficient characters who frequently have trusty sidekicks. Westerns often portray Native Americans in a biased and stereotypical way. *Broken Arrow* (1950) was the first Hollywood picture to take the side of Native Americans and emphasize peaceful co-existence, with a sympathetic portrayal of Apache chief Cochise by Jeff Chandler.

Westerns were among the slowest of the film genres to mature. Many westerns were unsophisticated, low-quality, action-packed B-pictures filled with familiar stock footage. At the end of the 1930s, however, director John Ford's landmark *Stagecoach* (1939) marked a turning point. He created a new kind of western film, which had standard B-picture action, but also epic scope and an intelligent emphasis on character and mood, transforming the western into A-film status. As the genre's popularity began to diminish, it was revived again in the 1960s and 1970s when the episodic TV western became popular, with series like *The Gene Autry Show*, *The Lone Ranger*, *Hopalong Cassidy*, and *The Roy Rogers and Dale Evans Show*.

Science Fiction

Science fiction films are visionary and imaginative fantasies that contain elements such as distant planets, impossible quests, improbable settings, fantastic places, dark and shadowy villains, futuristic technology, unknowable forces, extraordinary creatures from space, mad scientists, or nuclear havoc. Sci-fi tales have a prophetic nature and are usually filled with fantastic special effects.

Thematically, sci-fi films often deal with how to control the impact of technological change on society or the potential of technology to destroy humankind. There are often encounters with aliens and battles between good and evil, and the genre overlaps with horror films when technology or aliens become malevolent.

The first science fiction feature films appeared in the 1920s after World War I, when people were acutely aware of the destructive effects of technology. One of the most innovative sci-fi films ever made was a silent film set in the year 2000: German director Fritz Lang's masterpiece, *Metropolis* (1926).

By the 1990s, sophisticated digital effects were used in science fiction films, creating spectacular and monstrous creatures such as the living dinosaurs in Spielberg's *Jurassic Park* (1993), the stunning visual effects in Roland Emmerich's summer blockbuster *Independence Day* (1996), Tim Burton's *Mars Attacks!* (1996), a spoof of 1950s alien-invasion movies with bulbous-headed aliens, or the slow-motion/fast-paced and much imitated sci-fi hit by the Wachowski brothers, *The Matrix* (1999).

Horror

Horror films are designed to be scary. They invoke our worst fears and often have terrifying, shocking finales. Horror films center on the dark side of life, on forbidden, strange, and alarming events. They deal with our nightmares, our vulnerability, our alienation, our terror of the unknown, our fear of death, or our loss of identity. Fantasy and supernatural film genres also often use elements of the horror genre.

Horror films are generally set in fog-shrouded, dark locales, with "unknown," human, supernatural, or grotesque creatures, ranging from vampires, madmen, devils, unfriendly ghosts, monsters, mad scientists, "Frankensteins," demons, zombies, evil spirits, arch fiends, satanic villains, the "possessed," werewolves, freaks, and even the unseen, diabolical presence of evil. In this genre, the forces of chaos or horror invariably need to be defeated, and the films often end with a return to normalcy and victory over the monstrous.

Many horror films, particularly in earlier decades, were B-movies, inferior sequels, or atrocious, low-budget gimmick films, but horror films, when done well, can be extremely potent film forms, tapping into our fears of the irrational and unknown.

The character that appears in more movies than any other fictional character happens to be a character in horror movies—the Dracula character from the many Dracula movies. Examples of classic modern horror films include Tobe Hooper's *Texas Chainsaw Massacre* (1974) and Wes Craven's *The Hills Have Eyes* (1977).

Musicals

Musicals are films with full-scale song-and-dance routines that are usually part of the film narrative. Musicals often highlight various musical artists or dancing stars, with lyrics that support the story line. Musicals were one of the last of the major film genres to emerge because they were dependent on sound. With the coming of sound pictures, the musical film genre developed from its roots—stage musicals, revues, and vaudeville—and became extremely popular.

Hollywood musicals came into full flower in the 1940s, with an increased demand for escapist entertainment during World War II and increased budgets for the musical genre. One of the top musical teams in the 1940s were all-American kids Mickey Rooney and Judy Garland. Another famous musical team from that era was Fred Astaire and Ginger Rogers.

By the late 1950s and early 1960s, the public seemed tired of the long succession of musicals, so studios began to abandon the expensive-to-produce musicals. From then on, most musicals were adaptations of Broadway smash-hits or showcased particular artists such as Elvis Presley, who made a total of thirty-three musicals in his film career.

Script Notes

Actor, dancer, and singer Gene Kelly, in a continuing collaboration/partnership with choreographer-turned-director Stanley Donen, made what is possibly the most popular Hollywood musical of all time: the exuberant *Singin' in the Rain* (1952). The film is a parody of Hollywood's shaky transition from the silent era to the talkies. The most famous scene is when Kelly dances and sings the title song through a downpour.

Despite the decline in the quantity of musicals, great musicals continued to be produced. *West Side Story* (1961) featured a Leonard Bernstein-Stephen Sondheim score, dynamite choreography, and a sensitive depiction of the problems of rival gangs and juvenile delinquency. Rodgers and Hammerstein's *The Sound of Music* (1965), starring Julie Andrews as a spunky governess for the von Trapp family, was the greatest box-office success since *Gone with the Wind* (1939). *My Fair Lady* (1964), based on George Bernard Shaw's play *Pygmalion*, was also an enormous success. Finally, choreographer-director Bob Fosse produced two innovative and dramatic musicals: the stylish *Cabaret* (1972) with Liza Minnelli and Joel Grey, and the director's semi-autobiographical *All That Jazz* (1979) with Roy Scheider as New York choreographer Joe Gideon.

A sub-genre of musicals was the concert picture, including the rockumentary *Woodstock* (1970), the three-hour-long epic of the four-day 1969 rock concert in upstate New York; *Gimme Shelter* (1970), chronicling the Rolling Stones' late 1969 appearance at a free outdoor concert at Altamont that turned violent; and *The Last Waltz* (1978), Martin Scorsese's film of The Band's final concert appearance.

Animated Films

Animated films are both a technique of filmmaking and a kind of genre. Animated films were first created by using individual drawings, paintings, or illustrations that are photographed frame by frame with stop-frame cinematography. Each frame differs slightly from the one preceding it, giving the illusion of movement when the frames are projected at 24 frames per second. When filmed and projected, the illustrator's static art comes alive and creates imaginative cinematic images. With animation, animals and inanimate objects can become evil villains or heroes. The subject matter of animated films is frequently fairy tales, or children's or family stories, but not always.

The first feature-length animated film, *Snow White and the Seven Dwarfs*, was released by Disney Studios in 1937. The heyday of Disney's animation was from the late 1930s through the 1940s. Then, in the late 1980s and 1990s, Disney returned to those roots with advanced, more mature animations such as *The Little Mermaid* (1989) and the updated version of *Beauty and the Beast* (1991). The latter film was nominated for a Best Picture Academy Award, the first nomination ever received for a full-length animated feature. In 1992 Disney released *Aladdin*, which used computer-generated images and was designed for a more adult audience.

Pixar Studios and Disney then created the first completely computer-generated animated feature film with the landmark *Toy Story*. Three years later, DreamWorks and Pacific Data Images (PDI) released the second computer-animated feature film—the adult-oriented *Antz* (1998). The second collaboration of DreamWorks and PDI was for the immensely successful and colorful *Shrek* (2001), a computer-animated film that added elements such as fire, liquids, digitized humans, and clothing to computer-generated images.

Cutaway

Hollywood filmmaking has long been dominated by white men, and countless statistics show that the studios still discriminate in the hiring of women and minorities. In 1969, director-writer-producer Gordon Parks became the first black director to direct a feature film, *The Learning Tree,* financed by a major Hollywood studio. Parks's second feature was the successful, urban, action-oriented *Shaft* (1971). It was the first commercially successful film about a black private detective and the first in a series of "blaxploitation" films in that decade. In 1999, with her film *Peacemaker,* Mimi Leder became the first woman to direct an action picture. Despite some individual successes like those of Parks and Leder, however, both women and minorities produce, write, or direct far fewer Hollywood films than white males.

Taking Stock of Non-Fiction Films

So far, I have covered the genres of narrative fiction film, which are most of the films we view at a theater or on television for entertainment. Non-fiction films also come in many forms. A list of the types of non-fiction films follows:

◆ **Feature documentary:** This is a feature-length film about a real-life topic, filming real people rather than actors.

◆ **Docudrama:** This is a film about a real-life topic that is scripted and dramatized with actors.

◆ **Historical documentary:** This is a documentary about historical events or persons.

◆ **Social criticism:** This is a documentary that calls attention to social problems or criticizes the status quo.

◆ **PR film:** This is a non-fiction film used to promote a product, event, or company.

◆ **Educational film:** This film is used to teach children or adults, shown in schools, colleges, or training facilities.

◆ **Nature film:** This is a documentary about animals and nature.

◆ **Travelogue:** This is a film about travel experiences.

◆ **Industrial:** This is a film financed by corporations to explain and promote their products and services.

◆ **Documentary short:** A short documentary (usually less than 30 minutes) is about any subject that could also be covered by a feature-length documentary.

Calling Cards: Short Films

Many students and aspiring filmmakers cannot afford to make a feature film to showcase their talent so they produce short films. These short films are often called "calling cards" because they are made primarily to call attention to the skill or talent of the filmmaker. Short films can be live-action narrative films, animated films, or documentary shorts.

The Least You Need to Know

◆ All genres of narrative films are essentially dramas, but each genre has certain identi-fying characteristics.

◆ Study great films from the genre of the film you want to make.

◆ Learn the types of non-fiction films if you are interested in making a documentary or other non-fiction film.

Chapter 3

Mise-en-scène: Basic Elements of Films and Videos

In This Chapter

◆ Using the lens and camera to capture images
◆ Understanding what the film lab or online edit can provide
◆ Knowing your story and your film's purpose

You've learned a little about the history of film and are sophisticated enough to distinguish one film genre from another. Now it's time to learn how to make your own film but, unfortunately, making a professional quality film or video is not simply a matter of looking through the viewfinder of a camera and pressing the button. If it was, you wouldn't need this book. In fact, making a film requires a very high level of technical knowledge.

All films and videos share certain basic elements—picture, sound, style, story, and structure. I'll give you an overview of what you need to know in each of these areas in this chapter—so you can expect a lot of technical terms. Once you have a basic working knowledge of the elements of a film or video, you will be much better prepared to begin work on your own film.

Getting the Picture

Film and video are visual mediums. A substantial part of filmmaking is the ability to capture compelling, dramatic, interesting, artistic, beautiful, or stunning moving images. To do that, a filmmaker needs to understand how the tools available to capture those images work.

The Lens

One of the most important tools for capturing an image is the *lens* of the camera. Lenses are devices, often made of glass, that attach to a film or video camera and focus the light rays emanating from a scene or subject onto the film or videotape. The type of lens used in a camera during a shot will affect the type of image created. There are basically four types of lenses available—a "normal" or standard lens, a wide-angle lens, a telephoto or long lens, and a zoom lens.

All of these lenses are classified and described by their *focal lengths*, which is the distance inside the camera from the film to the surface of the lens. The focal length of a normal lens is about 35mm to 50mm. The normal lens is used most often because it gives the least distortion of the image and thus most closely imitates the way the human eye views a scene.

The wide-angle lens—which, as its name suggests, photographs a wide angle—is used when the camera is in a cramped location in relationship to the image to be photographed and the filmmaker wants as wide a view as possible of the scene. Any lens with a focal length shorter than 35mm is considered a wide-angle lens.

A telephoto or long lens is used to magnify distant scenes. The focal length of a long lens generally ranges between 60mm and 1200mm.

Finally, zoom lenses are lenses with variable focal lengths that allow the cinematographer to change focal lengths during a shot. Most zoom lenses have a focal length ranging from 10mm to 100mm.

The Camera

The camera, which houses the lens and the film or videotape, is the most important tool of a filmmaker. It is a mechanical device that controls the amount of light

> **Script Notes**
>
> The term "time-lapse" is used for extremely fast-motion photography in which the camera operates intermittently rather than continuously. Time-lapse sequences of flowers, for example, might contain 30 seconds of screen time that would reflect several days of the growth of the flower, revealing it opening and blossoming. This kind of filming has been helpful to scientists and is also often used in nature films.

that goes through the lens and strikes the film. In motion picture photography, the camera moves the film and can be moved itself to create different kinds of moving images.

As you have seen, films are a series of still pictures. The motion picture camera (or video camera) works by moving film (or video) into position for the exposure of a frame, holding it steady for approximately, 1/24 of a second, then moving the next frame into position. When the speed of the camera is adjusted to speeds much higher than the normal 24 frames per second, you get images in *slow motion*, revealing details of the action being filmed that could not be seen in real time. When the camera is adjusted to take many fewer than 24 frames, the images appear in *fast motion*.

 Verbal Action

lens   The optical devices used in cameras and projectors that focus light rays by the process of refraction.

focal length   The length of a lens, measured from the outside surface of the lens to the film plane.

slow motion   Action filmed at a speed faster than normal, which when projected at normal speed appears slower on the screen than in reality; also an optical that slows down the action by printing every frame more than once. (Slow motion produced by an optical effect will appear jerkier than slow motion achieved by running the camera at a high frame rate.)

fast motion   Action filmed at slower than normal speed, which when projected at normal speed appears faster; also an optical that increases the apparent speed of the action by printing every other frame to double the speed or every third frame to triple the speed.

Where the camera is placed in relationship to the subject or scene also affects the look of the film. Shots can vary in terms of camera-to-subject distance, camera angle, and camera (or lens) movement.

The distance between the camera and subject determines whether the shot will be close to the subject, a medium distance from the scene, or far enough away to include more of the scene. The basic types of shots used in filmmaking—in regard to distance from the camera—are described as follows:

- ◆ **Long shot (LS)** is a shot that gives the viewer the context of the setting by showing it from a greater distance and including at least the full figure of a subject. Long shots are also sometimes called wide shots or full shots.
- ◆ **Establishing shot,** also called a master shot or cover shot, is a type of long shot that orients the viewer by showing the general location of the scene that follows.

- **Medium shot (MS)** is a shot that provides approximately a knee to head view of a subject. Medium shots are further broken down into medium long shots or medium close-ups. Two shots or three shots are usually medium shots in which two or three subjects appear in the frame.

- **Close-up (CU),** also called close shot, normally indicates a shot of the head and shoulders of a person. Close-ups can also be focused on some small part of the scene—a hand or an object like a phone ringing, for example. The purpose of the shot is to draw the audience's attention to that element to create a dramatic effect.

- **Extreme close-ups (ECU)** are when the camera is very close to the subject.

The angle of the camera also affects the look of the film and the way the story is told. Camera angle can be used to establish a specific viewpoint, allowing the audience to share a character's perspective on the action. A *point-of-view* or *POV shot* places the camera in the approximate location of the character in relationship to some other action and is preceded by a shot of that character looking in that direction.

The normal camera angle is eye level but other angles include a low-angle shot, where the camera is lower than the subject and a high-angle shot, where the camera is higher than the subject. The low-angle shot exaggerates the size and importance of the subject while the high-angle shot tends to reduce the subject's size and importance.

A *reverse-angle shot* is when the camera is placed in the opposite direction from the previous shot. Finally, an *overhead* or *aerial shot* is a view from high above the action.

In addition to distance and angle, the other way the camera affects how images look on film is through camera movement. The following list covers the basic types of camera movement:

- **Pan:** Any pivotal movement of a camera around an imaginary vertical axis running through the camera. The pan is the most common camera movement.

- **Tilt:** Any movement of a camera up and down so that it rotates on an imaginary horizontal axis running through the camera.

- **Roll:** The movement of a camera around an imaginary axis that runs between the lens and the subject.

- **Dolly or tracking shots:** Mounting the camera on a dolly and moving the dolly on tracks during a shot.

- **Crane shots:** Mounting the camera on a crane and moving the crane during the shot.

In pans and tilts, the camera follows the subject as the subject moves. In rolls, the subject doesn't change but its orientation within the frame changes. In tracking and crane shots, the camera moves along a vertical or horizontal line and the subject may be either stationary or in motion.

 Verbal Action _____

point-of-view (POV) shot   A shot which shows a scene from the point of view of a character.

low- or high-angle shot   A shot that is taken at an angle below (low) or above (high) eye level.

reverse-angle shot   A shot from the opposite side of a subject. Two-party dialogue scenes are often constructed using alternating reverse-angle shots.

overhead or aerial shot   A shot from above, usually made from a plane, helicopter, or crane.

You've learned about using the camera but if that were all there was to it, then photography would be relatively simple. But it's not. A cinematographer can also create different images by adjusting the quality and quantity of light entering through the lens. The quality of light is altered by using *filters*, which are devices that absorb light and are attached in front of the lens. Filters are often used to establish a mood or tone.

As I explained earlier, adjusting the exposure time changes the quantity of light hitting the film and creates slow or fast motion. The other way to change the quantity or amount of light hitting the film during a shot is by changing the aperture, or size of the hole, through which light enters the camera. The size of the aperture is measured in *f-stops*, which are numbers derived by dividing the focal length of a particular lens by its effective aperture.

If you understood the last sentence immediately, you might consider becoming a cinematographer or photographer. If you didn't, don't worry. If you don't plan on shooting your own film, you don't need to understand everything about f-stops or focal lengths because your cinematographer will know how to use the camera to help you create the effects you want. You should, however, know certain terms to be able to communicate with your cinematographer, and you should understand the kinds of images the camera is capable of creating.

The term *depth of field* is used to indicate the range of distances in front of the lens that will appear in *focus*. If you want your film to strive for a sharp focus—giving it a very realistic effect—then your cinematographer will strive for deep-focus photography or a larger depth of field. If you want a more arty, expressionistic look to your film, you will have it shot in shallow focus with a smaller depth of field. Rack focus, a technique that is sometimes used, changes the focus from one subject to another during a shot in order to redirect the viewer's attention.

Cutaway

The ability to control the angle and movement of the camera gives filmmakers a wide range of choices of the images they wish to show and the impact those images will create in the viewer. For example, in Alfred Hitchcock's famous tower shot from the movie *Vertigo*, he used a carefully controlled tracking shot of a model of the stairwell of the tower, combined with a zoom lens. The camera was mounted on a track and aimed at the model stairwell, which was on its side. The shot began with the camera at the far end of the track and the zoom lens was set at a moderate telephoto length. As the camera tracked toward the stairwell, the zoom was adjusted backwards, eventually reaching a wide-angle setting. The effect that was created mimicked the psychological feeling of vertigo.

Film Stock

The basic chemical principle on which all photography is based is that some chemical substances such as silver salts change chemically—they darken—when exposed to light. The result is a negative image. When the negative is developed, by projecting it on similar film stock, a positive print of the image results. Also, when the negative is projected, the image can be enlarged, reduced, or otherwise altered.

The type of film stock used can affect the look of your film. Film can vary in gauge, speed, contrast, tone, and color. When motion pictures began, the standard gauge or width of film stock was 35mm and, for the most part, still is. 16mm film and 8mm film were originally introduced as a less expensive alternative for amateur filmmakers. Now, however, 16mm film and even "super" 8mm film are used for television and even feature films. Larger 70mm film stock is usually used in special films, such as those made for IMAX large-screen theaters.

The grain of film stock varies by how "fast" the film is. Faster film stock can often be used with available light so that scenes can be filmed more spontaneously without the necessity to carefully light them. This is particularly useful for documentary filmmakers. The disadvantage of faster film is that images may appear grainier. Slower film stocks give sharper, fine-grain images.

Film also varies by its *aspect ratio*, which is the frame size of the film when projected. The aspect ratio of widescreen films today is usually 1.85:1 for 35mm American films. For television the standard aspect ratio is 1.33:1.

Finally, film stock can be black and white or color and can vary in contrast and tone. Cinematographers often test a batch of film to check its contrast or color before ordering large quantities of it for a film shoot.

 Verbal Action

filter   A plate of glass, plastic, or gelatin which alters the quality of light entering a lens.

f-stop   The measure of the camera diaphragm's opening. A high f-stop number indicates a small opening and little light entering the camera lens.

depth of field   The varying range of distances from the camera at which an object remains in sharp focus.

focus   The clarity and sharpness of an image, limited to a certain range of distance from the camera.

The Lab

The laboratory develops the film and also gives you techniques for adjusting the final image so that it looks more like what you had in mind when you were shooting. One of the most critical functions of the lab in color film is the *timing* of the print, which means adjusting the colors of various scenes shot at different times and under varying conditions. The lab might also have to correct for exposure differences.

In addition, the lab can add certain effects, called *opticals*, to your film. The opticals that labs can provide include the following:

◆ **Fades:** This is a technique for gradually bringing an image up from black or another color to the full image (a fade-in) or gradually making the image disappear to a black or another color screen (a fade-out).

◆ **Superimposition:** Also called multiple exposure, this is an image printed over another one or several images printed over each other.

◆ **Dissolve:** This is a transitional device that superimposes a fade-out over a fade-in.

◆ **Wipes:** This refers to an optical process whereby one image appears to wipe the preceding image off the screen. This technique was a common transitional device in 1930s films but is used much less frequently now.

◆ **Freeze frame:** This is a shot that replaces a still photograph, achieved by printing a single frame many times in succession.

- **Mask:** This is a covering of some type placed in front of the camera lens to block off part of the photographed image. Also, the shield inserted behind a projector lens in order to obtain a desired aspect ratio.

- **Ghost image:** This is a type of double exposure in which one or more preceding frames are printed together with the main frame to give a multiple exposure.

- **Split-screen image:** This is a technique that shows two or more separate images within the frame, not overlapping.

Videotape

Video has been rapidly developing as a medium since its invention in the 1950s. Far less expensive than film, Betacam SP or Digital Beta video are used professionally in many productions, particularly for things like television news, daytime television shows, documentaries, and other non-fiction films. Most of my discussion so far about the way in which the lens and camera affect the image also applies to video. The difference, of course, is that videotape does not need to be developed at a lab but is immediately available for viewing and editing.

Counterpoint

Throughout this chapter, I have presented a lot of information about how one creates varied visual images for film or video. Sometimes, however, less is more. Using too many camera movements, unique angles, or effects can be distracting to the viewer. Be sure to choose shots not so they stand out for themselves but so that they illustrate or emphasize what you want to say in the narrative or story.

Even though videotape isn't developed like film, it can also have visual effects and color correction added after the shoot. Instead of this being done in a film laboratory, tape finishing is done in an "on-line" session after the "off-line" edit is done. On-line editing uses computers and electronic effects equipment to correct the color, create opticals or effects, clean up dirt on the tape, and add titles.

Mixing the Sound

I've spent a lot of time on the picture or visual elements of film because film and video are visual media, but other elements are also critically important to good filmmaking. One of those elements is sound. In a film shoot, the sound for the film is captured by microphones and a tape recorder that generally uses ¼-inch magnetic tape. After the shoot, this tape must be transferred to a magnetic tape format, which is then synchronized with the film and used in editing. A crystal clock device is used to keep sound and picture in proper relationship to each other.

In video, the sound is actually captured on the videotape so there is no need for a transfer after the shoot.

In both formats, the production sound person must determine the best type of microphone to use during a shoot and also the best position to place the microphone. On the set, the sound person also must set the tape recorder console to the proper loudness levels for each scene.

In post-production (see Chapter 19, "Finishing the Film or Video"), during the sound mix, levels can be adjusted and other recorded sounds, besides those recorded during the shoot, can be added to the film.

Telling the Story

So far, I have talked about the technical process of shooting a film and capturing visual images and sound. Before you run out and start doing that, however, it is essential that you know what you want to shoot and what you want to say with your film. All films, even documentaries, have scripts, with some sort of narrative or dramatic structure. In Chapter 6, "Act 1: Developing the Script," I go into detail about writing a script. It is important to note, however, that the script is the basic blueprint for a film production and any type of filming done without a script will usually lead to a lot of wasted time and money.

 Verbal Action

aspect ratio   The ratio of the width to the height of the projected film. In television the aspect ratio is 1.33:1, in U.S. films it is 1.85:1, and in most European films it is 1.66:1.

optical   An operation done in the film laboratory that creates an effect, such as a fade or dissolve.

timing   The process of correcting color values in various film shots and scenes shot at different times of the day, in different places, or under different lighting conditions.

Adding Style: Art, Information, or Entertainment

In addition to having a script as a guide or blueprint for your film shoot, you should also know what you want to accomplish with your film. Is it a film that will convey information, like a news segment, a documentary, an educational or industrial film? Or do you hope your film will be an artistic achievement, designed to illuminate something beautiful or to explore deep philosophical truths? If it's neither of these, then you probably want your film to be entertaining.

Most films and videos today are created as entertainment. But what is entertainment? The dictionary describes entertainment as "something that amuses, pleases, or diverts, especially a performance or show." Today, in film, the line is often blurred between information and entertainment as well as between art or "specialty" films and entertainment. You see news shows that entertain and so-called art films that are not that different from Hollywood movies. The distinction is often not whether a film is entertaining, but how "commercial" it is. Will it appeal to the masses of people that Hollywood films and television productions are designed to appeal to, or is it likely to have a more limited audience, such as those attending film festivals or art house theaters?

All of these decisions affect not only aesthetic questions involved in how you shoot your film but also how you will go about trying to finance it. Should you go the independent route? Or should you try to get your movie idea produced through the Hollywood system? The next two chapters give you a sense of these two different ways to proceed in making a film.

The Least You Need to Know

- Cameras can have normal, wide, telephoto, or zoom lenses.
- Shots can vary by the camera's distance from the subject, the camera angle, or its movement.
- Film labs or on-line editing in video can correct color and add special effects.
- The script is an essential blueprint for all types of films. Don't start without it.

Chapter 4

Making an Independent Film

In This Chapter

- ◆ Tips for packaging your script
- ◆ Raising money from industry sources
- ◆ Raising money from private investors

Is your dream to become an independent filmmaker, someone like John Sayles (*Passion Fish*) or Christine Vachon (*Boys Don't Cry*), filmmakers who raise the money they need to produce their films without the backing of Hollywood studios? As an independent filmmaker, you have more control over your vision for your film than if you make your movie though the studio system. That is the good news. The bad news is that you will be responsible for every detail involved in producing the movie, including raising the financing for it—which can take up a considerable amount of your time and energy, and may be exceedingly difficult unless you have access to investors and sources of film financing.

There are many reasons for making an independent film besides the increased control you have over the outcome of the film. The movie you want to make may be about a controversial subject that you don't feel the studios or networks would touch. It may be about subject matter that is likely to appeal to a smaller audience than most Hollywood films. Whatever the reason for going the independent route, if you aren't willing to beg, borrow, and plead for money for your film, then skip this chapter and go on to Chapter 5, "Making a Hollywood Film." Independent filmmaking is not for you unless you are willing to tackle the business of raising money and have access to resources.

Packaging Your Script

Let's assume that you have what you believe is a great, unique script. It's called *Complete Idiot* and is a dark comedy about an idiot who tries to find true love by reading *The Complete Idiot's Guide to Romance*. You don't really see it as a big Hollywood movie, but rather as a small film that you think would do well at the art house theaters. You've read Chapter 6, "Act 1: Developing the Script," and you really think the script is good. You're ready to make the movie. What do you do next?

One of the first things many independent producers do with a script is to try to *package* it, which means attach certain *elements* to the script. The elements of a film package include actors or actresses attached to play the lead roles and a director with a track record or screen *credits*.

 Verbal Action

package   A presentation, including a script and the elements attached to the script, such as the director and actors for the starring roles.

elements   The people who will play a major part in the production of the film, including the director, producer, and cast for the leading roles.

credit   Acknowledgment in film titles of work on a produced film in one's capacity as a writer, director, actor, producer, or a member of the crew.

How do you go about getting elements attached to *Complete Idiot?* First, you have to get the script to the people you hope will be interested in it. For *Complete Idiot*, let's say you want to direct it yourself but you'd like to bring in a producer who has made one or more successful independent films to work with you. You have to contact that producer and hope that you can get him or her to read your script. Then, if the producer reads it and likes it, you have to hope that she actually has time to work on *Complete Idiot* with you. The same is true if you are a producer and are looking for a director to work with you. It may take some time before you find someone who is even interested, much less as passionate as you are about *Complete Idiot*.

While you are looking for a producing or directing partner for *Complete Idiot*, you should also try to attach actors and actresses for the lead roles. Start by making a list of the actors and actresses you would like to see in the film. Don't bother with lists of people for supporting roles—that is just *casting* and won't help you get financing. If Julia Roberts or Brad Pitt is on your list, cross them off. You are not going to get major stars who earn $20 million or more a picture to star in an independent film. A recent film, *The Mexican*, actually started out as an independent film but when Julia and Brad got interested, it soon became a Hollywood film. If big stars do by some miracle happen to read and like your movie, so will the studios, and it will no longer be an independent film. It will cost too much. If that happens, do not pass "Go," but immediately go to Chapter 5.

Also make sure that the actors or actresses you are trying to reach are well known enough to "mean something" to potential financing sources. What you want is not a megastar and not the unknown that you saw do a fantastic scene at an actor's showcase, but someone in between, someone with a "name" that is recognizable to potential investors or potentially of interest to a domestic or foreign distributor. The term "bankable" is sometimes used to convey which actors or actresses are of interest to financing sources. It comes from the idea that you can take that person's name to the "bank" and get financing. You will probably need a casting director on your team to help you create that list. A casting director knows what actors are currently "hot" enough to mean something to financiers.

Sometimes you might be able to attach an actor or actress who isn't necessarily that meaningful to financing sources but who is someone that other actors or actresses want to work with. For example, in the film *Gods and Monsters* (Bill Condon, 1998), Ian McKellen was the first actor to become attached to the project, followed by Lynn Redgrave. The producers were then able to interest Brendan Fraser, a more bankable star, who in addition to liking the script was interested in working with great actors like McKellen and Redgrave.

Let's say that you've made a list of five actors and five actresses as your top choices for the leads in *Complete Idiot*. How do you get your script to them? If any of the actors or actresses have *managers*, you are in luck. A manager might read your script, and if she likes it, might get her client to read it. Light candles and organize prayer vigils while the actor or actress reads the script. Voodoo or hope is about all you can do. If there is genuine interest, a letter from the actor or manager expressing the willingness of the star to be in the film should be very helpful to you in raising the money you need. If there is a manager, you can expect that person to demand a producing credit. It's worth it if you want to get your movie made.

If the actors and actresses you are interested in are only represented by *agents*, not managers, you may have a more difficult time getting them to read the script or show it to their clients. Many agents are only interested in reading scripts with *offers* attached—which is only possible when the financing is already in place. An offer to the agent includes the amount you can pay the actor.

Some of the large agencies, such as the William Morris Agency, have begun divisions that specialize in independent films. If this division of an agency becomes interested in *Complete*

Idiot, for example, the agents may help package the film with actors, actresses, and a director who are also represented by the agency. Then, they may become involved in helping put together financing for the film. The agency may have contacts for getting financing through avenues like foreign pre-sales, which I'll cover later in this chapter.

The disadvantage of getting an agency involved is that their first interest is in representing their clients, not necessarily in making the best possible film. The agency's help is contingent upon the participation of an interested actor or director who is their client, regardless of whether or not you feel that actor is really right for the lead in *Complete Idiot*.

Script Notes

To find out who represents an actor or actress, call the Screen Actors Guild (323-954-1600), and they'll tell you the name of the representative of the person you wish to contact. Some actors and actresses only have an agent, some only have a manager, and others will have both. Get the manager's or agent's number from the *Hollywood Agents and Managers Directory*, published by the Hollywood Creative Directory. Order at 310-315-4815 or 800-815-0503 (outside California).

Another important part of your film package is, of course, your budget. You need to know how much money you have to raise to make your film. Chapter 8, "Show Me the Money: The Budget," provides more details on how to prepare the budget for your film, or hire a production manager or line producer to prepare a budget for you.

You also might want to prepare a marketing analysis of your project. To do that, you will have to decide who is the likely audience for *Complete Idiot*. Is it older adults, thirtysomethings, teens? Then you should research other similar films that appealed to the same audience groups and find out how much money those films made from all sources. This information may be very helpful in convincing potential investors in your film that they will ultimately get their money back or even make money on their investment in *Complete Idiot*.

Packaging your film can be a long and difficult process. It requires ingenuity and flexibility, and it teaches you the first big lesson of filmmaking—it is a collaborative effort.

Financing Through Potential Domestic Distribution

A film can earn back the money it takes to produce it from a number of sources—a domestic theatrical release, foreign theatrical and television sales, domestic television license fees, and domestic home entertainment, which includes video and DVD sales. The U.S. theatrical release (domestic distribution), however, is most important because the other income from the film is often based on how well the film does in the initial theatrical release. How do you secure domestic distribution for your film? You can wait until you make your film and then arrange screenings for distributors, or you can try to arrange a distribution deal before you shoot the film and use that as leverage to raise money.

Verbal Action

casting   The act of finding actors and actresses for roles in a film, usually done by a casting director; or, in film financing, actors or actresses whose names don't help get financing for the film but are needed to fill out the cast.

agent   A person who represents the interests of others. A "talent agent" represents actors and actresses and a "literary agent" represents writers and directors.

manager   A person who manages the careers of actors, writers, or directors.

Let's say you have put a package together on *Complete Idiot*. You are going to produce it. You've got a director involved who directed a fairly successful independent film a year ago, and you've got letters from an actress and an actor who are committed to play the starring roles—maybe it's Julianna Margulies (the former *ER* nurse) and Tony Danza (in the title role). You plan to shoot in May when Tony is on *hiatus* from his *Family Law* television series. Where do you go for the money?

You can try to arrange a *negative pick-up* deal with a major or minor studio at this point. If you are successful, you will get most if not all of your financing, but you may lose some control of your film. A negative pick-up is an agreement by the studio to repay you for the cost of the negative upon delivery of the film. You basically present your package to the studio and, if they like it, they will give you a commitment to distribute the film. Unless the distributor you get the commitment from is on the verge of bankruptcy (not uncommon with some of the smaller independent distributors), you can usually take the distribution agreement to a commercial bank and get a loan using that agreement as collateral. The bank will discount the amount it loans you by the amount of its fee. So if the studio deal is for the entire amount of your budget, you will receive that amount less the amount of the bank's fees. Hopefully, you have included bank financing fees in your budget. A negative pick-up deal is often very complicated, so you will need an experienced entertainment attorney to negotiate and make the deal for you.

You might also use a distributor's negative pick-up commitment to go to a group of private investors. It should reassure them that once the film is completed, some of their money will be returned, because the studio usually pays the negotiated fee at the time the negative is delivered. Also, the negative pick-up guarantees that the film will make it to the theaters and have an opportunity to earn back their investment and maybe even some profits.

Films that are financed by negative pick-up deals with the major studios are often big Hollywood films produced by large production companies with a lot of clout in Hollywood, rather than the kind of small film we think of as an "independent" film. These companies want to do negative pick-ups rather than straight studio-financed movies, because they are generally able to make a better deal with the studio and therefore make more money if the studio only releases and doesn't finance the film. These movies are independently financed but are not true "independent" films, because the studio that distributes them usually requires certain approvals—such as of script, cast, and director—before the film is shot.

The *Hollywood Distributor's Directory* may help you at this step in the process. It contains the company names and contact numbers for the principal executives of over 550 film and television distributors. It's available by calling 310-315-4815 or 1-800-815-0503 (outside of California).

Cutaway

Each of the major studios distributes about twenty films a year. Of those, perhaps as many as seven (depending on the studio) are acquired through a negative pick-up. There are many minor studios or smaller distributors that also make negative pick-up deals with independent producers. You have to make sure that the distributor is financially stable before you make a deal with them. The negative pick-up distribution agreement is typically a lengthy contract that should be negotiated by an experienced entertainment attorney. It includes such negotiable items as the pick-up price, the rights granted, the territory, the term of distribution, and the producer's percentage of net profits.

Money, Money, Money: Investor Financing

The stereotype of the independent filmmaker is that of a young guy who gets his wealthy relatives to invest their money in a film. In reality, private investor financing of films is usually only a small part of the financing of independent films, and generally for those films that cost under $1 million. Most sophisticated private investors know that investing in films can be a very risky business. Some investors are attracted to film investments because they relish the chance to meet an actor or actress, spend the day on a set, or see their name in the credits. Not very many people, however, either have, or are willing to risk losing, large sums of money for those privileges. And large sums—often in the millions—are what you need to make a feature film.

It definitely can be done, however. I have a friend who spent years—many more than it took to write or produce the film—going around pitching her film at small house parties organized by friends. She had structured an arrangement whereby the minimum investment was about $25,000 but people who had less to invest could participate by being a part of a small investment group that invested at least $25,000. Somehow, after scores of house parties all over the country, she managed to raise about $900,000 to make her film.

It made most of its money back in its theatrical release and did a brisk business in video, so her investors were eventually paid back and probably made some money. The producer/director, who had the time to spend years raising money because she lived off a trust fund, went on to a career directing television movies.

The federal government's Securities and Exchange Commission (SEC) has rules for how one can raise financing through investments. Do not go out and start telling people you have a hot movie idea and begin collecting their checks without getting an attorney who specializes in SEC law to help you with what you need to do. And be forewarned—it costs money to raise money. It will cost you attorney's fees, various filing fees, and may also cost you consulting fees, all of which could add up to $100,000.

Verbal Action

offer   A proposal for work on a film in exchange for money, credit, and a share of profits. At minimum, an offer includes the actor's fee and the start date of the production.

hiatus   A gap in television series production—the time of year when a series is not in production, usually sometime between May and July, giving the actors in the series time to work on other projects.

Creating a Structure to Receive Funds

There are many ways to structure your company in order to be able to receive investments. Unless you plan on getting all the money you need from a single investor, you will have to create a company for either a *private placement* or a *public offering*. This is an area where you will need legal advice and help, but the following will give you a general idea of the types of structures available for receiving investments:

◆ **Limited partnerships:** This is a business agreement that includes at least one general partner (such as the film producer) and one or more limited partners. The general partner makes decisions and is usually liable for breaches of contract, and so on.

◆ **S corporation:** This is a corporation that is taxed differently from a regular corporation. It is limited to 35 individual shareholders and is often used for the purpose of raising money for a single film since the profits will not be reinvested in the business, but will be distributed to the shareholders.

◆ **Limited liability company:** This is a business structure that is often used in raising money for films that combines the tax benefits of limited partnerships with the limited liability benefits provided by a corporation.

◆ **Small corporate offering registration:** This is a form of public offering designed to reduce the costs and paperwork involved in public offerings. This offering requires the completion of "Form U-7," which sometimes can be done without the assistance of an attorney. The form can only be used, however, when the amount of money being raised does not exceed $1 million.

Counterpoint

It generally costs from $50 to $1000 in state filing fees to set up a limited partnership or corporation. Attorneys' fees for the preparation of a feature-film offering memorandum in accordance with SEC guidelines and related work may range between $10,000 and $50,000, depending on the experience of the attorney. In addition, you should expect costs for printing and binding the offering memorandum, a very formal document.

◆ **Regulation A offering:** This is a small public offering that allows the corporation or limited partnership to raise up to $5 million.

◆ **Regulation S-B and S-1 offerings:** These are types of complicated public offerings used for raising large amounts of money from the public.

Creating a Business Plan

A business plan that you create will be the basic selling tool that you will use to entice investors into putting their money into your film. Portions of your business plan can also be used by your attorney in his or her preparation of the more formal offering memorandum. The business plan is similar to the package discussed earlier but is more appropriate for those investors who are not part of the film industry.

Your business plan should include a synopsis of the script, narrative biographies of the key persons attached to the project and a "use of proceeds" section, which is essentially the top sheet of the film budget. It should also include a market analysis, financial projections, and any letters or guarantees of financial support already obtained.

The business plan might be used to raise the seed money that you will need to pay for the next step of creating a legal structure and doing a private or public offering.

Approaching Potential Investors

Depending on the type of offering you are doing, you will have to approach either a limited number of people (whom you know and who have a certain net worth) as part of a private offering or many people that you may or may not know in a public offering. It's generally a good idea to know that you have a few people interested in investing before you go to the expense of preparing an offering memorandum. Once you have some people committed to investing in your project, it will be easier to find others. Ask your investors and everyone you know if they know other people who might invest.

The important thing to remember when approaching people is that you are offering them an opportunity. If your film is successful, they could earn a lot of money because of your talent, skill, and creativity, and the talents and skills of your collaborators. On the other hand, it's also important that you do not attempt to hide the very real risks of investing in a film. Even though you don't intend it, your hard-working uncle could lose his shirt.

Verbal Action _____

negative pick-up   A financial deal made with a film distributor, usually before the start of production, to distribute the film when it is completed.

private placement   The sale of securities or limited partnerships through private contacts to a limited number of investors.

public offering   The sale of securities to the public, usually with the services of an underwriter, in a transaction that must be registered with the Securities and Exchange Commission.

Financing Through Foreign Pre-Sales

Another way of raising money for your film is through pre-sales or commitments by distributors in foreign territories to handle your film. Most of the foreign pre-sales are done at film markets such as the American Film Market (AFM), held annually in Los Angeles. Using the package you have prepared, you, your sales representative or your U.S. distributor if you have one, tries to sell *Complete Idiot* to a buyer in each foreign territory and medium (video, theatrical, television, and so on). When someone wants to buy a territory or medium, they give you a guarantee that they will pay a specific amount upon delivery of the completed film to that person in exchange for the right to keep the revenue from that territory/medium for a certain length of time or until a certain amount of revenue is reached.

It is usually wise to use foreign sales representatives to help you with foreign pre-sales. This area is very specialized and a sales representative will not only help you prepare the most attractive package—usually including full-color pictures of your stars and other attention-grabbing graphics and photos—but will also know the going rate for different territories and can therefore negotiate you a better deal for each area she sells. The sales rep will, of course, take a percentage of the revenue she brings in to the project.

You can locate a foreign sales agent in the *Hollywood Distributors Directory*. The *International Film Buyers Directory*, published by the same company, will also be helpful at this stage. It lists the names and contact information for film buyers from 45 countries.

As with a negative pick-up guarantee, you can use the contracts from foreign pre-sales as collateral for a loan from a commercial bank that deals in film financing. Piece by piece, dollar by dollar, you will begin to put together the money needed to make your film.

If making an independent film sounds too overwhelming, you can always try the studio system. But, as you'll see in the next chapter, breaking into Hollywood's film and television industries is not easy, no matter how you approach it.

The Least You Need to Know

- ◆ The most important thing you can do to raise money for your independent film is to attach well-known actors or actresses to the project.

- ◆ Once you have an attractive package, including stars and a director or producer with credits attached to your project, you may be able to arrange the financing of your film through a negative pick-up arrangement with a domestic distributor.

- ◆ Raising money from private investors can be a complicated and costly process, but it is often done by first-time filmmakers with very low-budget films.

- ◆ Foreign pre-sales are another method of raising financing and should be done with the help of a foreign sales representative.

Chapter 5

Making a Hollywood Film

In This Chapter

- ◆ Getting an agent
- ◆ Getting a production company interested in your project
- ◆ Making film and television deals
- ◆ Navigating the development process

Hollywood is basically a closed shop. It's difficult to break into and requires more than simply talent for success. You must have perseverance, total dedication, and usually a bit of insanity to succeed in Hollywood. The odds are against you, but if you have the guts, stamina, and gambling instinct to go for it, then this chapter is for you.

Why is Hollywood so difficult to break into? You always hear studio and television executives say that they are looking for new talent. If that's the case, then why don't they want to make your movie or even read your script? Because there is enormous competition—so many people want to make movies, and there are a limited number of movies made each year by the studios and television networks. Compared to other industries, there is a lot of money to be made if one does succeed in Hollywood, so everyone has a script they hope to sell.

Hollywood is also not immune from nepotism, favoritism, cronyism, or sex and race discrimination. The saying, "In Hollywood, it's not what you know, it's who you know" is still very much a reality. So if you aren't first cousins with Steven Spielberg or Michael Eisner, read on. It will help to at least know something about how Hollywood works.

Selling the Script

Everything starts with a great script—one that is fresh, unique, and at the same time commercial enough to appeal to a large audience. Hollywood film studios are simply not interested in making "small" films. They have too much overhead to be able to afford to make films that they don't expect will earn back a lot of money. The companies are also thinking about whether or not the potential film will have an appeal not just domestically but around the world.

Television movies also have to have a wide appeal, both in the United States and globally. Although there are a few cable networks that may air more off-beat, eccentric, or art house films, those films are usually acquired by television after they have been completed, not financed or produced by those networks.

Even though writers in Hollywood are treated worse than any of the other key players in making a movie—they are frequently replaced and "rewritten," blamed when the film fails but not mentioned when it succeeds and generally paid less than directors—a writer is nevertheless the most essential person in the process. Without a script, there is no movie. If you are a good writer and have written a particularly good script, you have a better chance of making it in Hollywood than if you simply want to direct or produce a film.

Script Notes

There are a number of very good screenwriting contests into which you can enter a script. If the script then wins a prize, it may help you get an agent or production company interested. There are hundreds of minor contests, but the two that are particularly respected by Hollywood development executives are the Nicholl Fellowships in Screenwriting and the AFI/Maui Writers Conference International Screenwriting Contest. For a complete list of all screenwriting contests, go to the Movie Bytes website at www.moviebytes.com.

If you are a first-time producer or director but not a writer yourself, you still need to start with a script. If you can find a first-time writer who has written a script that you love, you should "attach" yourself to that script, usually through an *option/purchase* agreement. An option gives you the right to attempt to set up the script with a studio or other financing. The writer, for consideration—which could be as low as one dollar or as high as many thousands of dollars—grants you an option for a period of time that can be as short as a month or as long as several years. The agreement is usually renewable for another period of time upon paying an additional sum.

Generally, it's a good idea to have an entertainment attorney negotiate the agreement. It has to contain an ultimate purchase price and all the deal points, including what the writer will receive when and if the project gets financed by a studio or other financing entity. Occasionally, however, some producers without much money negotiate and draw up agreements themselves, based on a sample option/purchase agreement.

Getting an Agent

The first step in getting a script read by a studio, television network, large production company, or even by a smaller producer who might have enough clout to help get the movie made is to get a literary agent or manager.

How do you do that? It's not easy. You can get a list of agents from the Writers Guild (213-782-4502) or you can buy the *Hollywood Agents and Managers Directory*. But even with a list of agents and managers, you can't just start sending your script out because most of them will not accept unsolicited submissions. If you know someone who is represented by a particular agency, you can ask if she will ask the agent to read your script.

You can also try to get an entertainment lawyer to help you find an agent. Agents will often accept submissions made through entertainment lawyers, but you have to find one who has good contacts with agents. You will also usually have to pay the entertainment lawyer. Sometimes an attorney likes your work and figures if you succeed you'll come back to him or her with more work, but generally you will have to pay an hourly fee. Some attorneys in Hollywood will accept 5 percent of what you ultimately make instead of their hourly fee, but that is only if they really believe in your project's success.

Finally, you can simply query the agent with a letter asking that she read your script. Your query letter should be short, with just the basics: a *logline* describing the script, a short paragraph about the script and a short paragraph about you. Do not waste the agent's time by talking about your cat or your hobbies. Only include information about yourself that is relevant to the agent—if you went to film school, have won an award, or placed high in a screenwriting contest, for example. Your query should also have a self-addressed, stamped envelope to make it easy for the agent to reply.

If you are successful in getting interest from an agent, don't sign an agency agreement, which will commit you to paying the agent a commission (generally 10 percent for the sale of a script) for a particular period of time, until you meet with the agent and feel reassured that she is someone you can work with. Don't be afraid to ask questions of the agent in the meeting, such as the following:

◆ Who are some of your other clients?

◆ May I speak with one or more of them?

◆ What are your plans or ideas for my script?

◆ Who are some of your contacts in the industry?

Ask the other writers who are represented by the agency what they think of the agents. Also try to find out what kind of reputation the agency has in the industry. They may be known as agents who take on clients indiscriminately and do not have high enough standards for the material they represent. You don't want to be represented by an agent with that kind of reputation. You do want an agent who is excited about your script and has good relationships with the executives of studios and large production companies, so that your script will be read by them.

If you are lucky enough to have a choice between going with a large agency like Creative Artists Agency (CAA), William Morris, or International Creative Management (ICM) or with a smaller "boutique" agency, what should you do? Most writers or producers would jump at the chance to be represented by one of the large agencies because they have tremendous access to the studios and networks, but there is a possible downside. It's easy for you and your script to get put on the back burner as the agents deal with their established clients who will most likely earn them a much larger commission. So the decision is one you must make carefully, based on how you feel about the individual agents involved.

 Verbal Action _____

option   The exclusive right, obtained for an option fee against a purchase price, to sell a script, book, or life story rights within a specified period of time.

logline   A pithy, one-sentence description of a script or story, often using other movies as a reference, such as: *Rambo* meets *Gone with the Wind*: the epic story of a hard-driving confederate commando in love with a high-strung Southern belle.

trades   The film and television industry trade papers, *Daily Variety* and *The Hollywood Reporter*.

Once you have an agent, don't just sit by the phone and wait for the offers to come in. Anything you can do to help your agent sell your script will be appreciated. Go out and meet people in the industry and read the *trades* (*Variety* and *The Hollywood Reporter*) to learn who is doing what. It can be depressing to read the trades because it may seem like everyone in town but you has a million deals going. In fact, much of what is in the trades is just hype—everyone wants everyone else to think they are really busy and important—but every once in a while, you might find out that a production company just got financing and is looking for material or that a studio has a deal with a particular actor or director that you think might be interested in your script.

Depending on your agent, you might find that she will always want to contact a production company on your behalf—so it's best if you just forward your suggestions or ideas to your agent. Try to do so in a short fax or e-mail so as not to use too much of your agent's precious time. Or, your agent may not mind if you send out some initial queries about your project to production companies and then, if the company wants to see the project, the agent will take over from there. Whatever the arrangement, just make sure you and your agent agree on the strategy.

Getting a Producer

Let's say you've tried but failed to get an agent. How else can you get access to the people who make movies in Hollywood? Even as an unrepresented writer, you can query production companies about your project. To get a list of producers working in Hollywood, you need the bible: *The Hollywood Creative Directory*. Updated three times a year, this book contains a list of over 1,700 companies and includes the names and titles of their top executives, the company's credits, and whether the company has a film or television deal with a studio or a deal with a larger production company that has access to financing.

Based on the company's credits or anything else you might learn about it, make a list of the companies that you think might be interested in your script. You can query them by mail, fax, or e-mail, but however you do it, make it easy for them to respond to you. If you do an e-mail query, don't expect the executive to open a long attachment or go to a website. Simply write a short, polite letter addressed to a specific individual at the company that gives a logline and has a short paragraph describing your project—one that will make it stand out from the dozens of other queries the company receives each day. If you send a letter by snail mail, don't forget to enclose a self-addressed, stamped envelope (SASE) so it's easy for the executive to reply.

I don't really recommend faxing the company unless you live in the same city as the company and it's easy for them to fax or call you back. It's also not a great idea to pitch your project on the phone. Much of the business of Hollywood producers and executives is done on the phone. They have to talk to agents, network and studio executives, writers, directors, and actors they are already working with, so a call from an unknown, unrepresented writer is simply an annoyance. You usually won't get an executive on the phone anyway—just a very busy assistant. On the other hand, a letter, e-mail, or even a fax can be responded to at the convenience of the executive, not in the middle of his or her busy day.

CAUTION

Counterpoint

Writers often worry about their work being stolen. To protect your material, copyright your script by putting a copyright symbol (©), your name, and the year on the cover page of the script. Also, you can register it with the copyright office in Washington, D.C. (202-707-3000), and with the Writers Guild Registration Service (213-783-4540). Most important, learn your craft. If your script is well-executed, a company is more likely to buy it than to hire another writer to rip off the idea.

If your query is successful and the company wants to see the script, send it with a nice cover letter repeating the information in your original query and indicating that you are sending the script at a particular individual's request. Don't write: "Hi Bob, Here's my script, Best, Joan" as though you expect the executive to remember you. Producers get too many queries to recall yours.

It's also a good idea to enclose a synopsis of your story that is no longer than two single-spaced pages. A good synopsis simply tells the whole story, without hyping it and without cliffhangers. For example, the beginning of the synopsis of your script, *Complete Idiot*, might be: "Tony is a complete idiot. He wakes up one morning, ..." It should not be: "The funniest, most heartwarming story since *Forrest Gump*, *Complete Idiot* is the story of Tony, a complete idiot who wakes up one morning ..."

A synopsis is valuable because in Hollywood most scripts are initially read by script readers rather than by executives or producers. Readers prepare *coverage* for the executives, which includes a synopsis of the story as well as the reader's comments, criticisms, and recommendation. If you have provided a good, clear synopsis of the story without a lot of hype, you will make the reader's job easier. She may use it in her own coverage, in fact.

Cutaway

Occasionally today and more frequently in the past, films have been sold on a verbal "pitch" of an idea to an executive. Successful screenwriters with lots of credits may take a meeting with an executive, tell the story of the film in a 15- to 20-minute pitch, and get a contract to write the script. That is not likely to happen to a novice writer. You should nevertheless learn how to pitch a story because your agent may be able to set up meetings for you with executives once they have read your script. They may like your writing style but feel that your script is not commercial enough or just not right for them. They may want to meet you and hear your other story ideas in a pitch meeting.

Making the Deal

So far, you've been pounding the pavement with your script under your arm. Perhaps you've found an agent or perhaps a production company has optioned your script. Now the moment you've dreamed of happens—the agent or producer calls and says the studio or network loves the project and wants to make a deal.

What can you expect in that deal? First, if you have given a production company an option on your script, it was probably negotiated by an attorney, and all the basic points of your deal, including the purchase price for the script and your fee for writing another draft, will already be outlined in the option agreement. The studio will generally take over that option and put your script into *development*.

If there has not been an option and your agent is negotiating a deal directly with a studio, then she will negotiate the price for the sale of your script and the fee for you to do another draft of it based on the studio's notes—if there is to be another draft, and there almost always is at least one, if not many more drafts. Your agent should also negotiate a production bonus, profit participation, and the price for sequel rights and rights in other mediums. The deals are fairly complicated, and writers who are represented by agents should also have an entertainment attorney look over their deals.

 Verbal Action _____

coverage   In the film industry, a written synopsis, critique, and recommendation prepared by a script reader employed by a studio or production company.

development   In the film industry, the term used for the process of getting a script ready for production.

signatory   A production company, studio, or network that has signed the negotiated Writers Guild Minimum Basic Agreement (MBA).

Staying Attached

The important thing to realize when you sell your script to a studio is that you are giving up your baby. You no longer own the pages that you agonized over. They now belong to the studio to do with as it wishes. The studio may decide to pay you off and not even let you do the rewrite that your agent or attorney has negotiated for you to do. They have the right to pay you but not "play" (read: use) you. Instead of letting you take another crack at the script, they may bring in another, more established, writer to rewrite your work. How can you prevent that?

There are a few things you can do to stay attached to your project, but it's often difficult. First, you can have your attorney try to negotiate some sort of associate producer or consulting position on the film so you can stay involved even if other writers are brought in.

Script Notes

When you sell a script to a studio or production company that is a *signatory* to the Writers Guild, you will be eligible to join the Guild. It's important to join the Guild for a number of reasons, including: Members of the Guild are respected more than non-members, you will get health insurance and pension and welfare benefits, and the Guild's legal department will take your side in any dispute you have with a studio or production company.

Most important, in your first meeting with the studio executives—a meeting that usually takes place before the deal is made—you need to appear absolutely terrific and indispensable to them. Show that you are cooperative and genuinely interested in all of their suggestions—even when there are three executives or producers in the room all making different, often contradictory, comments on and suggestions for the script. Everyone likes to feel that their ideas are heard and considered by the writer. Be relaxed and fun to be with even when the executives or producers are saying things that make absolutely no sense or seem like they will totally ruin your script. Unlike people from different sides of the aisle in Washington, D.C., for example, the culture in Hollywood is not really confrontational. People like to have a good time when working and don't like it when you are upset, defensive, or argumentative.

Surviving Development Hell

If you are successful enough to stay attached for one or more drafts on your script, you will have officially entered what is known in Hollywood as "development hell." Development hell is what often seems like a never-ending process of rewriting and rewriting a script to please everyone involved (except, of course, the writer)—the studio executives, the producer, the director, and any stars who might have signed on to the project. Everyone will want to give his or her input and you, the writer, will be tearing your hair out trying to please them all.

The other dreadful thing that happens during development hell besides endless rewrites is when people who have already become attached to the project—like a director or star—drop out or when the studio decides for whatever reason that it doesn't want to go forward with the film. If your project is still in the option period (usually one to three years), they will simply let the option period run out and neither extend the option nor exercise it by paying the required price. Sometimes you will wait for days, weeks, or even months to find out whether the studio will be going forward with your project or will be giving up on it.

If the studio has already exercised the option (purchased your script) and decides not to go forward with making the movie, they will put it into *turnaround*—try to get some money back by making it available for another studio to buy. Development hell is called development hell because there is always a very real possibility that, even after years of work, a script may never get made by the studio that optioned it, or by any studio.

Why, despite complaints from everyone involved, does this process remain so awful? The answer is partly because movies cost so much to make. The studios can lose a lot of money on a movie that fails at the box office, so a lot of time is put into trying to make sure that the script is good. Unfortunately, it often turns out that a decent script may get worse during development hell.

Of course, every once in a while the process does work. A script that was optioned by the studio may actually turn into a better script after a period of development. The movie may be greenlighted, and it will then emerge from development hell and go into pre-production.

Developing Television Movies

If you feel your script or idea is better suited for television than for film, you will go through basically the same steps of trying to find an agent or a production company first. The difference is that you will be looking for an agent who specializes in television rather than motion pictures and generally for a production company that specializes in television projects.

In particular, you should take your project to a large television production company that does *deficit-financing* or one that has a deal with the network on which you want to see your movie aired. Deficit financing is when the company advances a portion of the cost of production of the film (usually not more than one-third) and is paid a license fee by the network for the balance of the cost of producing the film. A license fee gives the network the right to air the film a certain number of times over a certain number of years.

 Verbal Action _____

turnaround   In the film industry, when a script that was purchased by a studio is no longer being developed by said company and is available for purchase by other companies.

deficit financing   The partial production financing of a television movie or series episode by a production company, giving the company the ownership of the copyright of the film and the ability to make money through foreign television or other distribution sales.

treatment   An initial written narrative telling of a story, which a writer or production company wishes to develop into a script.

Unlike feature films, television movies can sometimes be sold without a script. If you have, for example, the rights to a life story ("life story rights") that would make a good television movie, you and a production company may be able to sell the idea based on a package that includes a *treatment*—a telling of the basic events of the story in narrative rather than script form.

The good thing about television is that your movie has a better chance of actually getting made if a TV network puts it into development than it does when it is being developed by a film studio. The downside, of course, is that it will be shot on a much shorter production schedule and for a much smaller budget than a studio film.

The Least You Need to Know

♦ Because of overwhelming competition, it is not easy to sell a script in Hollywood, but it helps to know how the business works.

♦ To query an agent or a production company, make it easy for the busy executive. Keep your letters short and include an SASE.

♦ You can try to survive development hell by being a mensch and writing your heart out.

♦ The chance of a movie getting made that is sold to television is generally greater than one that is being developed by a film studio.

Part 2

Opening Sequence: Script and Pre-Production

You've established the fact that you want to make a movie. So now let's get down to the nitty-gritty of filmmaking, which includes three basic phases: pre-production, production, and post-production.

This part of the book covers everything that must be done before you start to roll the camera, or pre-production—and that's a lot. First and foremost, you have to write or hire someone to write a good script. Then you need to prepare a shooting schedule and budget. Next you must hire your cast and crew. Finally, you need to choose your locations and make all the arrangements for equipment and taking care of your team during the shoot.

Chapter 6

Act I: Developing the Script

In This Chapter

- ◆ The elements of a story
- ◆ The creation of complex and interesting characters
- ◆ Common reasons scripts are rejected
- ◆ Documentary and short film scripts

Screenwriting is a difficult art form or—as some call it—craft. Yet many people think that they can knock off a script and sell it for big bucks. Some feel it's so easy that they write a script without even learning the basics of screenwriting. Others read books and spend a lot of money taking screenwriting courses. It's certainly very important to learn the craft, but even with knowledge, you still have to have talent. You must have a good story sense, a good visual memory and imagination, a snappy, clear, concise writing style, and a good ear for dialogue to write a good script. You can develop into a better writer through learning more about your craft if you have those writing skills. If you don't have some basic talent, however, you won't be able to write a script that sells.

If you can't write very well but you want to make a movie, you should still learn the elements of a good screenplay because you will need to evaluate scripts by other writers. Does a script have good dramatic structure? Does it open strongly? What about the ending? Everything in filmmaking starts with a script—even documentaries and short films. No matter what role you plan to play in the making of movies, learn as much as you can about what makes a good script and what makes a terrific one.

As in any business, there is an element of luck involved in achieving success in Hollywood. A friend recently sold a pilot for a television series to a major production company. She had met one of the executives of the company when she was getting a manicure—a bit of serendipity. But beyond luck, serendipity, and persistence, the only real rule in Hollywood is that a great script might sell, a good script might sell, and a bad script will not.

What's the Story?

All scripts start with a story idea or concept. How do you come up with a good concept for a film? Writers are usually most successful when they write about what they know or what interests them. That's because what separates good writing of all kinds from bad writing are the details. Writing that is broad and general is boring, whereas novels, nonfiction books, and scripts filled with interesting detail fascinate us. It's the small details about a character that tell us the most about him or her.

For example, which sentence is more interesting? "The dog's owner was an anxious 40-year-old woman." Or, "The dog's owner, 40, hid behind sunglasses and fidgeted with her bangle bracelets." The second sentence conjures up an image of an anxious woman, but the first sentence only tells us that the woman is anxious—we don't see a very clear picture of her in our minds. The second sentence is visual, the first one isn't. The second sentence gives us details, the first one doesn't.

The above example illustrates not only the importance of detail but also the other basic maxim of good fiction writing, which is "show, don't tell." In writing for film, a visual medium, it is not just important—it is essential—that you find ways to show visually the emotions and feelings of characters in the plot's action rather than by having characters convey that information in dialogue.

Bad dialogue in screenplays is filled with exposition, which is background information that helps us understand the characters and the action. In good scripts, the writer finds ways to show or reveal expository material without simply telling it. For example, let's say it's the

> **Script Notes**
>
> You are more likely to be able to show the details and create pictures in the minds of the reader if you are writing about a subject you know and love, rather than about a subject you do not know so well but think you should write about because it is "commercial." What will make an obscure subject more commercial is your ability to bring it to life with interesting detail.

moment in the story when one character, Joe, realizes that his wife, Susan, has killed his rich father. An unskilled writer might write:

> Joe
>
> (looking at Susan)
>
> Susan, it was you. How could you have killed my father?

Whereas, a more skilled writer might write:

> Joe looks at Susan. His eyes widen and a wave of nausea comes over him. He knows.
>
> Joe
>
> My God, Susan. How could you?

So, the first step is to find an idea for a story that involves something you know about or are fascinated by enough to research and learn about. Let's say you want to write about the world of perfume-making and, in particular, people who work in that world who have a heightened sense of smell. Next, decide what genre you plan to write. Is your movie about this world and its characters a comedy? A thriller? A serious drama? You happen to think perfume-making is funny, so you will be writing a comedy set in the world of perfume-making. Once you have this great idea for a script, what do you do next?

From Concept to Script

All good stories start with the characters, so your first step should be to get to know your characters. Begin with your main character, or *protagonist*, and write a short biography of her. How did the character get to the place where she is at the beginning of the story? That is the *backstory* on the character. The lead character in your script—let's say it's called *Something Is Rotten*—is a woman who smells perfumes for a living. Some questions to answer about her include:

- How did she get that job?
- What is her age, her race, her ethnic background?
- What kind of education does she have?
- What are her favorite things to do for fun?
- What has her life been like so far—has it been happy, sad, eventful, or uneventful?
- What about her special ability to distinguish smells—are there downsides to that?
- Who are her friends, relatives?
- Is she married, single, divorced, gay, or straight?
- Does she have children?
- Is she pretty or plain?

You get the idea. Learn as much as you can about her because out of her character will flow your story. All good plots are really a development of the main character as she moves toward a goal and is stymied or blocked by conflict with an opponent or *antagonist*.

In the same way that you have just gotten to know the main character, next develop the opponent's backstory. Let's say that the opponent or antagonist in *Something Is Rotten* is a robber who has a disease that gives him a particularly bad body odor. This smelly guy, like our main character, also has a heightened sense of smell. He, too, has become an expert in perfumes, which he uses to hide his offensive body odor. He is known as the "perfumed robber" because wherever he strikes, the air is filled with the scent of beautiful perfumes.

A good story has an interesting antagonist or a "worthy" opponent. She must challenge the main character and make the achievement of the protagonist's desires more difficult, therefore making the story more interesting.

 Verbal Action _____

protagonist   The main hero or heroine in a screenplay, play, or other literary work, whose actions drive the plot.

antagonist   The opponent in a screenplay, play, or other literary work, who opposes the main character.

backstory   Facts and background information about a character that make the character who she is. The details in a character's backstory may or may not come out in the story.

So far, in writing your script, you've been working on creating your main character and the opponent. As you work on the backstory for each of them, you also will begin to imagine and develop the secondary characters who are part of each of their lives. Now, it's time to start thinking about the structure of your story.

Three-Act Dramatic Structure

The concept of dramatic structure goes back to Aristotle and the ancient Greeks. You don't have to read Aristotle, however, to understand it. Essentially, all good stories have a beginning, middle, and end. The beginning is the first act, the middle is the second act, and the end is the third act.

As George M. Cohan, a famous old-time writer, producer, singer, and dancer, and the subject of the movie *Yankee Doodle Dandy*, put it: "In the first act get your man up a tree, in the second act throw stones at him and in the third act, get him down out of the tree."

Those are the three essential stages in the structure of all films, TV dramas, and plays. The main character will be confronted with a problem or crisis in the first act, then that problem will be intensified in the second act and finally resolved in the third act.

The crisis comes out of the conflict between the main character's desires and the desires of the opponent. The main character wants something and the opponent either wants the same thing or wants something that will make the main character's desire impossible.

Character Arc and Premise

The other important aspect of the structure of a good script is the growth and evolution of the main character in the story. Often described as the *character arc*, the main character must grow or learn some moral lesson in the course of the story. The moral lesson she learns is usually something that is a universal theme—a lesson that is relevant to us all.

Script Notes

It's helpful to watch movies and identify the plot points or turning points as they occur. In most movies, particularly Hollywood films, you will notice that something happens about 25 to 30 minutes into the film that complicates, changes, and intensifies the action, ending the first act and beginning the second. Then, perhaps an hour later, as the end approaches, another surprising twist occurs, causing a change that sends us into the final act of the story.

In Ibsen's famous play *A Doll's House*, for example, the main character, Nora, moves from being a very childlike, immature person who, in conflict with her paternalistic, stubborn husband, develops into a much wiser, grown-up woman by the end. We watch the crisis that forces her to grow and change—her character arc. As she tragically loses her relationship with her husband and children, she learns that there cannot be true love between unequals. Her husband loved her as a kind of perfect little "doll." As a woman with flaws, even those flaws she deeply regrets and has grown to see were wrong, he cannot accept her. She must therefore leave and live life on her own.

Closely related to what the main character learns is the *premise* of the story. The premise is the theme or what the author of the script or play wants to say to us about life. The premise of *A Doll's House*, for example, like what Nora learns, is that "inequality between men and women leads to tragedy or unhappiness." This play, written in 1879, is still frequently produced, in part because we are still dealing with the inequality of the sexes in our own society. Women who marry very rich men even today often become dependent "trophy wives." Of course, Ibsen's use of the language, his development of the characters, and his building of the conflict throughout the play is superb and that would make the play enjoyable even if its message was outdated; in fact, it still strikes a chord with contemporary audiences.

Plot Points, Climax, and Resolution

If the beginning of the story, the first act, sets up a problem or crisis, the second must build that crisis to an even higher level, ending at the plot point at the end of the second act and paving the way for the climax and resolution of the crisis in the third act. The crisis or problem can often be stated as a question that will then be answered at the climax of the story. In our script, *Something Is Rotten*, the question might be "Will our heroine catch the perfumed robber before he catches her?" In a play like *A Doll's House*, the question is "Will Nora's husband discover her actions and, if so, will he forgive her?"

The climax is the point where the tension created by the drama is over because we now know the answer to the question we have been following from the beginning of the story. After the climax, you only need to write a resolution—a few more pages to end the story and show the audience where the characters are at now that the conflict is over. Since the main character has grown in some way through the experience, we will see evidence of that growth by something she does in the end.

 Verbal Action

character arc A term used to describe the growth and development of a character throughout the course of a story.

premise The theme, thesis, central idea, or motivating force of a film or play. A premise is also a thumbnail synopsis of the story.

plot point An event or turning point in a story that spins the action in another direction. In three-act structure, there should be a plot point at the end of act one and act two.

In the recent thriller *Don't Say a Word* (Gary Felder, 2001), the crisis is set up when the daughter of an upper-class psychiatrist played by Michael Douglas is kidnapped. The turning point or plot point at the end of the second act is when it looks like the young mental patient has remembered incorrectly the number of her father's grave and they will all be killed. The climax is when the bad guys are killed and Douglas and his kidnapped daughter are finally safe. In the resolution, we see how he has grown from the experience as he goes to the young patient and brings her into his family circle.

Build It Visually

You now have most of the basic tools you need to start writing. You know your characters and your genre. You have a vague idea of the beginning, middle, and end of the story and the plot points at the end of acts one and two. As you begin to sketch out your story, imagine it visually. Think of the images that will help create the world in which your screenplay takes place.

If, for example, you are working on *Something Is Rotten*, about the world of perfume, even though it's primarily a world of smells, you have to think of images that will convey that to us. You might open with an image of women from all walks of life spraying themselves with perfume and then cut to noses smelling little vials, until you land on the nose of your perfume-testing heroine and widen out to the pleasure on her face as she finds a particularly wonderful odor.

A Scene Outline

Some screenwriters like to write out the beats or scenes of a script before actually starting to write. I think it's a good idea, but not everyone does it. If you do make an outline, do it by acts and scenes within acts. Your first act will usually have about 20 scenes. The second act will have about 40 to 60 scenes and the third act, the shortest, will only have about 10 scenes.

Each major scene is like a microcosm of the whole script. The scene should have a beginning, middle, and end and should have conflict between the characters. Each scene should also move the story along. Never include a scene, no matter how interesting, if it is irrelevant to the story or plot.

CAUTION

Counterpoint

Scripts must be professionally formatted. Don't fudge with the margins or fonts if you want to sell your script. When typed in Courier 12-point font and with proper margins, each script page averages out to about one minute of screen time. An average two-hour movie script is therefore about 120 pages. Action movies, with less dialogue and more description of action, are usually shorter. There are several screenwriting software programs available that will enable you to format your script properly.

Top Ten Reasons Scripts Get Rejected in Hollywood

So far I've described some of the basic elements of screenwriting. How can you learn whether a script you are working on will sell? You can't, but you can learn the reasons why it might be rejected.

I have worked as a writer in Hollywood for over 15 years, and although I have been fortunate enough to have worked in both television and film, it wasn't until my partner and I started our own literary management company and sister production company that I really learned what makes a "salable" script. It took reading hundreds, if not thousands, of script submissions to understand the standards that a script must meet for it to have a chance in the extremely competitive market. I developed these "top 10" reasons why scripts are rejected for myself and for readers who work with us. The following list can only predict rejection, not necessarily success. Nevertheless, if you don't make sure your script is free of these common reasons for rejection, you will be wasting your time trying to get it sold in Hollywood.

In David Letterman style, the top 10 reasons scripts get rejected are:

10. **Bad dialogue:** This is the easiest to spot of all the reasons for rejection. Your script will quickly be recycled if the dialogue is full of exposition or just doesn't sound like the way people talk.

9. **Unprofessional formatting:** A script is a blueprint for a movie. There are very specific standards that have been developed over time for writing a script so that the script, when shot, will average approximately a minute per page. The font type and size, the width of the dialogue, and other standards are all designed with that in mind. A script that is formatted improperly gives a bad first impression. Companies often reject such scripts without even reading them.

8. **A familiar story:** Very often scripts are submitted that are not bad, but there is nothing new or original about them. It seems like we have seen this movie many times before on television or at the theater. You may wonder then: Why are there so many movies that seem the same? The answer is that those movies or TV movies are written by established writers rather than by new ones trying to break in, usually from ideas of established producers. They might be able to get away with a lack of originality for a while because they are a known quantity in the industry, but you can't.

7. **A small or esoteric story:** Scripts with esoteric subjects that will interest only a few people, not the masses of moviegoers, are usually rejected, even when the script is well-written. "Small stories," such as a sweet little tale about a lovable main character, will also be rejected if there is nothing in the script to make it a big enough event for people to pay $8 or $9 to see on the large screen. It may not be right for the small screen either, maybe because it's got too much humor or because it just isn't what the networks are looking for. If you have written a small or esoteric story, you may be lucky enough to find a producer equally passionate about the story. If she has enough connections with talent, your script might one day be made into an art house film. But that is a very long shot.

6. **No conflict or a weak antagonist:** All good scripts are driven by conflict and stand on two legs: that of the hero and opponent. The problem of a weak opponent often surfaces even in some otherwise well-written scripts. Although the story is commercial, the writer can write decent dialogue, and has created a great hero/protagonist, the bad guy or gal is not a worthy opponent for the hero. It's too easy for the hero to win, and that takes away from the suspense and the drama—and the script gets rejected.

5. **Episodic structure:** Good structure is the essence of good drama (and good comedy). The three-act structure is a must in Hollywood. The story, set up by the hero's desire, which is opposed by the opponent, cannot just be a series of episodic events. It can't be "this happens and then this happens and then this happens." The story must have plot points that end each act and build to a climax and *resolution*. The characters must have arcs that take them from one place at the beginning of the story to a new place at the end. Mastering good dramatic structure is not easy and separates the good writers from the mediocre ones. Not mastering it is perhaps the most common reason a writer's script is rejected.

4. **Weak character development:** Some writers are very plot-oriented and neglect their characters. As readers, we don't feel like we really know these characters. They seem to be doing things for the sake of the story only—things that are inconsistent with who we thought they were a few pages earlier. Characters should drive the plot. Characters are the plot. They can and must change, but their change should come out of who they are rather than arbitrary changes necessary for what the writer wants to happen in the plot. This is a common reason for rejection.

3. **A weak middle:** Often a script will start out great, but by the middle we're bored. We peek ahead to the ending and it looks exciting, but we just don't feel like having to trudge through the middle to get there. This is a very common problem. The middle or second act is one of the hardest parts of a script to write and keep interesting, but if it isn't compelling, the script goes into the rejection pile.

2. **A weak third act:** Not infrequently, an otherwise good writer seems to have tired by the time she reaches the end of the script. The level of good writing that kept us interested in the rest of the script is suddenly gone. Either the story is hastily and unsatisfactorily resolved, or it has several endings, as though the writer didn't know when to quit. Good endings and good beginnings are essential to a great script.

   Which leads us to the final reason scripts get rejected:

1. **A slow start:** If your script does not grab the reader in the first few pages, it will not get far. There has to be an inciting incident in the first several pages, something that wakes the reader up and gets him or her interested enough to read the whole script. Even if it later turns into a brilliant script, if a reader gets to page 10 and nothing much has happened, no one will ever know. The script goes into the rejection pile.

Sorry, that's show business. If you want your script to have a chance to rise above the masses of material submitted to producers and studios, make sure it does not have any of the above common flaws of inexperienced screenwriters.

Verbal Action

resolution   The final pages of a story in which the complications of the plot are resolved and the main character's growth or change is evident.

narration   In either a dramatic or non-fiction film, the telling of a story, either spoken by an on-camera narrator or by voice-over, to provide information not already evident in the story.

The Non-Fiction Script

Most non-fiction films, particularly documentaries about social issues, should be constructed by following the same kind of dramatic structure as fiction films. The opening should define what the film is about and where it is going. It should grab the viewer's attention, presenting a question, conflict, or problem that will be explored in the film. In a documentary, the writer's job is to find ways to dramatize the film's point of view, premise, or theme.

For example, a number of years ago, before the Clarence Thomas/Anita Hill uproar, I was asked to write a film about sexual harassment on the job. As I began researching the topic, I soon realized that men and women generally have very different attitudes toward the workplace behavior that is legally considered sexual harassment. Women see it as scary, a threat to their livelihood, and humiliating, while many men feel it's just good office fun.

For the film, we decided to gather a group of women to talk about their experiences of sexual harassment on the job and a group of men to separately talk about the problem. The differing stories and viewpoints of the men and women in the two groups created conflict and increased the drama in what could have been a much drier informative film. We also filmed, in detail, the story of a bank manager who had been sexually harassed and then sued her company. Finally, we used actors to dramatize some scenes of typical sexual harassment scenarios. That was the basic material we had for the film.

Next, we pulled it all together with *narration*, which is common in non-fiction films. (Although less common in feature films, narration can also be effective in telling some dramatic stories.) Narration, unlike interviews, is scripted and can be either spoken by an on-camera narrator or by voice-over. In a documentary, a narrator can clarify images and provide important additional information that is not already captured in the sound and images of what has been filmed. It can also emphasize important themes of the film.

Returning to the example of our film, *The Workplace Hustle*, about sexual harassment, we decided that the most effective narrator would be a man, since it would be more powerful listening to a man explain the women's viewpoint, in contrast to the other men in the film who didn't seem to understand how women felt. Actor Ed Asner, well-known as the curmudgeonly editor on *The Mary Tyler Moore* TV show, was chosen as the narrator. The film was very popular—it was shown in schools, workplaces, and on television. When the Clarence Thomas hearings took place, Lifetime television began running the film frequently. The film probably did better than others on the topic because, like a dramatic movie, it set up a conflict—in this case, between the views of men and women—and resolved it through the course of the film and the words of a male narrator.

The Short Film Script

A short film is usually about 30 minutes or less, in contrast to the 90 to 120 minutes of most feature-length films. A short film script is to a feature script as a short story is to a novel. It is not simply shorter, it is also a unique form. In writing a short film, you have to choose characters that can be developed quickly and a story that can be told briefly. Not every idea will fit well into that form.

Most people who make short films do so because they eventually want to make feature films. Their short film becomes a "calling card" for them, an example of their skill and talent that they hope will get them an agent or, even better, a deal to make a feature film.

What makes a short film stand out from the many others that are made? Again, it starts with the script. The short film must, in very little time, introduce us to a compelling, unique main character who lives in a particular world and is confronted with a crisis, which she must resolve in 30 minutes. An antagonist and conflict must also be part of the film, just as in a feature film.

The Least You Need to Know

- ◆ Good writing shows rather than tells and is filled with details rather than generalizations.
- ◆ The main character's desire, action, and growth should drive the story.
- ◆ Conflict is built by having a strong opponent who challenges the main character.
- ◆ The most common reason scripts are rejected in Hollywood is because of the lack of good dramatic structure.

The Set-Up: Script Breakdown and Shooting Schedule

In This Chapter

- ◆ Breaking down a script
- ◆ Working with computer scheduling programs
- ◆ Using the production board in scheduling
- ◆ Important factors in estimating shooting time

Somehow, through your own talent and hard work or that of a writer you have hired, whose screenplay you have optioned or to whose screenplay you are attached as the creative producer, you have a script that you feel is ready to be made into a movie. Next, you need to know how long it will take to shoot the film and how much it will cost—you need a schedule and a budget. You may have a commitment for the financing or you may not yet have the money. In either case, you need the budget and you can't do a budget without first breaking down the script and doing a shooting schedule.

On an independent feature film, the production manager or the first assistant director generally prepares the schedule during pre-production. An estimated or preliminary schedule may have already been done, assuming a budget was needed to secure financing. If your film is a studio film, a draft of the breakdown and schedule might be done by people in the studio's production department. On a smaller shoot, such as a documentary, there may be only a very small crew and the producer or director may have to create the schedule. Whether you do the work or someone else does it, as a producer or director, you should still know the basics of the process.

Breaking Down the Script Manually

What exactly is breaking down a script? Essentially, it is the process of isolating the different parts of a script and analyzing those parts to see what will be required during production. If you are doing a breakdown and are not the writer or someone who knows the script well, your first step should be to read the script to get familiar with the story and the action.

The different elements or categories you will be dealing with in a script breakdown include the following:

- Cast
- Extras
- Stunts
- Exterior locations
- Interior locations
- Action props
- Special effects
- Sound effects
- Wardrobe
- Vehicles/animals
- Make-up and hair
- Special equipment

Each of these elements or a script will play a role in constructing both the schedule and the budget.

The purpose of the script breakdown is to help create a schedule that will minimize the amount of time it takes to shoot the film by grouping together shots that are similar. Most films are shot out of sequence. The end of the story, for example, may be shot before the opening scene. Some directors, particularly when filming emotional dramas, may want to shoot the film at least somewhat in sequence to help the actors. But, nevertheless, the schedule is generally arranged in the most efficient, cost-effective way.

Verbal Action

stunt   In filmmaking, an action that appears different and more incredible than the actual action filmed.

prop   In filmmaking or in a play, any physical object that is needed in a scene, such as chairs, books, paintings.

special effects   In filmmaking, a broad term for a range of shots and processes, including model shots, matte shots, rear projection, or other effects that are artificially created for the camera.

Marking Up the Script

Start a breakdown by "marking up" the script, which simply means underlining the different categories in the script in different colors. Color-code each of the different categories above with different color pencils or ink. The cast, for example, may be red. Go through the script and underline in red every member of the cast. (Underlining is better than highlighting if the script might later be copied.) The cast includes anyone with a speaking part. Later you will break down the cast further into those with major parts and those with "bit" parts. But for now, go through each category and mark the script with the color for the item.

Marking up the script has to be done very carefully. You don't want to miss any important props or a cast member with a bit role. Every element of the script must ultimately be reflected in the breakdown, schedule, and budget.

Filling Out Breakdown Sheets

The next step is to transfer the information from the marked up script to "breakdown sheets." There are essentially two kinds of breakdown sheets. The first will list each element in a certain category such as cast or exterior locations. These breakdown sheets provide critical information for doing the budget, so make sure everything from the script that will take time or cost money is transferred to the appropriate breakdown sheet.

To fill out these breakdown sheets, go through the marked-up script page by page and transfer each underlined item onto the appropriate breakdown page. All the cast members will eventually be listed on the cast page, all the exterior locations on another sheet, and so forth. Set these breakdown sheets aside for now. You will be using some of them in doing a schedule and others in preparing a budget.

The second kind of breakdown sheet is a scene breakdown sheet, and these breakdowns are used in preparing the production board and schedule. Stores like Enterprise of Hollywood Printers and Stationers (on the Internet at www.enterpriseprinters.com) sell pads of scene breakdown sheets, or you can create your own. The header information that is required on a breakdown sheet includes:

- The date you prepare the breakdown sheet.

- The production name and company name.

- The scene number—also called the breakdown page number—from the script. (If the script is revised later, new scenes are generally indicated by using letters, like 19A and 19B, for example.)

- A short scene name, such as "Perfumed Thief's Capture."

- A brief, concise description of the main action of the scene.

- The physical address of the location where you will be filming.

- An indication whether it is an interior or exterior scene. ("INT or EXT" is usually denoted by circling one or the other.)

- An indication whether the scene takes place during the day or night. ("DAY or NIGHT" can be circled.)

- The page count by one eighth of a page. Calculate this by dividing each script page into eighths of a page—each eighth is about an inch.

- A space for the cast members in the scene.

- A space for the "bits" or cast members with bit roles in the scene.

- A space for the extras needed in the scene.

- A space for the props and animals needed in the scene.

- A space for any special effects needed in the scene.

- A space for any music or audio effects needed in the scene.

Script Notes

Most scripts that are ready to be broken down and budgeted will have scene numbers on them. Almost all computer programs that format and print out scripts have an option for printing out a script with scene numbers. While the script is still a reading script, during the writing and development phase, it should not be printed with scene numbers. Only when the shooting script is ready and you are beginning pre-production should it be printed out with scene numbers.

Fill out a scene breakdown page for each scene in the script by transferring the information you have underlined in the marked-up script from each scene to a breakdown sheet. Some people combine short scenes that will be shot in the same location. For example, in *Something Is Rotten*, let's say there is a daytime scene that establishes the exterior of the main character's home and another daytime scene in front of the main character's home when the perfumed thief, posing as a mailman, delivers a letter to the main character's mail box. You could list both of these scenes on the same breakdown page. If you do, make sure you write all the scene numbers on the sheet.

Be careful to list all props that are needed and, of course, any stunts or special effects that are necessary for the shot or scene. Special effects are those things that are artificially caused on cue, for the camera. For example, a car swerving off the side of the road and crashing into a tree is an action special effect. A stunt coordinator or special-effects person will probably be needed to plan and carry out that scene.

Once you have filled out your breakdown lists and have a breakdown sheet for each scene in the movie, you are ready to transfer the information to a production board in order to create your schedule.

Breaking Down the Script on the Computer

Although there are other programs, Movie Magic Scheduling is the most widely used computer program for breaking down a script and creating a schedule. The program simplifies and takes some of the tedium out of the time-consuming and often complex process of preparing a script breakdown and schedule.

Movie Magic provides an import feature to extract breakdown information from scripts written in "Final Draft" and two other script-formatting programs published by the same company that makes Movie Magic. If the script isn't written in one of those three programs, the program also has a quick-entry feature, which can be used to break down the script scene by scene without retyping information from the script.

The program creates a breakdown sheet that contains scene information such as cast, crew, props, and other data, just as in a manual breakdown. You can navigate between breakdown sheets and merge two breakdown sheets into one. The merged sheet includes information from the top part of the breakdown sheet—such as location and script page. Elements on the bottom part (cast, props, vehicles, and so on) are merged and all the information is included on the new breakdown sheet.

You can also customize your categories by modifying or deleting any existing category or creating a new one. Once you have completed your breakdown pages through the program, they will serve as a complete database, giving you information you will need later for your budget (see Chapter 8, "Show Me the Money: The Budget"). The information in the breakdown pages can also be sorted and organized for any kind of report that you may need. You can export this data directly to Movie Magic Budgeting and Movie Magic Wireless AD. The latter is a program that prepares call sheets and production reports. And with the scheduling program, you also will not need to handwrite production board strips (see the following section).

Preparing a Production Board

The preparation necessary to make a schedule is done—either manually or by computer—and now it's time to begin constructing a shooting schedule. The schedule gives you the total number of days needed to shoot your film. This is a very critical piece of information for your budget and for all phases of pre-production planning.

The tool you need to create a shooting schedule is a *production board*. The production board is a board on which the essential elements in the script (from your breakdown sheets) are converted to moveable strips that fit into the board. A production board enables you to quickly see all of the scene elements so you can determine the most appropriate way to schedule your shoot. Once you have transferred all your data in a particular way to these moveable strips, you can move the strips around, grouping scenes that should be shot on the same day.

For example, it makes sense to shoot scenes together that will be done at the same location. Scenes that need to be shot at night also should be grouped together. Scenes that have certain cast members in them have to be shot together if the actors are only available for a particular number of days. Scenes that use certain special props such as vehicles or animals or require special effects might have to be grouped together.

Cutaway

Just as scheduling a feature film has certain challenges and problems, so does preparing a schedule for a documentary film. Documentaries often do not have a full script available at the beginning of a shoot, but only an outline. Also, interviews with real people and covering real events may run much shorter or much longer than estimated. And sometimes something unexpected happens that is relevant to the film that the director will want to take the time to film. Many documentaries are shot by simply having the camera and crew in a place where you expect something interesting to happen—and it may not happen in the time frame you hope it will. Documentary producers and directors with experience, however, get better at estimating the unknown and creating realistic schedules.

Whenever the production must move from filming at one location to filming at a second location on the same day, a great deal of production time will be lost and a lot of money will be wasted. Therefore, always try to minimize moves as you set the order of the scenes.

Player (or actor) scheduling is also an important cost factor. Whenever possible, the player's time should be scheduled to limit the number of days she will be working. Don't, for example, schedule an actor to work on days 1, 4, 7, and 14. Try to pull the scenes together for four continuous days if possible so you only have to pay the actor for one week rather than two or more.

A production board can be done manually, with handwritten strips (both the board and strips are also available at Enterprise of Hollywood), or can be done by using a computer program like Movie Magic Scheduling. If it is done by hand, you manually transfer the information from the breakdown sheets to the strips. If it is done by computer, you can view strips on the computer and move them around on the computer. Or some programs allow you to print out the information on strips that can be attached to blank strips for the production board, and those strips can then be manually moved around to create the schedule.

Movie Magic Scheduling's "sort and select" feature gives you a quick way to do rough drafts of schedules. You can see how a schedule lays out with certain locations being shot first, for example, or you can see what happens if all exteriors are grouped together. With the program, you can save your first pass at a schedule, then try another strategy and compare the two schedules.

The most common ways to sort scenes are by location, by interior or exterior, by day or night, or by cast members in the scene.

Whether you do the schedule on a computer or manually, you will be using:

- ◆ **A strip board or production board:** Either a manual board or a computer facsimile of an actual production board.
- ◆ **Strips:** Either actual strips or a computer program's version of the strips.
- ◆ **Strip colors:** In both manual boards and computer boards, the colors of the strips instantly give you information. Usually the colors are white for day interior; green for night interior; yellow for day exterior; blue for night exterior; black and white for day dividers; orange for week ending; red for holidays; and black for separating locations from each other.

Determining the Schedule

Once you have the strips arranged in an order that seems efficient and logical, you can then determine your shooting schedule. To decide how many scenes can be shot in a day, you have to estimate the number of *set-ups* that will be required to film the scene. A set-up is the actual setting-up of the position of the lights, camera, props, and so on in order to get the desired shot. Each time the director wants a different shot, the crew will have to move or change the lights, the camera, and the props, all of which takes time.

Shot Lists

If the director has already prepared a *shot list*, it will tell you exactly how many set-ups you will need for each scene. A shot list is a listing of every shot to be filmed in every scene to be filmed. The screenwriter does not list the shots. Even though the writer may indicate certain shots in the scene, it is up to the director to decide how to cover a scene. For example, one director may want to shoot an entire scene in a long or master shot and then shoot it again to get close-ups on one actor and yet again to get close-ups on another actor. This gives the director a lot of options in the editing room. Another director, on the other hand, may know exactly how she wants the scene on film. She knows she wants the master shot and just a single close-up on one of the actors during a particular line. Clearly, the latter director will be able to shoot more scenes in a day and her shoot will be shorter.

Because of differences in the director's style and in the nature of the story itself, a typical 90-minute shooting script may have as few as 300 or as many as 1,000 or more shots.

 Verbal Action _____

production board   A board with moveable colored strips that show the schedule for every day of a shoot and list the actors, locations, and elements needed for each day. Traditionally put together manually, production boards can also be created and assembled through computer programs.

set-up   The position of the camera, lights, sound equipment, actors, and so on for any given shot.

shot list   A director's list of every shot that will be needed in the film.

Other Scheduling Factors

There are a number of factors that will affect how many scenes you can shoot in a day. How quickly does the director work? Does she tend to stay on schedule? How long does she like to work? Do the actors who are working on the shoot have a reputation for needing a lot of "takes"? How quickly does the cinematographer work? How long does he take to light? Also, consider whether anything can be done concurrently while a scene is being shot. For example, could the art department dress the set for the next location while the rest of the crew is shooting a scene? Or should a second unit shoot some exteriors while the primary shooting is taking place?

Another consideration is whether the scene to be shot is an important or key scene. If it is highly dramatic or has a lot of physical action, the director will need enough time to handle the performances or make sure the action is captured correctly. Some scenes are more critical to the story, and you will have to schedule enough time to make sure they are done right.

Start actually making the schedule by placing a strip between each day of the shoot after calculating the number of scenes you think can be shot on each day. This is your shooting schedule. It should be shown to everyone involved. The director and cinematographer should both feel it is feasible. If you are the film's director or producer, it is important for you to check the schedule a studio may prepare. You may want to try, for example, to shoot part of the film in sequence. Or you may want to get the difficult action shots done first before you shoot the more dramatic scenes. There is usually some flexibility in making the schedule, and there may be a way to meet your concerns while still arranging the production in the most efficient way.

CAUTION

Counterpoint

There is a rule of thumb for the number of pages that can be shot per day—but don't follow it blindly because a lot depends on the director. With action sequences, you may be able to shoot between five and six script pages a day. For scenes that are mostly dialogue, you might be able to cover nine to eleven pages. The number of set-ups that can be shot each day may vary from seven to thirty, depending on the complexity of the set-up change.

Using Storyboards

Another item that may help you decide on how long it will take to shoot is a storyboard. Storyboards, different from production boards, are drawings that can be used as visual aids on a shoot. They are usually prepared by the director, often with help from the art director. Some directors create storyboards for every scene and every shot of the shoot. The crew can then see each shot illustrated and can get an idea of how the director is visualizing the shot. Accurate storyboards often mean less time and fewer reshoots and therefore fewer expenses, and they are great for scheduling purposes. On feature films, storyboards are particularly important for difficult or action sequences.

There is also software, such as StoryBoard Quick and BoardMaster Storyboard, available now to help non-artists create storyboards.

The Least You Need to Know

- ◆ Script breakdown is a listing of all of the critical elements of a script—such as cast or locations—that will impact the schedule and budget.

- ◆ Computer programs such as Movie Magic Scheduling can make the scheduling process easier and less time-consuming.

- ◆ The director's style, the cast, and the number of shots or set-ups necessary all affect how quickly a scene can be shot.

- ◆ The production board—either a manual or computer-generated board—is the main tool for creating an efficient, cost-effective schedule.

- ◆ When completed, the production board shows visually the order in which the film's scenes will be shot and the number of days the shoot will take.

Chapter 8

Show Me the Money: The Budget

In This Chapter

- ◆ Choosing the format in which to shoot
- ◆ Cost-cutting ideas for low-budget films
- ◆ Selecting budget tools
- ◆ Estimating budget line items

How much does it cost to make a feature film? That's like asking "How much does a necklace cost?" You can get costume jewelry for a few dollars or can pay many thousands for exquisite pearls. In the same way, Hollywood studios can spend $200 million on a film—like the *Titantic*, so expensive that it took two studios, Fox and Paramount, to finance it—while independent producers may spend $200,000 or less, scraping together money from credit cards and rich relatives.

Unlike with a necklace, where the price and the quality of the piece of jewelry are usually linked, the size of the budget doesn't necessarily predict how good the film is or how successful it will be. We all have seen big-budget movies flop because they were so bad, and have seen equally terrible low-budget movies. This chapter won't help you make a good movie, but it will give you tools for determining how much the movie you want to make will cost.

Choosing the Medium

The first major decision you have to make in the budgeting process is what kind of camera you will be using to shoot the film. Will you be using film or video, and what format of film or video? It is a very exciting time right now in the world of filmmaking because there are so many new options for shooting a movie. Some of the options may save you a great deal of money on your film, money that you won't have to raise or money that could be better spent on some other aspect of the production.

35mm Film

Most feature films distributed by the major and minor Hollywood studios for theatrical release, with a few exceptions, are shot in 35mm color film. The cost of film stock and processing 35mm film is more expensive than any other medium you might choose. Many filmmakers, however, feel that the quality of the 35mm image is so much better for the ultimate movie that will be projected in a theater that it remains the film stock of choice for most productions.

16mm Film

Until the development of video, 16mm film was the standard film stock used in documentaries and for television news and other shows. The problem with 16mm film for movies for theatrical release is that the area of a frame in 16mm film stock is four times smaller than a frame of 35mm film. Therefore, when it is projected, in order to fill the same size screen, it has to be "blown-up" and thus looks grainier than a film shot in 35mm. If, on the other hand, 16mm is transferred to video for television broadcast or is projected in smaller venues than the average widescreen commercial theater, it will look fine.

16mm film is far less expensive than 35mm film, and is an option for documentaries both for cost reasons and because the lighter-weight camera allows the cinematographer to shoot handheld or "*cinéma verité*" style. As we'll soon see, however, video has largely replaced 16mm film in television news and other documentary and non-fiction films. Sometimes, short films for film school classes or for "calling cards" are shot in 16mm, and for that purpose it is still an excellent choice.

Hi-Eight

Hi-Eight is 8mm film. It was initially introduced as a format for amateur filmmakers to make home movies. It has been used somewhat in commercial filmmaking, especially in television news before video and in making educational or industrial films. Since the introduction of video and digital video, however, this film format is used less and less.

Beta SP Video

The standard professional video camera for many years was the ¾-inch video camera. Then the Beta SP camera—"SP" stands for "superior performance"—was introduced. Like its forerunner, it records sound and images in an *analog* rather than *digital* format. Beta SP videotape is only ½ inch and is made of a higher-grade videotape than that used by earlier Betacams. The camera is smaller and easier to use than earlier video cameras. It is still used widely in the television industry for *broadcast quality* productions, which actually means the quality or strength of the video signal that is broadcast but has also come to mean the quality of the image that is captured by the camera.

In all forms of video, as opposed to film, not only will the stock be cheaper because videotape is less expensive than film, but because video can be instantly replayed; there is no cost for developing videotape as there is in film. Also, the director can instantly see how a scene looks, without waiting for *dailies* to be printed and screened. This often allows a director to require fewer "takes" to feel satisfied she has gotten the shot, thus cutting down on the number of shooting days.

 Verbal Action

analog   A device or signal that is continuously varying in strength or quantity, such as voltage, audio, or video.

digital   The conversion of an analog signal into a binary form with regular strength as opposed to varying strength.

broadcast quality   A term that originally meant the quality of the signal that broadcasts television shows to television sets. It has now come to mean the image quality of a show made for television.

Digi-Beta Video

Digital Betacam or "Digi-beta" is the digital version of Beta SP. It is becoming the camera of choice in the industry for documentaries, television, and even some small features. The quality of the image is barely distinguishable from Beta SP, but there are editing advantages because the tape is already in a digital format (see Chapter 16, "Preparing to Edit").

There are other digital video cameras such as Digital-S, DVCAMS, Mini-DV, and Digital 8. The major advantage of all digital formats is that you do not lose a *generation* when you make copies of your video if you are doing your post-production in a facility that has digital editing equipment.

Verbal Action _____

> **cinéma verité**   Literally, "cinema truth," originally a term to describe filmmaking that utilized lightweight equipment, small crews, and direct interviews; now used to refer to any documentary technique.
>
> **generation**   In film or video, when there is a loss of quality of an image as a result of transferring from one format to another or copying.
>
> **dailies**   Prints of takes that are made immediately after a day's shoot ends so that they can be examined before the next day begins.

24p High Definition Video

The new thing in filmmaking today is the 24p Digital High Definition video camcorder. It is called 24p because the format's progressive 24-frames-per-second rate exactly mimics the frame rate of 35mm film. Other digital video formats produce 30 "interlaced" images per second. When converted to film, 30 frames worth of information are then jammed into 24 frames and the transfer causes some "stuttering" and unnatural blurs of color.

The 24p HD digital video camera produces images, according to filmmaker George Lucas, that are "indistinguishable" from film. Lucas shot "Star Wars Episode II" entirely in this format and saved about $12 million dollars in the overall budget of the film by using 24p instead of 35mm film. (The film premieres in the summer of 2002.) The savings were a result of the ability to shoot more scenes during each day because they did not have any costs of developing and shipping dailies and because the cost of the tape is so much cheaper than film. A 52-minute digital video cartridge costs about $75 versus about $4,000 for 50 minutes of film.

Cutaway

Both Hollywood and independent filmmakers are experimenting with 24p. George Lucas, whose company has invested in the new format, thinks it should replace 35mm as the industry standard. He and others feel it is so good that there is no reason not to use it. Other filmmakers, however, feel 24p has a look that is too "perfect" and lacks the depth, richness, and detail of film. Some filmmakers are using it in selective parts of a movie and find that it cuts well with film. Still others find it appropriate for some types of movies but not others. Although it seems unlikely that it will replace 35mm film soon, it definitely could at some point. Now, theaters are all geared for film, so even if a movie is shot in digital video it has to be released on film. Digital distribution and projection is probably several years away.

Shooting for No Budget to Low Budget

Now that you've decided what medium to use, the next decision to make is whether or not the film you are shooting will be a normal- to high-budget film, a low-budget film, or an ultra-low "no-budget" film. If you need to film at a low budget or "no budget" level, you are going to have to find ways to beg and borrow to get what you need for the film. Most extremely low-budget films, for example, do not use union crew members. Some are not even filmed under the Writers Guild or Directors Guild contracts. (Both of those unions have "low-budget" contracts for films under a certain budget and your film might qualify for that. Check with the signatory department of each guild to learn the latest rules.)

Even low-budget films are usually signatory to the Screen Actors Guild contract, unless they are filmed using all unknown actors who aren't members of the union (SAG also has a low-budget contract). In addition to deciding whether you will be signatory to the various unions and exploring each of their low-budget contracts, there are other ways to keep the budget low or even to add money to the coffers.

Cast and Crew Deals

Actors sometimes will make deals to be in films that interest them that include accepting different payments or increased profit participation in exchange for cutting their up-front fee. Another way that low-budget producers work with actors is to offer all of the lead and co-starring roles payment on a *most favored nations* basis. That simply means that everyone gets the same fee as the *most favorite*, or the person who would normally get the highest fee. This also applies to any profit participation that the actor will receive.

Remember that credit is also a negotiable part of your deals with actors. A bigger star may accept a most-favored nations fee if she has her name above the credits, for example.

Crew members may also accept deferred payments or may cut their regular fee for a low-budget production. Also, students and others who want to get experience in the film business will often work as interns for free or for school credit for low-budget productions. Interns make great runners and can play valuable roles on a film shoot.

Equipment and Post-Production Deals

You might be able to make very helpful deals with a film laboratory or other post-production house before you begin the shoot. Some smaller film labs have made deals to defer their fees up to a certain amount in exchange for participating in a film's net profits. If you do make a deal with a lab, be sure to investigate the quality of the lab's work first. Equipment houses might also give you a discount if you explain that it's a really low-budget film and ask for a break.

Location and Film Commission Incentives

You might be able to save money on your film if you shoot it in one state or country as opposed to another. For example, at one point, Arkansas offered a nickel back to a production for every dollar spent in Arkansas. If your budget is several million and you were planning to spend one million at the location for hotel, food, location, and local crew expenses, then you'd save $50,000 shooting there. Other states may offer a break on hotel or other necessities. Some states have film-production facilities and those facilities may offer deals in order to attract business.

The best way to find out about these opportunities, which change frequently, is to contact the film commissions in the areas where you might possibly shoot. All states and many large cities have film commissions. To find out more about film commissions and locate one in the area you want to shoot, go online to The Association of Film Commissions International at www.afci.org or call the AFCI at 406-495-8045.

The exchange rate between the dollar and a country's currency can also make a difference to your budget. Many network television shows and parts of many studio films are shot in Canadian locations, such as Toronto and Vancouver, largely because of the savings the favorable exchange rate brings. Another advantage of those particular two cities is that there are a large number of skilled potential crew members who can be hired, and it saves the production money to hire local people.

Product Placement

You might also want to approach certain companies about "product placement" to help add money to your coffers. If, for example, in shooting *Something Is Rotten*, you have a number of scenes where perfumes are featured, maybe you can get Chanel or Calvin Klein or another perfume maker to donate money to the film from their advertising budget in exchange for prominently displaying their products in certain scenes in the film. This is even done in studio films. When you see certain brands of soft drinks, cars, and other products prominently displayed in a shot, you can be fairly certain that the production has gotten advertising money from the product's maker. Unfortunately, studios also often take money from tobacco companies for displaying brand-name cigarettes in movies.

Selecting Tools for Budgeting

You've made several decisions—in what format to shoot your film, which unions you will become signatory to, if any, where the film will be shot—and you have a general goal for or limit on the size of your ultimate budget. Now it's time to start recording and tallying the numbers and seeing where you can cut corners.

Computer Programs

Budgets are often done today using a computer spreadsheet or a special software program for film budgets, such as Movie Magic Budgeting. A program like Movie Magic Budgeting can handle budgets of any size, including the $200 million it took to make *Titanic*. A major advantage of using a computer program over doing a budget manually is that you can instantly see the effects of any changes you might make to your budget. For example, if you think you will need two extra weeks of pre-production but aren't sure if you can afford it, you can add two weeks and re-calculate your budget instantly to see what the cost will be.

With Movie Magic, you simply enter an unlimited number of lines of detail for each line item in the budget. All lines of detail are then totaled into sub-accounts, which are then totaled at the top level, which becomes the top sheet of your budget. The top sheet and sub-accounts are calculated instantaneously as changes and additions are made. There is no limit to the number of categories on your top sheet, accounts per category, or lines of detail per account. There are also more than 25 standard film, television, and video budget forms that the program generates and customizes for your production.

A computer program is also very useful in calculating often time-consuming and complicated union fringe benefits (see the section "Fringe Benefits" later in this chapter). It also allows you to do your budget in one currency and convert it into another by simply providing the exchange rate, which you can get from a database provided by Movie Magic on the Internet at www.moviemagicproducer.com.

Movie Magic also has a database that works within Movie Magic Budgeting of all union and guild pay rates in the United States and Canada. Once downloaded from www. moviemagicproducer.com into your program, you can easily find a pay rate by clicking on the Labor Rates icon on the toolbar.

CAUTION

Counterpoint

If you are hiring a writer, director, or actor who is a member of a guild, your company must become a signatory to the guild or the individual you want to hire could risk a fine or even expulsion from her guild. The guild will then require minimum payments for each guild member you hire and the payment of fringe benefits into the guild's pension and health funds.

Industry Directories and Word-of-Mouth

If you are not using Movie Magic Budgeting and you are not using union crew members, how do you know what the going rate is for various crew members or for equipment? Basically, you just have to call around and find out. If you are able to hire an experienced line producer or production manager, she will know what the going rate is in almost all categories. If you can't hire someone, see if you can find a friend of a friend who will show you a recent sample budget of a film that is in the same budget range as yours. The rates reflected in that budget should help you. Potential crew members also can usually suggest equipment houses that give good rates. If you still don't have any leads, use industry directories and production guides to find phone numbers of equipment houses and labs. Then, call for the rates and compare. If you are filming on location and using local crew members, ask the film commission in that area for help with the rates for crew and equipment.

Adding Up the Above-the-Line Elements

Budgets for films are traditionally divided into two parts—the *above-the-line* and *below-the-line* elements. The above-the-line elements are the writer(s), director, producers, and cast. The below-the-line elements are the costs for other people, supplies, and equipment needed for the actual physical production and post-production. The division probably originated because of the widely varying salaries of certain above-the-line elements—such as particular actors and directors—versus the actual cost of a production, which might be somewhat consistent from film to film.

If, for example, you get Julia Roberts instead of Molly Shannon to star in *Something Is Rotten*, it will add $20 million to your above-the-line budget. A star like Julia will also probably insist that her "producer" become one of the above-the-line elements. She also might require some things that will change the below-the-line budget, but not nearly as significantly. For example, she might require that you hire her make-up and hair people or an assistant, and their salaries will no doubt be more than what you had originally budgeted for those categories.

By dividing the budget into those two categories, someone familiar with film production can immediately see whether the budget is reasonable, since the high salaries of major stars or of star directors won't affect the below-the-line total.

Writing

This category, also called "Story and Rights" is usually the first category on most budget forms. It includes not only the writer's salary but such items as writer's secretaries, the cost of copying the script, and mailing or sending scripts by messenger, as well as research expenses to verify aspects of the script and avoid libel or plagiarism suits. (There are companies and/or attorneys that can be hired to do the latter.)

If yours is a location shoot and if the writer will be going on location, you can include the writer's travel and per diem expenses here or in a separate category for all above-the-line travel.

Verbal Action _____

most favored nations   In film deals, when everyone in a category accepts the same fee as the "most favored" person.

above-the-line   In film budgeting, costs associated with writing, directing, producing, and performing, listed in the top section of a budget.

below-the-line   In film budgeting, labor and other costs associated with physical production and post-production, listed in the lower section of a budget.

per diem   The amount of spending money given to a production member for daily living expenses.

Producer and Staff

The producer is, of course, at least nominally the boss of the entire production, even though the director runs the set. Although producers' fees can vary widely, the producer will usually receive a substantial fee, often as much as the director. There is frequently more than one producer, as well as associate producers, executive producers, and line producers. The executive producer may be someone who is instrumental in securing the financing for the project. Sometimes, in studio films, an executive producer credit is given to the person who line-produces the film. A line producer may also get credit as the production manager or the unit production manager, depending on the production. She is the expert in physical production, while the producer is the central creative figure who has brought all the above-the-line participants of the film together, such as the writer, director, and major cast.

An associate producer credit is sometimes given to writers or others and is often negotiated in exchange for lower fees. Also in this category are the travel and living expenses for those who will be on location, if the shoot is a location shoot.

Director and Staff

This category includes the director's salary, the cost of any secretaries, and miscellaneous expenses related to the director's role. If your production company is signatory to the Directors Guild contract, there will be a minimum salary required for the director, as well as a minimum per diem for the director if you are filming on location.

The director may receive a flat fee for directing the movie or may be paid a weekly rate. The director's weekly rate for pre-production or "prep" work and for post-production supervision will generally be less than her weekly production rate. This pattern is the same for many of the below-the-line crew.

Talent or Cast

From the breakdown sheets that you prepared after marking up the script (discussed in Chapter 7, "The Set-Up: Script Breakdown and Shooting Schedule"), you should have one sheet that lists all of the cast members. Either you have already negotiated a fee for each of the leads and members of the supporting cast or you can enter in the category the maximum you can pay. Sometimes it will only be the minimum weekly or daily rate as required by the Screen Actors Guild, plus 10 percent for the agent's commission. ("Minimum plus 10" is usually negotiated by agents so that the agent's 10 percent commission does not force the actor, writer, or director to receive less than their guild's minimum fee.)

Included in this category are any stuntmen or -women, bits, and extras. The fee for a casting director—whose job it is to help the producer and director cast the film—should be listed here as well. Finally, travel for the actors and their per diem should either be here or in a special above-the-line travel budget item.

Fringe Benefits

You are now almost through with the above-the-line category, but not quite. You must add up the total taxes and fringe benefits required by the state and federal government and each union—WGA, DGA, SAG, and possibly the Producers Guild—for your above-the-line talent. You will need to find out the amount each union requires according to their contract. The taxes are generally about 18 percent of the total salaries.

Filling in the Below-the-Line Elements

Now that the above-the-line budget is complete, you need to estimate the cost of the production and post-production phases to complete the budget. If your film is signatory to unions, including the Directors Guild, IATSE, and the Teamsters, then the rates for many of the crew categories will be set by those unions. If not, you will have to negotiate with each crew member, based on the amount of money you are willing to allocate to each category and the going rate in the area you are shooting.

Production Staff

The first below-the-line category includes the production manager or unit manager, the first assistant director, the second assistant director, and the script supervisor. If you are signatory to the Directors Guild, the production manager, 1st AD, and 2nd AD will all be covered by their contract. Also included in this category is a production secretary if there is one and the cost of doing the schedule and budget.

Camera

The next big department in your budget is the camera department. In addition to your director of photography or DP, you may or may not need, depending on the size of the production, a camera operator and/or several assistant camera persons. This category is also where you will enter the cost of the camera rentals, including lenses, tripods, batteries, and other miscellaneous items.

Other Production and Post-Production Budget Categories

If you are using Movie Magic Budgeting or another computer program, or if you purchase standard budget forms (available from Enterprise of Hollywood Printers and Stationers at www.enterpriseprinters.com), you will have listings of all potential budget line items that you will have to consider and attach dollar amounts to. The important below-the-line budget items that are necessary for most feature films include the following:

- **Art direction** includes the production designer and/or art director and supplies.
- **Set construction** includes the cost of labor and materials to build sets.
- **Set operations** include the people who keep the set running: the grips, greenspersons, craft services people, police, or fire persons. Also includes any special effects needs.
- **Electrical department** refers to the lights and everyone responsible for the lights, including the gaffer and best boy (or girl).
- **Set decoration** refers to the set decorator and the props needed to dress the sets and includes any action props you need, such as vehicles or animals.
- **Wardrobe** includes the costume designer and assistants and the cost of wardrobe rentals or purchases.
- **Make-up and hair** includes the make-up and hair artists and their supplies.
- **Production sound** includes the production sound mixer, a boom operator or other helpers, and sound equipment. If shooting in film, also include the cost of transferring sound from ¼-inch tape to magnetic strip stock.
- **Location expense** includes all site rentals, location scouting costs, hotels, meals, travel, shipping, office rentals, etc.
- **Transportation department** includes a transportation captain and staff and vehicles for moving equipment and crew around.
- **Raw stock** refers to the cost of film stock or of videotape. If film, include the costs of developing a negative and dailies.
- **Editing** includes the editor, an assistant, the editing equipment, and facility.

- **Music** includes the composer or music supervisor, music purchases, and recordings.
- **Post-production sound** includes looping, sound effects, the cost of a sound mix, and music editor.
- **Titles and opticals** include the cost of creating titles and optical special effects.
- **Insurance** is mandatory, in case of disasters or loss of a key person.
- **Fringe benefits** for below-the-line members of guilds and unions.
- **Publicity** includes the cost of a publicist and a still photographer's expenses.
- **General expenses** include attorney's fees, accountant's fees, office rentals, etc.
- **Contingency** is customarily added to film budgets as a fall-back in case of delays or other problems. Typically, the amount is 10 percent of the budget.

Whew! Now you know why it costs so much to make a movie.

Estimating Documentary Budgets

Documentary film budgets are generally much smaller than feature-film budgets. First of all, the cast in a documentary is comprised mostly of non-actors who do not need to be paid at all—or at least not as much as actors. In addition to saving the cost of the cast, you don't usually have wardrobe or make-up and hair expenses. Also, the crew for a documentary is usually far smaller, enabling the production to move quickly. Documentaries use real locations rather than constructed sets, and money is saved there. Finally, documentaries are usually shot in far fewer days than features, so that also lowers the cost. And, as we have said, documentaries are almost never shot on 35mm, but rather either 16mm film or a video format, all of which are cheaper.

The Least You Need to Know

- If you are shooting a feature film and want to save a lot of money, consider using 24p High Definition video.
- Movie Magic Budgeting or another computer spreadsheet program can save you a lot of time in estimating your budget.
- Potential crew members often know the best and cheapest equipment houses.
- In various estimates of a film's budget, the above-the-line budget items can vary widely depending on the fees of stars and the director, but the below-the-line elements usually remain relatively constant.

Collaborators: Hiring the Cast and Crew

In This Chapter

◆ Working with a casting director to cast the film

◆ Hiring the key department heads

◆ Bringing on the rest of the crew

Making a movie is a team effort. At first the team of collaborators is small—usually just the writer and a producer and/or director. Then the team gradually expands, finally including the entire cast and crew. The producer, director, and line producer/production manager are responsible for assembling the key members of the team. The skill, talent, and spirit of the team members will make a difference—not in winning or losing as with an athletic team—but in the quality of the film and whether it will be finished on schedule and within its budget.

Before you hire your collaborators, however, you should know something about what each team member's role is going to be in the film. What are the responsibilities of the key people on a film shoot? How do you find the best people for your movie? What kind of experience should you be looking for? This chapter helps you answer those questions.

Casting the Leads and Supporting Actors

For many films, particularly independent films, the stars of the movie may already be attached to the project before the film is financed (see Chapter 4, "Making an Independent Film"). The commitment of the star(s) who will be playing the leading role(s) often enables independent producers to get their movies financed.

With studio films, the script may have been put into development without stars attached but, before it is *greenlighted* for production, the director and the lead roles are set. This is also true of most television movies today. Studios and networks don't usually make the commitment to invest money in the production of a film until they know who will be playing the leads. A list is made of stars the studio or network will approve in the roles. The script, with a financial offer and starting date attached, is then submitted to those stars one at a time, in order of the actor the studio wants most for the role. Waiting for the stars to respond may take a while. Also, there is the problem of a star's availability. If she likes the script but isn't available on the dates proposed, either another star must be found or the production dates will have to change to accommodate the actor's schedule. If a well-known director is interested in the film, she might be very busy and the production dates also would have to also be adjusted for her schedule.

Let's say, however, that the headache of casting the lead actors and getting the production dates set has already been accomplished. Now it's time to surround the principal actors with a strong supporting cast. How do you go about casting the rest of the roles?

 Verbal Action _____

> **greenlight**   The term for when a movie studio decides to produce a film it has been developing.
>
> **sides**   In casting, the pages containing a scene or parts of scenes from a script that actors must read or act out in an audition.
>
> **cold reading**   A reading of a scene or part of a scene by an actor who has not had a chance to memorize the dialogue or otherwise prepare for the performance.

Casting Director

You may or may not have had a casting director involved in casting your lead roles but, if so, her job has only just begun. The casting director will be responsible for setting up meetings or auditions with actors to play all the co-starring roles, as well as the bit parts.

A good casting director will have a wide range of knowledge about actors and actresses, what they have done, and the kinds of roles in which they are particularly good. She will also have good relationships with talent agents and acting coaches.

Casting directors often use the *Player's Directory*, published by the Academy of Motion Picture Arts and Sciences, to find people who may be right for the roles in your movie. The directory, which is available in most libraries and through the Academy at 310-247-3000, consists of several volumes of leading women and men, character actors, and child actors. Another source of information frequently used by both producers and casting directors for getting information on possible cast members is The Internet Movie Database at www.imdb.com.

The casting director will also use a service that disseminates casting information for features, television, and plays to actors' agents and personal managers. The service, called "Breakdown Services" (in LA at 310-276-8829, New York at 212-869-2003, or online at www.breakdownservices.com) writes synopses of the story and a description of each character in the film at no charge to the production. It is only available, however, to films that are already financed and in pre-production.

Finally, a good casting director will also have seen tapes of up-and-coming performers and may know of people not listed in the directories.

Auditions

The casting director will usually schedule meetings or auditions with the director for the potential cast members. Sometimes the producer will also sit in on the meeting or audition. If it is a significant role and the actor is a well-known one, most of the meeting may be devoted to talking about the script and the actor probably won't even be asked to read a scene from the script. Sometimes, however, the actor may want to read, to show you her take on the character.

Most actors (excluding famous stars), however, are asked to audition by reading a scene or parts of scenes for the director. The casting director often reads the role opposite the one for which the actor is auditioning. Sometimes the actor will only get a copy of the scene to be read at the time she arrives for the audition. When that happens, the actor will have to do a *cold reading*—a reading of a scene when the actor has had very little time to prepare. More often, the *sides*—pages that have the scene or scenes to be read—are sent to the actor's agent the day before the meeting and, in those cases, most actors are quite prepared for the audition.

You may like to see actors work spontaneously in cold readings rather than seeing prepared scene readings. Some actors who aren't good at cold readings, however, might still be very good when given the chance to prepare.

How do you decide between one actor and another? Sometimes it is obvious—an actor just seems to become the character you envisioned as you read the script. Other times, you may be torn between several actors who seem right. One way to resolve that dilemma is to think about how each of them might complement and work with the actors who will be playing roles opposite them. You might be able to bring in another actor you have already cast to read opposite the actor in question. Or, one of your lead actors might have an opinion about one or another of the actors under consideration for a role. You can also check with people who have worked with the particular actors in the past to get an idea of their style and how easy they are to work with on a film.

Bits and Extras

Sometimes an assistant casting director may be auditioning actors for minor or bit parts and casting extras while the casting director and director are focused on filling the major speaking roles. If the shoot is a location shoot and you will be casting extras and some small roles in the local area, you may have to bring the casting director and her assistant on location.

CAUTION

Counterpoint

Trouble can occur if the producer, for example, wants one actor because she is better known, but the director feels another actor is better for the part. Because a production is a team effort, people are usually willing to compromise to end a conflict and get decisions made. When people can't work together to come to agreement on things, it's not a good sign. That is when you hear about a key person leaving the production for "creative" reasons.

Unit Production Manager or Line Producer

One of the most important persons you will hire on the shoot will not have a single word to say about any of the "creative" issues such as which line in the script to change or which character actor to hire for a role. Yet that person, on some film shoots called the production manager and on others called the line producer, could make or break your production. (Sometimes one person will get both credits and sometimes on large features there may be both a line producer and a production manager.) The production manager or line producer is really the below-the-line producer. She comes on board several weeks (or even several months on very large features) before production is to begin and will stay on to wrap things up after the shoot.

A good production manager or line producer will have experience on productions the size of yours and also often in the state or country where your film is going to be shot. She will have relationships with people who work in various production capacities, will know going labor rates, and will know the labs and transfer facilities. She will have authority to spend the production's money and make deals for the production. Your line producer must be someone you feel is responsible, exceedingly capable, and trustworthy.

When interviewing a line producer or production manager, ask a lot of questions about previous shoots and how she handled problems that came up. Is the person's problem-solving style something you are comfortable with? Do you feel calm around this person or on edge? Can you communicate well with him or her? It's important that you get along well with the individual because she will be your direct link to many others on the crew.

Sometimes a studio insists on a particular line producer that they have worked with in the past, particularly with an inexperienced producer or director. All you can do in that instance is try to get along with and learn as much as you can from him or her.

Director of Photography

Your cinematographer or director of photography (usually called "DP" for short) is a very key person on the shoot, someone who will be working as closely with the director as the production manager or line producer will be working with the producer. The DP will help the director plan the shots and set-ups, will be responsible for lighting each shot, and will provide ideas and suggestions for the overall look of the film.

Never hire a DP without first seeing a reel of samples of her work, usually a film the DP has shot. Even if the DP is well-known, it is important that you know something about her work. Make sure your director doesn't judge the work by the content of the reel, but by the style of lighting, particularly interior lighting or night scenes that may be difficult to light. After you and your director have seen a DP's work, meet with him or her to discuss the script and possible visual styles. Make sure that you and the director share a similar vision for the film with the DP *before* you hire him or her.

You can get names of potential DPs from your line producer, from other producers, from agents who represent DPs, and from the unions or the

Script Notes

On large features, directors of photography usually do not operate the camera. They oversee the lighting, decide on the lenses and camera settings, and, with the director, compose the shot; but the actual operation of the camera is the job of a camera operator. On documentaries and smaller shoots, however, the cinematographer operates the camera. She also may frequently shoot handheld scenes with the camera on her shoulder.

American Society of Cinematographers. The DP will need to begin work on the shoot a number of days or a number of weeks before production begins, depending on the length of the shoot. She will also need to be involved in location scouting to determine lighting requirements or lenses that might be needed for the intended location shots.

Production Designer

Film is part story-telling, part technical skill, and, like photography, part a visual art form. The person on your team who will, with the director and DP, help create the visual style of the film is the production designer. (On smaller films the production designer might be called the art director, and on larger shoots the production designer supervises an art director.) She can make the difference between a mediocre film and a good one. Like a painter, the production designer sees the script as a series of visual images. She may create storyboards in collaboration with the director, which as we have seen are basically drawings of key scenes in the film.

The production designer works closely not only with the director in imagining the look of the film, including color schemes and the design of sets, but then oversees the execution of that look by working with the people who are building sets and decorating them with props. The production designer also works with the costume designer and make-up and hair artists to make sure the actors look like they fit in with the overall visual style of the film.

In hiring a good production designer, both the producer and directors should meet with her after she has read the script and talk about any ideas she has for the film. Look at her previous films or a reel and consider the amount of experience the potential production designer has had. As with other key team members, your final decision about who to hire will probably be based on your gut instinct that one person will help you make a better film than other candidates.

Editor

Don't wait to hire the editor for the film until after you have finished production. The editor is a very important member of the team, and she will be overseeing assembling the dailies if you are shooting on film and doing some rough assemblies of scenes while you are still in production.

Editors, like film directors, have signature styles and tastes. They can make an ordinary or even dull picture better or they can make it worse. When hiring an editor, look at her reel or a film she has edited. Talk to her about your script and what kind of style the editor envisions is right for the picture. See if she seems imaginative and try to get a sense of how you will get along with her. You will be spending many more weeks working with the editor than with any of the production crew, so she should be someone you like and with whom you can communicate easily.

Production Sound Mixer

I've been focusing on the visual aspects of film and the people behind creating and capturing visual images, but sound is also critically important to a film. The person in charge of recording the sound on your production is the sound mixer. If she is not competent, then your production may have to spend extra money in post-production *looping* or dubbing lines of dialogue. The recommendation of other directors or line producers is the best way to find and evaluate potential production sound mixers. A reel might be great, but you have no way of knowing how much the production sound was cleaned up in post-production, thus adding to the cost of the film.

Other Departments and Crew

The heads of many of the other key departments on a film shoot may be people who are suggested by or who frequently work with either the production manager/line producer, production designer, or director of photography. Although as the producer or director you may not be involved directly in selecting these people, you should know their basic responsibilities.

Gaffer or Lighting Director

Because the lights and their placement is one of the most important tools of a cinematographer, the DP will usually suggest you hire a *gaffer* or lighting director whom she has worked with in the past and likes. A good gaffer knows all the lighting equipment well and can communicate easily with the DP about where the lights need to be placed to not only adequately light the scene but also to create a particular mood or feeling for the scene. A lighting director must be able to move quickly in response to the DP's direction.

The sexist term "best boy," now sometimes called "best person," is the gaffer's right-hand person. Often she may be working ahead, getting lights ready for the next set-up as the gaffer adjusts the final lighting for a shot.

A slow gaffer or best person or one who can't communicate well with the DP can cause the production to lose precious time, possibly have to shoot more days and ultimately to go over budget. If, however, you are confident of your DP's ability to keep the production on schedule, you should be able to trust the lighting director she wants to work with.

Verbal Action

looping When an actor attempts to match dialogue to her performance while watching a short piece of film formed into a loop. Looping is usually required because of faulty dialogue recorded under noisy conditions.

gaffer A film's lighting director and electrician, who sets up lights and makes sure there is adequate power for the lights and equipment.

continuity The necessity for the details of a scene to match the order of the scenes in a final edited film.

Grips

The key grip and her staff may be suggested by the gaffer or by the line producer. This person works closely with the DP and gaffer and is responsible for maintaining and operating all the equipment needed on the set. On large shoots, some grips such as a "dolly grip," who operates the camera dolly, only handle specialized equipment.

Assistant Directors

The first AD is the person who controls activities, keeps order on the set, and sees to it that each person is getting her job done. The second assistant director does all the call sheets and production reports. She also makes sure that actors are on the set when it is time for their scenes. On union shoots, the first and second assistant directors are both members of the Directors Guild. They are usually hired by the production manager.

Location Manager

If you are shooting a feature on location and not simply on a sound stage, you will probably need a location manager, although sometimes the production designer and line producer together may be able to handle the functions of a location manager. She will be responsible for scouting locations, securing permits for filming in public places, negotiating agreements with owners of location sites, and maintaining good public relations with the community in which you are shooting. Your production manager may know a good location manager or one may be suggested to the production by the film commission for the area in which you will be filming.

Transportation Captain

The transportation captain is usually hired by the production manager or line producer. She is responsible for coordinating the movement of all the cast, crew, and equipment from one location to another and she is also responsible for all the "show cars" or vehicles used in the film. If you are going to have Winnebagos for your stars, the transportation captain is also responsible for them. It is not an easy job and you need someone who is super-organized. All you need is for a car you are using in a shot not to be there or to run out of gas at a crucial moment in the scene. As with other key crew members, when transportation captains are good at what they do, things run smoothly. When someone is not good, however, it can cost the production a lot of money.

Costume Designer

The costume designer is the head of the Wardrobe Department and she will be responsible for choosing, cleaning, soiling, or altering the clothes all the actors will be wearing in every scene. In period pieces, the costume designer must research the historical period and design clothes that are right for that era. Even in contemporary films, however, the costume designer must carefully select the clothes for each character. For example, the script may only describe our lead character in *Something Is Rotten* as a female perfume company executive. But does she wear a tailored Armani pantsuit at work or a short, sexy Donna Karan suit? The choice of her clothing will make a difference in the viewer's attitude toward or expectations of the character. Therefore, the costume designer needs to confer with the director and the production designer to create the appropriate look for each character.

The production designer may, in fact, suggest that the production hire a particular wardrobe person or costume designer whom she has worked with in the past. Or, the line producer may suggest a good costume designer.

Make-Up and Hair

Make-up and hair artists are responsible for the make-up and hair of every actor prior to her going on the set to perform. Then, they must continue to touch up the actor during various takes of the scene. Sometimes lead actors insist on having their own make-up and hair artists. The skill of both crew members are very important to how the actor will look on film. In contemporary films, they can do things like change skin tones or cover blemishes. On other more complicated shoots, they may need to provide artificial beards, hairpieces, wigs, or teeth.

Cutaway

How many crew members do you need for a documentary shoot? You can do a small shoot where you may be filming in a hospital or other location that you must maneuver with as few people as possible with only the director, cinematographer, sound person, a gaffer/grip, and a production assistant. On the other hand, a larger documentary shoot might have more than one cinematographer and at least one assistant camera person, both a sound mixer and a sound assistant or "boom operator," as well as a gaffer, grip(s), and one or more PAs. No matter what the size of the crew, however, when hiring for a documentary, make sure your crew members have experience doing documentary films.

Script Supervisor

Another important member of the crew is the script supervisor. She is in charge of the *continuity* of the film—making sure that the details in one scene will match details in another, even though the scenes may be filmed out of sequence and filmed days or weeks apart. When the script supervisor makes a mistake, it is very visible on the screen. For example, you've probably noticed films where a character was beaten up in one scene and ends up with a cut or a black eye. In the very next scene in the film, supposedly the next day, the character suddenly doesn't have the cut or black eye. Then the cut or black eye might appear again in a later scene. A good script supervisor will keep those embarrassing mistakes from happening on your film.

He or she is usually hired by the line producer and may have worked with the line producer on other productions. The script supervisor also is responsible for keeping a record of the scene numbers and takes for each scene and the director's comments and decision on whether or not to print a take (if the movie is shot on film). Her notes can be very valuable to the editor.

Production Assistants

Finally, the people who really can help or hinder a production are often the lowest-paid people on the set. Production assistants, or PAs, are the runners and "gofers" of the production. A cheerful, energetic PA who knows her way around a set and gets things done can lift the spirits of your hard-working crew. So don't hire your investor's nephew, unless you really think the guy won't complain about the long hours and hard work and will actually get the job done.

The Least You Need to Know

- Making a movie is a collaborative effort and the experience and talent of your team members will make a difference in the quality of your film.

- The production manager or line producer is the below-the-line producer who will be most responsible for the smooth operation of your shoot.

- Since the director of photography, production designer, and editor will all contribute creatively to the visual style of the film, make sure you share a similar vision for the film with each of those key crew members.

Foreshadow: Planning the Shoot

In This Chapter

- Finding locations or using sound stages
- Securing the necessary equipment and supplies
- Arranging the food and hotel for cast and crew
- Determining the insurance coverage for your film

As you begin to hire your cast and crew, you are officially in pre-production for your film, the stage of filmmaking that occurs just prior to actually shooting the film, or production. Besides bringing your team on board, a number of other important tasks must be accomplished in pre-production. Thorough planning in pre-production can prevent costly problems during production.

As a first step, go back to the breakdown sheets you made when preparing the schedule (see Chapter 7, "The Set-Up: Script Breakdown and Shooting Schedule"). In addition to your cast list, you have prepared a list of all the interiors and exteriors you will need, all the special effects, vehicles, animals, or whatever else your production requires. Pre-production is the time to start finding or building those locations and arranging for everything else you will need when it's time to roll the cameras.

Arranging for Sets and Sound Stages

In the first several decades of movie-making, most Hollywood films were shot on sets constructed on the huge sound stages on studio lots. Today, most episodic television shows are filmed on sound stages, but many feature films are shot on location rather than on a sound stage or on a combination of real-world locations and constructed sets. Shooting on location generally gives the film a more realistic look, and most filmmakers prefer that.

There are many advantages of filming on sound stages, however. Sound stages offer a controlled environment so you don't have to deal with traffic or other random noises; they provide all the electrical power you need; you can hang lights from the ceiling; floor surfaces are smooth for dolly moves; and, because sets are built with *wild walls* that can be moved, you will have plenty of room to move the camera around. There are also dressing rooms for the actors and places to feed the crew.

> **Counterpoint**
>
> Sound stage rentals require careful planning. You need the large empty space for a period of time that includes not only the time to shoot the film but also time to build the sets and strike them. Because of their high overhead, studios like to keep their sound stages booked most of the time. Therefore, if you run behind schedule you may find that the space you need is not available for even an extra day.

If you decide to shoot some part of your film on a constructed set or sound stage, unless it is a studio film shooting on the studio's lot, you will need to make arrangements during pre-production to rent a sound stage and hire a set construction crew to build the necessary sets. The cost of renting a sound stage is usually very negotiable, especially if you can plan to shoot during a slow period, such as when episodic shows are on hiatus.

Scouting Locations

If you have decided to shoot your film on location, you need to find the places in the cities, towns, or rural areas in which you want to shoot. The Film Commission for that city, state, or country can usually be very helpful. Often they will find possible locations and send you photos of them before you even arrive for a location scout. They may also recommend a local person who has worked on other productions shot in the area to be your location manager. She will find a number of possible sites and arrange for people from the production including, at minimum, the director, director of photography, and production designer to view the sites. Usually the producer or line producer will also go on the location scout.

Light and Space

The director and director of photography will be evaluating the space at the possible location to see, if it is an interior, whether it is big enough to get the desired shot. Will there be enough room to set up the lights, to move the camera, and to provide the kinds of shots and images the director wants for the scene or scenes to be shot at that location?

Second, the team will evaluate what the light is like, for both interiors and exteriors, and what type of lights will be needed. If it is an exterior, what time of day is the production scheduled to shoot? If it's supposed to be early morning on the farm, make sure you know what time you will need to be there to set up so the time you are actually shooting will still look like early morning.

Is there room, either at the location or very nearby, for a *staging area* where equipment can be stashed and the crew can take a break and have a snack? Is there adequate parking for all of the vehicles bringing cast, crew, and equipment?

Next, what will the art department have to do to make the location look like the scene described in the script? What kinds of props are needed? Are the owners of the location agreeable to the temporary changes the production must make, including possibly moving their furniture out and bringing in different furniture?

Finally, where is the location? Is it a long way from other locations, so the production will lose a lot of time making a move? Can the location be dressed to look like one or more different locations in the film so that it can be used for more than one scene? Remember, your goal is to limit as much as possible the number of moves the production must make, while still trying to get the best possible sets for the film.

An important consideration in selecting a location is also the sound in the area. Is the location right underneath a flight path or on a bus route so that valuable time will be lost every time an airplane flies over or a bus roars by? Is it in an office building where the air conditioning sound is a loud buzz that can't be turned off without making people working on 30 stories suffer from the heat? Someone on the location scout should be listening to the sounds of the place so that a sound problem that will cause either delays or expensive fixes in post-production isn't discovered after you have already arrived on the location.

Cover Sets and Alternate Locations

Cover sets are places where you can shoot if the weather turns bad and you can't film the exteriors you planned on a particular day. Try to make sure that some of your locations will have the flexibility of letting you arrive on a number of different dates. You should also line up alternative locations in case of last-minute problems with a particular location's availability.

Adjustments to the Schedule

Once you have determined the locations where you will be shooting, you may have to make adjustments to your shooting schedule in order to accommodate the requirements of the different locations. A certain location may not be available on the day you originally planned to shoot the scene. Or you may want to move the days certain scenes are shot so that you will not have to move the company in the middle of the day.

 Verbal Action _____

wild walls Walls in a theater or on a sound stage that can be moved to create a set.

staging area An area near a set where crew members can set up and store equipment and supplies.

cover set A set that is available on a flexible timetable so that it can be used for filming on a day when weather or other problems prevent filming at the scheduled location.

Permissions and Permits

The production will need to negotiate with the owners of the property at each location for their permission to use the location, usually in exchange for a payment. Sometimes, with documentary and low-budget features, you can get the use of locations without paying for them. In either case, your location manager, production manager, or line producer should have a standard location agreement that both the owner or manager of the location and a representative of the production should sign.

If you want to shoot on public property, you may also have to obtain certain permits. Once again, your trusty film commission representative can help you navigate the various local bureaucracies to get the necessary permissions and permits.

Equipment

Pre-production is also the time for you to make deals with equipment and supply houses for all of the supplies and equipment you will need for the shoot.

Each department head will make a list of what they are going to need and will try to get everything that is needed with the money available for that item in the budget. For larger-budget items, the department head will work with the line producer or production manager to negotiate the best price. On a documentary or very low-budget feature, the producer will usually negotiate all the purchases and rental agreements.

Camera Package

The most important piece of equipment you will need is, course, your camera. As I discussed in Chapter 8, "Show Me the Money: The Budget," you have the choice of a number of film or video formats in which to shoot. Once you have decided whether you are filming in 35mm film, 16mm film, or a video format, the specific camera package will usually be determined by the director of photography, and the line producer or production manager will negotiate with equipment rental houses for the best price for the particular package.

Prices are usually for the day or the week and they really do vary among equipment houses, so you will save money if you shop around. In addition to price, however, it's important to know the supplier's reputation for maintaining, servicing, and replacing gear quickly if something breaks down. Your director of photography will generally know if a supplier has a reputation for reliable equipment and for solving problems quickly.

Script Notes

If you are filming at a distant location, your camera equipment may be shipped to you in a few dozen cases. Make sure that everything you ordered is there and that everything is working properly in enough time to get replacement equipment to the location if there is a problem. The assistant camera person or the DP should test the camera and lenses by shooting and developing some test film during pre-production.

Lights and Grip Equipment

If you are shooting on film, you will need a fairly extensive lighting package. Again, the director of photography will develop the list of what is needed. Sometimes a gaffer may own some lights and you can rent them inexpensively from him or her. There are a number of different types of lights that will help the DP create the look that the director wants to get in various scenes of the film. Most of the time lights come with stands, *barn doors*, and *silks*, but be sure to check that your package includes those items.

Grip equipment is all the stuff that you need to make everything work on the set. It's better to get plenty of grip equipment, even if you never use some of it, because costly delays can result from not having a simple clamp or C stand that is needed for a shot. Grip equipment covers a wide range of items including such everyday things as apple boxes, ladders, and sandbags to more film-specific items such as silks and *flags* for directing or shading light. Equipment like walkie-talkies, first aid kits, flashlights, and a director's chair can also be ordered from rental houses dealing in grip equipment.

Some grip equipment, such as gaffer's tape and plastic gels, are called *expendables* because they have to be purchased rather than rented. On small shoots, your grip might have the needed expendables and you can just buy them from him or her.

Sound Equipment

A basic sound equipment package for film includes the sound recorder and various microphones that are needed for different kinds of shots. Often, the sound mixer you hire will have her own equipment, which you can rent. It's usually a better deal than getting equipment from a rental house. You may have to purchase batteries and ¼-inch tape if you are recording on film. Also, you may have to rent any special microphones or extra sets of earphones (for listening to the sound exactly as it is picked up by the recorder) that are needed for the production.

Stock or Tape

In pre-production, you need to order the raw film stock or tape for the format in which you are shooting. While doing your budget, you estimated your shooting ratio, which is how many feet of film you plan to shoot for every foot of film in the final cut. A two-hour film is 10,800 feet of 35mm film. Most films are shot at ratios ranging between 5 to 1 and 20 to 1. So if your shooting ratio is 10 to 1, you will need 108,000 feet of 35mm film.

Be sure to also take into account the inevitable waste that occurs with film. In 100,000 feet of film, for example, as much as 20,000 to 23,000 feet can be wasted—such as when the camera is rolling but performances haven't started or have already stopped. Film waste can also occur because of *short-ends*, which are bits of film left in a *magazine* that are too short to be used for the next scene. There is a similar amount of waste that occurs with videotape.

Most productions order film stock directly from the manufacturer, such as Eastman Kodak, or from various film supply houses. If you are operating on a very low budget, you can buy film stock from film exchanges that buy unused, unopened cans of film from major studio productions and resell it at a reduced cost to independent producers. If you buy from a film exchange, try not to buy bits and pieces from several productions with different emulsion numbers, but see if you can get enough leftover stock for your film from one production. It's also a good idea to buy one can of film first and test it to see if it's okay before purchasing the entire lot.

Verbal Action

barn doors Hinged, solid black doors that fit on lights and are used to control light during filming.

silks White cloths used for modifying the amount and quality of light during filming, often used to "bounce" light in a particular direction.

flags Devices placed in front of lights to cast shadows.

Special Effects Planning

You can save money on special effects and avoid costly locations when you plan carefully during pre-production. With proper planning, there are many inexpensive tricks for filming in moving vehicles—trains, planes, buses, automobiles—or for creating jungle and forest scenes, for example. You can also create extraordinary visual effects such as car crashes, explosions, or a burning city by using miniatures. Your art director or production designer will be able to create the miniatures or you may be hiring a special-effects coordinator or studio. Any effects that use fire will require the attendance of a fire marshal and should always be done by a certified explosives expert.

Laboratories and Sound Facilities

During pre-production, you will be making arrangements with a laboratory and sound facility if you are shooting on film. If you are shooting on video, you will only need to make arrangements for having the tape transferred into a format (such as VHS) for convenient viewing of what you have shot.

If you are shooting a feature film, you should definitely use a laboratory that has handled feature films in the past. Your DP may suggest several labs that she has worked with. The price you will be paying the lab for developing the film and making the various types of prints is generally very competitive and negotiable. Find a lab you feel is good and then call around for prices so you can negotiate a good deal with the lab you want to work with.

Finding a good sound facility for transferring your $1/4$-inch tape during production and for post-production sound services is another important pre-production task. Your production sound mixer will usually know good facilities. You might save money by making a package deal to do all of your sound work at one facility or by using a smaller, less expensive facility.

Food, Drink, and Accommodations

Never underestimate the importance of food and beverages to your cast and crew. In pre-production, you will be lining up a catering service for the shoot and also hiring a craft services person to be responsible for beverages, breakfasts, and afternoon snack food on the set. Don't cut corners on the food and drinks or you will have an unhappy, disgruntled crew. It is a sign of your respect for the hard work you expect from the crew that you see to it that they have plenty of good stuff to eat and drink.

If you are a small production shooting at different locations during the day—such as a documentary shoot—rather than using a catering service, you may find it more efficient to

Script Notes _____

Unless you have reserved office space elsewhere in the location area for your production offices, hotel rooms often make very convenient offices. They can be reserved for a production office, an accounting office, a wardrobe room, a room for camera and sound equipment, and so on. A hotel banquet or conference room might be reserved for screening dailies, for production meetings, or even for rehearsals.

simply get menus from a local restaurant and take the crew's orders in the morning for your production assistant to pick up at lunch time.

Also, for all shoots, make sure that the cast and crew have a comfortable place to sit and eat. Don't expect them to huddle on the floor while wolfing down a sandwich, even if that is how you usually eat lunch.

When you are shooting on location, you will have to make arrangements with a hotel to put up your cast and crew. Your production office will become the middle-person between the hotel and your cast and crew. You need to find out each individual's preferences—such as king-size bed or no smoking—and give the information to the hotel, along with the date of arrival and departure for each person. Also make sure the hotel has adequate parking for all the production's vehicles.

Insurance

Insurance requirements are different for different types of films. A movie with lots of action sequences requiring special stunts may cost more to insure than one without those sometimes dangerous or costly shots. You may need some or all of these types of insurance coverage:

- **Cast insurance** insures the production against the death, injury, or illness of any insured cast member (usually just the leads) and/or the director.

- **Film and tape insurance** insures against the loss, damage, or destruction of raw film or tape stock or exposed film, tape, or soundtracks.

- **Faulty stock, camera, or processing** insures against the loss, damage, or destruction of raw film stock or tape or exposed film or recorded tape due to faulty equipment or accidental erasure of videotapes.

- **Props, sets, and wardrobe** insurance covers props, sets, scenery, costumes, and wardrobes against loss, damage, or destruction.

- **Extra expense** reimburses the production for any extra expense caused by the damage or destruction of property or facilities used by the production.

- **Miscellaneous equipment** covers the loss, damage, or destruction of equipment owned or rented to the production company.

- **Property damage liability** covers the damage or destruction of the property of others while the property is being used by the production.

- **Errors and omissions** insures the production against lawsuits alleging the unauthorized use of titles, format, ideas, characters, plots, plagiarism, unfair competition, or breach of contract, as well as alleged libel, slander, defamation of character, or invasion of privacy.

- **Worker's compensation** provides medical, disability, or death benefits to any cast or crew member who becomes injured while working on the production.

- **Comprehensive liability** covers claims for bodily injury or property damage liability arising during the production, including covering all non-owned vehicles.

- **Completion guaranty bond** provides completion funds for up to 100 percent of the total budget.

Most of the above insurance coverage has deductibles. Worker's Compensation insurance is required by state law; rental houses usually require that you have Miscellaneous Equipment coverage; and Errors and Omission insurance is usually required by a distributor prior to the theatrical release of a film or its airing on television.

The cost of the insurance coverage you choose for your film could amount to up to 3 percent of the total budget, depending upon the location site, length of the shoot, any dangerous stunts, or the need to insure performers who have had health or other problems. It's important to be properly insured and all of the insurance coverage should be secured during pre-production.

 Verbal Action _____

expendables   Small items needed for a film shoot, such as gaffer's tape or plastic gels, which must be purchased rather than rented from equipment houses.

short-ends   Ends of a can of film that are too short to be used for the next scene to be shot.

magazine   A container that fits into a motion picture camera that does not admit light and feeds and takes up the film.

The Least You Need to Know

- When filming on location, be sure to arrange cover sets and alternative locations in case of weather or other problems.
- It's better to have more equipment than you need rather than losing time if you don't have a necessary item.
- Check out all equipment before the shoot and test the film stock.
- Make sure your cast and crew are well-fed and treated with respect during the production.
- Get the necessary insurance coverage for your film.

Part 3

Roll Camera: Production

You've made it through script development and pre-production. Now it's time for the second phase of filmmaking—production.

This part of the book covers that critical and expensive stage of the filmmaking process. It focuses on working with the crew, directing the actors, and directing yourself to make a professional-looking and emotionally-effective film. This part also deals with potential production problems and the things you must know if you are making a non-fiction film.

Chapter 11

Directing the Crew

In This Chapter

- ◆ Doing your homework
- ◆ Communicating what you want to the crew
- ◆ Knowing the basic rules for shooting and editing
- ◆ Staying on schedule

It's time to roll the camera, and the leadership of the team shifts from the producer, who has been hiring everyone and making sure everything is ready for production, to the director. The director is responsible during production for making sure each scene of the script is captured on film in such a way that the entire film can be cut together to make a movie.

The first time I directed a film, the producer, who was also a first-timer, told me that he was worried initially that I wasn't living up to his image of a director. His image of a director was that of a person who rules a set with an iron fist, always certain of her vision and never wavering. Instead, he watched me change my mind about a camera angle at the suggestion of the cinematographer or embrace other suggestions made by the crew. The producer was concerned that I wasn't in control of the set. Then, on a weekend day off, he happened to watch a documentary about the "making of" one of Steven Spielberg's films. He watched Spielberg behave as I had—he, too, was flexible and often took suggestions from his team. My producer relaxed about my style, and together he and I and a great crew finished the film without a glitch. When I later heard this tale from the producer, I was, of course, pleased to be compared to Spielberg.

Different directors do, in fact, have different styles of working with their crew and cast, usually reflective of their different personalities. Some may rule the set more strictly and others may seem more relaxed and easy-going but, generally, to make the best possible movie, a director should be flexible enough to take advantage of the experience and creativity the members of the team can bring to the shoot.

Be Prepared

A director inspires confidence in her crew when it is obvious that she is prepared for the day's shoot and has a vision of what she wants to capture on film each day. That preparation includes knowing what shots you, as the director, want for each scene and therefore what camera set-ups will be needed. For complicated scenes, you may need to prepare a storyboard, often with the help of the art director. A simple drawing of the floor plan of the scene may also be helpful in scenes that are not storyboarded.

It's not enough for a director to have a vision of what she wants unless the director is also able to easily and clearly communicate that vision to the crew. Shot lists, storyboards, and floor plans are the tools the director can use to show the crew what it is that she wants in a scene. Doing homework and preparing those items is very important to having a smooth shoot.

If you are a first-time or inexperienced director and are unsure of what you want to accomplish in a scene, the crew may feel you don't know what you are doing. Worse, the producer and production manager may lose confidence in you, fearing that you won't be able to keep the production moving on schedule and therefore on budget. If, however, you know what you want and can communicate it clearly, then both the producer and crew will relax. When people are relaxed, they are more creative. A relaxed crew may help you find a better, easier, or more interesting way to capture the kind of image you want and will feel free to make suggestions to help you get the best possible shot.

> **Script Notes**
>
> A director should never hesitate to ask questions or solicit advice from members of the crew. On many films, when the DP and director have already discussed the scene, the DP will take on the task of selecting the angles and choreographing the action while the director concentrates on the content of a scene. When a director knows when to ask for help from members of the crew, the scenes can be shot in less time and with better overall coverage.

Prepping the Crew

Many directors find that it works well to have a production meeting before the shoot begins, in which you can explain to the entire crew your vision of the film and what you hope to accomplish during production. That way everyone feels they are part of a team with a specific goal, rather than just hired hands. The result is usually increased creativity and enthusiasm for the work in every department.

If you can't afford to have a large production meeting before the shoot, then make sure that you communicate with as many crew members as you can before you begin shooting. Each crew member needs to feel like a part of the production and needs to understand what you are going to want each day.

In addition to prepping the entire crew, it is also essential that you have in-depth discussions with the director of photography prior to shooting so that your work together on the set will go smoothly.

Set Walk-Throughs

When possible, it can also be a very helpful step toward creating a smooth shoot for the director and key crew members to walk through the sets and locations before production. Unlike during a location scout when the purpose is to evaluate whether or not the location will work, the purpose of this walk-through will be to discuss the mood and feel of the scene that the director wants to capture on film. During a walk-through, crew members will not only locate problems and thus be prepared to solve them before the shoot, they may also make suggestions that will change the shots the director envisions in some way.

When the Shooting Begins

When you arrive on the set for the first day of principal photography and each day thereafter, your first task is to again go over the shots for each scene and the order of the shots with the crew. Next, bring the actors on the set before they go to wardrobe and make-up and have them walk through the scene. Not only will this familiarize the actors with the set before doing their scene, perhaps even more importantly, it will show the crew the action that will be taking place in the scene—where the actors will stand and how they will move. The members of the crew can then do their jobs with the knowledge of exactly what is going to happen in the scene.

Knowing What Will Cut

To work well with the entire crew and especially with the DP, the director needs to know the basic types of shots, how different shots in a scene cuts with each other and how different scenes will cut together. This is often referred to as "editing in the camera." You need to know some basic rules for making sure shots cut together, even though your DP hopefully won't let you make mistakes. Also, the script supervisor will alert you to potential problems, such as when you haven't kept a consistent direction of movement.

Although the DP should not expect you to know everything about lighting, she has more respect for you if you know the basic rules for what shots will or will not cut together well in the final film.

A basic rule of thumb in Hollywood is that anything that makes the viewer aware of the camera will take the audience out of the story and therefore is generally discouraged in Hollywood movies. Viewers can be distracted by clumsy camera moves or jerky cuts or fascinated by beautiful camera movement—in either case it takes the viewer's attention off the story and puts it on the technique.

Cutaway

The most efficient way to shoot a scene is to shoot the longest or widest shot first and then capture the medium or close shots. The longest shot usually requires the most lighting and is therefore the most time-consuming set-up. If you do it first, the lighting crew will then only have to make small adjustments for closer shots. Also, if you shoot the long shots first, the basic look of the scene will already be established and the DP won't have to worry about matching the light in the scene as she would if the close shots were filmed first.

Consistent Direction of Movement

When actors, or any moving objects on film, move in a consistent direction, the action is easier for the audience to follow. For example, imagine a scene where an actor walks up a sidewalk, moving from left to right in front of the camera, and then knocks at a door. When the door is opened the shot is cut. Then, if a subsequent shot of the actor entering through the door into the room is shot with the actor crossing from right to left in front of the camera, when the two shots are cut together, the cut is more noticeable or jarring for the viewer. If, on the other hand, the actor maintains the same left-to-right movement in front of the camera as in the earlier shot, then there is a smooth, less noticeable transition. Therefore, most of the time, maintaining a consistent direction of action is a good idea.

Consistent Direction of Looks

An even more important shooting rule is to maintain a consistent direction in terms of where the actor is looking between shots. If, for example, two actors are speaking to each other in a scene and the camera is placed so as to get a master two-shot of the actors, when it is time to do medium shots or close-ups on one or both of the two actors, each actor must be looking in the same direction as in the master shot.

This rule is a fairly simple one, but filmmakers make mistakes and break it all the time, causing headaches in the editing room. When such mistakes happen, it is referred to as "crossing the *imaginary line*." The imaginary line is a line that runs through the actors, parallel to the camera. The camera should always be placed on the same side of that line, for the master shot as well as for the closer shots, and the actors should each be looking in the same direction for all medium or close shots that are intended to be cut with that master shot. If not, when the scene is cut together, it will not seem as though the actors are looking at one another.

The vertical direction of the actors' looks must also be consistent. If a master shot, for example, has one actor looking up at another, in the close-up, the one who is looking up should continue to be looking above the camera lens.

Matching of Shots

Certain kinds of shots will match or cut together better than others. The goal in shooting a scene is to get several different angles or shots of the scene—or *coverage* of a scene—that will match or cut together well in the editing room.

One type of shot that will be easier to match in the editing room is a shot that is cut on action. It gives the editor more flexibility in making the cut when there is movement in a shot rather than a static shot.

Also, shots that have enough overlap will cut together better. You should always shoot the action past the point where it will be cut by the editor and start the new angle with part of the action that was completed before the first cut. This will give the editor several feet of overlapping action with which to make a smooth cut.

Cutaways and Transitions

A *cutaway* is a term for a shot that is inserted into a scene to show action at another location or to show a face or an object. It is usually a very brief shot and is most often used to bridge any awkward cuts or edits. We have all seen the stock shot of a full moon stuck between a couple of scenes or even in the middle of a scene. That's a cutaway. A wise director will get plenty of interesting cutaways to cover shots that are not matched well enough, so that the various cuts in the film are not awkward.

Other shots that are used as a bridge or transition in a film are simply called *transitional shots*. There are several different kinds of transitional shots—those that bridge the action from one location to another, from one picture size to another, or from one camera position to another.

Verbal Action _____

imaginary line   In film production, an imaginary line parallel to the camera that is drawn through the actors. With rare exceptions, the camera should always be on the same side of that line in filming a particular scene.

coverage   In film production, getting enough shots to cover transitions or cuts within scenes and from scene to scene, or simply enough different shots in a scene to pick up the pace of the movie and make it visually interesting.

cutaway   A brief shot that takes the viewer out of a scene for a moment. Cutaways are often used to bridge cuts within a scene or between scenes.

For example, in cutting between picture size, never cut directly from a full shot to a close shot. Either zoom in slowly to the close-up or use a medium shot as a transition and then go to the close-up.

Even when cutting from one location to another, it is better to bridge the cut with a transitional shot unless you are cutting on action or movement. For example, in *Something Is Rotten*, if you have an establishing shot of a field of flowers (from which perfumes are made), don't cut directly to an establishing shot of the perfume factory unless you have some movement like our heroine driving past the field of flowers, perhaps with a closer shot of her smiling as she sniffs the fragrant air, then driving her car up to the perfume factory.

The key to understanding when you will need a transition is to simply imagine the picture in your mind. Usually you will come up with a set of shots that will flow easily on film.

The First Take

When the shot set-up is ready and the actors are brought back to the set in costume and with make-up, most directors like to rehearse the scene at least once before rolling the camera. This gives the DP the opportunity to check the lighting and make last-minute camera adjustments. The sound mixer can also use the dress rehearsal to adjust sound levels, and, if a dolly is used in the scene, its moves can be practiced by the dolly grip.

When you are ready to go for your first *take*, the first assistant director will ask for quiet on the set and then say, "roll sound and camera" on a film or "roll tape" or just "roll camera" on a video shoot. When the camera operator indicates that the camera is rolling at full speed by saying "I have speed" or just "speed," you need to say "action" to tell the cast to begin their performances. When the scene is over—or before it is over if there is a problem—you need to say "cut" to stop the camera and sound recorder.

Some directors always print their first take unless there is an obvious technical problem. For both cast and crew, there is often a sense of anticipation or excitement in filming the first take that isn't always sustained through several takes. If you are not satisfied with the first take, then you may require several more takes to get the shot or performance you want. Even if you do feel satisfied with the first take, it is usually a good idea to get at least one more take as "insurance"—there could be technical or performance problems that no one noticed in the shot that might become evident when the film is developed and screened.

Pick-Up Shots and Wild Tracks

If you are shooting a long master shot, doing one or more *pick-up shots* may be necessary. Let's say, for example, that our heroine in *Something Is Rotten* is taking a police detective on a tour of the room where potential new perfume scents are being tested by employees who have extraordinary senses of smell. As they walk through the area, the heroine and the detective are talking about the case of the "perfumed robber." If you get a take of your master shot in which the dialogue is acceptable in the first half but there is a problem in the second half, you could shoot a pick-up shot starting from the place where the dialogue wasn't so good rather than starting the shot over again from the top of the scene.

If you decide to do a pick-up shot, you will need a cutaway or a transitional shot: perhaps a medium shot of our heroine studying the detective, or perhaps a point-of-view shot of the whole area as viewed by the heroine and the detective, or perhaps a shot of one of the employees in the room smelling some perfume. Any of these types of shots will allow you to cut between the beginning of the master shot and the pick-up of some portion of the end of the shot.

Even if a long master shot seems acceptable, it's a good idea to get extra cutaways and medium or close-up shots just in case you decide in the editing room that you want to pick up the pace of the scene. As I'll discuss further in Chapter 13, "Directing Yourself," more frequent cuts will accelerate the pace of a film and give it more visual variety.

If a master shot was pretty good except for a problem with a line an actor says or a word or two that wasn't clear because of sound problems, rather than doing another take of the whole scene, a *wild track* can be made by having the actor record the line without the camera running. This wild track can later be cut into the scene.

CAUTION

Counterpoint

Not every rule for shooting is iron clad and must be followed at all times during a film shoot. Great directors such as John Ford, for example, have experimented with changing the direction of movement in scenes that have to be cut together. More recently, Steven Soderberg used jump cuts effectively in *The Limey* (1999). Directors, however, should know the basic rules and should know the effect that will be created in the viewer if a rule is broken.

Preventing Crew Fatigue

As the director, you are responsible for staying on schedule and on budget. If you are unsure of yourself and can't decide if a take is good enough, you may require many extra takes and slow the production down. The already long shooting days will be even longer and, as the days go on, your crew will usually become fatigued and disgruntled. Tired crew members are then more likely to make mistakes that will slow down the production even more.

The way to prevent this escalating cycle is for the director to be prepared, to be decisive, and also to be willing to compromise when she has to. Even though you may be a perfectionist, there are times when, as a director, you will have to accept a less-than-perfect shot or performance simply to keep the production moving, keep it on budget, and prevent your crew from burning out.

Verbal Action

transitional shot   A shot, such as a cutaway, that bridges two scenes, shots, or camera angles within a scene.

take   An individual piece of film with no cuts, or one shot of a scene. A shot may be filmed several times until a satisfactory take is achieved.

pick-up shot   A continuation shot of a scene that is picked up before a point where there is a problem.

wild track   A sound recording of a line of dialogue or other sound made independently of the camera.

Respect for the Locations and Community

Most crew members are very respectful of the location sites on which they work. When striking a set, they put a site back to the condition in which they found it—and sometimes in better condition than they found it. The producer and line producer are concerned about how the location is treated because it costs extra money if anything is damaged. The director, however, also sets a tone for the shoot, and if she is respectful of the locations, the crew generally follows suit.

Because a production often is on location in a community for weeks or months, word gets around if the location owners or people in the community aren't treated well by the members of the film production. A bad reputation can cause not just headaches but costly delays, so it's important that everyone on the crew is respectful, keeps agreements, and is generally polite and friendly with people at the locations and other members of the community whose lives may be disrupted by the presence of the film production.

The Least You Need to Know

- ◆ A director who is prepared and can communicate clearly her vision will win the respect of the crew.
- ◆ Directors can often benefit from listening to the ideas and suggestions of the crew.
- ◆ Directors should have a basic knowledge of how well shots are likely to cut together in the editing room.
- ◆ The best way to keep a production on schedule is for the director to be prepared, decisive, and willing to compromise.

Chapter 12

Directing Actors

In This Chapter

- ◆ Knowing what you want from an actor
- ◆ Communicating with and rehearsing actors
- ◆ Understanding different styles of acting
- ◆ Directing actors on the set

So far you've learned how important it is for the director to know the technical requirements of filmmaking, including the fundamentals of cinematography and editing. Perhaps even more important, however, is for a director to create the proper atmosphere for actors in order to elicit good performances. An audience will forgive most technical inadequacies if the film's performances are strong and believable. But perfect camera angles, camera movement, and lighting will mean nothing if the acting isn't good.

In working with actors to elicit believable performances and in deciding on when those performances are right for the film, directors must use intuition and feelings rather than their artistic eye or knowledge of lighting and editing. To make the best possible film, a film director must have what author Daniel Goleman calls "emotional intelligence" and must also know something about actors and acting techniques.

For their part, actors are unique in what they add to the film. Unlike other artists on the set who use cameras, sound recorders, props, and designs to make their contribution to the film, actors use themselves in their art—their bodies, minds, and life histories. As a director, you can help actors best make their contributions when you understand the methods and techniques actors use in their craft.

Knowing What You Want

One of the first tasks of the director is to analyze and get to know the characters in the film as they fit into the tapestry of the entire film. Each actor will be focusing primarily on her character. As the director, your perspective on the character may not be exactly the same as the actor's because you will be focusing on the entire story and each character's part of that story. Through discussions and rehearsals, however, you and the actors will hopefully come to a closer vision of each of the characters.

> **Script Notes** _____
>
> It may be a good idea for those who are serious about directing to take acting classes. I did, and what I learned by actually acting out scenes in classes was far greater than I could ever have learned in books or even in directing classes. Acting is being in the moment, it is reacting naturally, and it requires a lot of intense energy. Taking acting classes will help you appreciate and respect the actor's art.

Most of the problems between actors and directors are caused by directors who don't know what they want. As the director, you must know the point of each scene. You must know how each scene is part of and contributes to the emotional lives of your characters. In general, you must know what your characters want, what they get in each scene, and how these experiences set them up for the next scene.

Knowing the Characters

Some of the questions about each character that you, the director, will be asking and answering for yourself include:

◆ What are the basic facts about the character— her age, occupation, education, background, environment?

◆ What is the character like physically—how does she move and react?

◆ How does the character think about things—what are her beliefs and attitudes?

◆ What are the character's dominant emotions, feelings, or emotional attitudes?

◆ Is the character a simple one with a dominant character trait or a more complex character with contradictory traits?

◆ What is the character's arc throughout the story?

◆ What is the character's predominant desire in the story?

◆ In each scene, who is the character with and how does she feel about him or her?

♦ What does the character want from the other person or persons in each scene?

♦ What is the character doing to get what she wants in the scene?

If you know the answers to the previous questions, you know a character's attitude and motivation in a scene and will be able to give your actors the necessary background to the scene and the essential information she needs to experience the emotional moment of the scene.

It's important that you don't stray too far from the characters as depicted in the script and that you keep your actors from straying from the script. It is the job of the actor to breathe life into the character, but it is your job to make sure that the character that comes to life isn't a different character from the one depicted in the script. A good writer intentionally writes every moment and every line of dialogue in a script. Directors and actors must interpret the script, not rewrite it, because even the slightest changes in a character can throw the movie off balance and make a good script turn into a bad movie.

Sometimes actors suggest changes in the lines of dialogue and you will have to evaluate those suggestions. If the change is something that is perhaps easier to say and doesn't change the meaning of the line much, and if you like the change, there is probably no reason not to agree to it. If the new dialogue affects the meaning of the line in some way, however, make sure that it doesn't cause the character to change even in a very subtle way or you may end up with inconsistencies in the character in other parts of the film.

Communicating What You Want

Once you have the information you need about the characters and know what you want, you have to communicate that to the actors. In general, you don't want them thinking about their characters as much as you want them to be feeling their characters' emotions and thoughts. Directors are most successful in working with actors when they don't talk about the results they want to see in a scene but instead about the characters' process. Directors who talk about results say things like, "In this scene you should be really furious with Jim." When you give an actor direction like that, you make her think about trying to achieve those results, which means that instead of inhabiting her character, she remains in her head, thinking about how to achieve the results you want.

On the other hand, if you say something like "Make Jim stop treating you like you are a fool," you are talking about the character's intention or motivation. The actor no longer has to think, "Now I'm supposed to be getting mad." Instead, she can concentrate completely on her life as her character and can pursue the character's objective in the scene. And she will probably end up giving you the results you wanted—getting furious at Jim— or maybe something even better than you imagined.

Simple directions such as how to move in front of the camera during the scene or paraphrasing the character's desire or motivation in a scene is far more helpful to an actor than giving specific instructions on how to behave. And worse, those specific instructions might produce a stilted, forced performance.

Rehearsals

Once you have done your own homework on each of the characters and perhaps have had some preliminary discussions about the characters or individual scenes, you are ready to begin rehearsals with actors. Some film directors and actors do not like rehearsals except limited ones on the set because they feel that rehearsals can kill the spontaneity of the scene. As a director, you should definitely be sensitive to the problem of over-rehearsing. Rehearsals, however, often do help illuminate problems in scenes prior to production that can be worked out in pre-production, rather than wasting costly time on the set.

Cutaway

The great film director John Ford, famous for his westerns, had unique ways of working with actors. For one thing, he would create a little world off-camera that was similar emotionally and physically to the world he wanted the actors to create on camera. He would bring his cast on location before the shoot, and the location would be set up so that the actors lived in a similar way as in the film. For example, if the characters were part of a family, the actors portraying those characters would be housed together as though they were in fact living together. This is one of the techniques that enabled him to get superb performances out of his actors.

A First Script Reading

Some directors find it helpful to assemble the whole cast in a room for a reading of the script. The director or perhaps the producer can read the descriptions of the action during this reading. The purpose of a read-through of the script is to give the director an opportunity to make notes about particular scenes and to watch the interplay among the characters. The rehearsal also gives the actors, who may have been focusing primarily on their own characters, a sense of the whole story and how their roles fit into it.

Scene Work and Blocking

In addition to a script reading by the entire cast, it is important to rehearse individual scenes. By spending some time on key scenes, the director and actors can come to mutual understandings about the scenes and the characters. Also, scene rehearsals give the director an opportunity to stage or "block" the action. The *blocking* of a scene should further the story or contribute visually to the scene's purpose. For example, if the scene is a three-person scene where two of the people are new lovers and the third is an unhappy outsider and former friend to both, you might have the two lovers seated together on a couch and the other character pacing nervously around the room rather than having all three standing or seated together.

Many directors don't want to block scenes during off-set rehearsals, not wanting to make actors move until they are actually on the set in front of the camera. Blocking the action during an off-set rehearsal, however, does accomplish two things. First, it allows the actor a chance to incorporate the moves she will need to do on the set into her performance so they become second nature. Second, if the scene is not working well during rehearsal, the director may want to change the blocking or try out a few different blocking patterns.

When to Stop Rehearsing

It's important that you do not expect to see a finished, polished performance in your off-set rehearsals. Actors need time to explore and experiment with their characters. Also, if the scene becomes too perfect in rehearsals, you may never get to the same place again and the actual on-set performances may lack the magic and spontaneity of the earlier rehearsal. Once you feel that you and the actors both know and agree on what you are going for in a scene, stop rehearsing. Wait for the real magic to happen in front of the camera.

CAUTION

Counterpoint

Never demonstrate to an actor how you would play a scene. Although you may be tempted to do so because you are not getting what you want in the scene, it's important to re-member that you are a different person with different facial ex-pressions and a different voice than the actor. You don't want the actor to try to mimic you, you want him or her to bring her own creative talent to the role.

Respecting the Actor's Style

Actors are professionals and they almost all have some degree of training. The kind of training an actor has usually affects how she works on the film. A director should be familiar with the different kinds of training an actor may have and should respect the way an actor works. After all, the actor and the director have the same goal—achieving the best possible performance—so the director should not try to impose a method of how to get to that performance but rather encourage and help the actor in using the methods that work for him or her.

Method Acting

The acting style known as *method acting* is the most well-known and widely used acting technique in the United States. It was initially developed in Russia in the early 1900s by Constantin Stanislavski, the director of the Moscow Art Theater. The method first became popular in the United States in the 1930s in the Group Theater of New York, a theater group formed as a government-sponsored project during the Depression. One of the founders of the Group Theater was Lee Strasberg, who, with other teachers involved with the project, interpreted Stanislavski's work for American acting students. In the late 1940s, Strasberg began to teach at the Actors Studio, which became well-known for producing many great film actors, including Marlon Brando, Paul Newman, Anne Bancroft, Montgomery Clift, and Shelley Winters. More recent practitioners of the method style of acting include such renowned actors as Al Pacino, Dustin Hoffman, and Robert DeNiro.

In addition to Strasberg, other prominent acting teachers who came out of the Group Theater and emphasized different aspects of the Stanislavski method included Stella Adler, Robert Lewis, Elia Kazan, and Stanford Meisner. These and other teachers have many variations on how the method is taught and interpreted. Strasberg, for example, focused on the importance of emotional memory, while Stella Adler stressed the importance of imagination, and Meisner emphasized the need to stay in the moment. In general, however, method acting focuses on internal means the actor can use to access her emotions and get to the emotional truth of a character in a scene.

One of the techniques used by method actors to access their emotions is relaxation. There are a number of specific relaxation exercises that actors use to get their bodies and minds to relax. Once relaxed, the performer can generally access her emotions more easily.

Perhaps the most well-known of the method-acting techniques are sense memory exercises in which the actor seeks to stimulate a feeling required by a scene by reliving or recreating a similar emotion. In sense memory exercises, the actor concentrates on a particular sense (taste, smell, sight, touch, or hearing) and then recalls an incident using that sense. For example, if the actor is trying to recall an event that took place at the ocean, she might use the smell of the ocean to trigger the scene and take herself back to the event. By using the senses, the actor doesn't just remember the event, but instead experiences it emotionally.

Emotional memory is another technique that is sometimes used by method actors. With emotional memory, the actor will relive an event that triggers a particular emotion that is needed in the scene. Sometimes the relived experience is painful to the actor and she will need some time after a scene to come out of the emotional state.

Other Acting Techniques

Although method acting is the most widely used acting technique among American actors, it is certainly not the only kind of training that your actors might have. Some actors are trained in what is loosely referred to as *technical acting*. Unlike method actors, who believe it is necessary to feel a role during a performance and give themselves over to a character, other actors feel it is better to rely on acting techniques to make the character meaningful. These actors have the details of a performance carefully planned, with nothing left to chance. This type of acting is also called classical training. Instead of the performance coming from the inside and from the feelings of the actor, with technical or classically trained actors, the performance will come from the outside and her analysis of the character and the scene.

The audience should not be able to tell whether a performance was obtained by using emotional techniques or simply analytical techniques, because the distinction between the two styles is a difference of means rather than ends. Some actors, of course, combine elements of both technique and the more emotionally oriented acting styles in their work.

Directing the Actor on the Set

Knowing your actor's training and background will help you to communicate and develop a rapport with your actor. The actor and director are collaborators in a very creative process, and it is important that there is trust between them. The director needs to create a safe space on the set for the actor to work and respect the actor's creativity and sensitivity. At the same time, the actor must attempt to fulfill the wishes of the director.

On the set, there are many important things you, as the director, need to guard against in performances and other things you need to encourage. For example, you need to make sure that the actor does not force or inflate emotions in the performance. You also need to make sure that an actor doesn't stereotype the character by any gestures or mannerisms that aren't really consistent with the character as it is written. The following sections detail other common ways you have to watch and assist actors during production.

Technical Assistance

Unlike stage acting, film acting requires precision. Because the camera lens has a narrow view, the actor has to be at her *mark* or designated position. Make sure the crew has clearly marked the floor with tape or chalk so the actor knows exactly where she must be and must move to in the scene.

It is also helpful for the actor to know the size of the shot you are filming. If it's a close-up, for example, she obviously can't make broad gestures. The actor also has to be sensitive to the sound levels. She can't shout one minute and then whisper or it will cause problems for the sound person.

 Verbal Action

method acting   A style of acting that focuses on reaching the emotional truth of a character through using internal methods such as relaxation and sense memory exercises.

technical acting   A style of acting that uses external acting techniques to create the character.

mark   The place on the floor of a set which the actor must move to or stay at during a scene in order to stay within the frame of the shot.

Dealing with Camera Fright

Even experienced actors sometimes have stage fright, or in film, camera fright. Professionals know how to deal with the problem and how to use their anxiety to fuel a good performance, but less experienced actors may sometimes need the director's help. If you sense that an actor is blowing lines or missing marks because of nervousness, take him or her aside and discuss the problem directly. Explain that even great actors like Laurence Olivier suffered from stage fright, so she is not alone. If you can make the actor smile or laugh, it is often very helpful—nothing eases anxiety like laughter. Be reassuring and let the actor know that the world is not ending because you have had to take a little extra time.

Maintaining Energy Levels

One of the main things that film actors must learn to do is to keep their energy levels high at all times. A conversation that might seem on the set to be normal and even energetic can seem flat and lifeless on screen. Performers need focused, intense energy at all times. Even when playing a laid-back person, the actor needs to be filled with energy. It's your job to make sure that in each successive take the actors keep their energy levels high.

Avoiding Overacting

Actors who have been trained for the stage but who have a limited amount of experience in front of the camera may tend to overact. What you need to do is to bring down the performance, or as some say, make it smaller. Remind the actor who is overacting that simplicity is the key to an effective screen performance. In front of the camera, the actor must create the illusion that she is not acting at all.

Handling Difficult Actors

Occasionally actors will be difficult to handle both on and off the set. It's rare because most actors, even stars, are very professional. Sometimes, however, you may run into a young star who is full of himself or herself and hasn't yet developed the professionalism usually characteristic of good actors. He or she may be taking drugs or drinking heavily, or may simply be demanding and obnoxious. Or, occasionally, there may be an older actor in the cast who is eccentric and has a reputation as "difficult." How do you get him or her to behave? In these situations, you will have to use all the emotional intelligence you can muster. You will have to be both child psychologist and kind but stern mother/father figure.

I was a producer on a small feature and one of the supporting cast members was an older, very talented and respected method actress with a reputation for being difficult. In pre-production, she was giving everyone a hard time—from the wardrobe department to the director. The director was tearing his hair out and didn't want to deal with her. I paid her a visit and listened to her complaints. They were actually very reasonable and could easily be accommodated. It was just that no one was really listening to what she wanted but only reacting to her demanding tone. Once I assured her that what she needed could easily be taken care of, she and I became fast friends.

Other times it isn't so easy. An actor's demands may be unreasonable and she may be out of control in some way. You may have to call the actor's agent or manager for help. In most cases, it's better that the producer deal with any serious problems rather than the director since the director will have to work with the actor more closely on the set and resentments could develop. Or perhaps there is someone else among the cast or crew who knows the actor better and can help handle him or her.

The Least You Need to Know

- A director needs to focus on the characters and the story in order to be able to direct actors.
- A director should know something about an actor's training and background to help him or her achieve the best performance.
- A director should never tell an actor how to behave or show an actor how to do a scene but instead should remind the actor of the character's motivation or intention in the scene.
- Directors should watch for and try to adjust certain common problems when the actor is performing on the set, such as stage fright, low energy, or overacting.

Chapter 13

Directing Yourself

In This Chapter

◆ Bringing movement to your film

◆ Controlling the pacing of your film

◆ Understanding the principles of good shot composition

◆ Using sound and music effectively

◆ Telling the story visually

As the director, you have to be motivator and cheerleader to a wide variety of technicians and artists. Even before you step onto the set, you have to be prepared for both the crew's needs—your shot list and storyboards—and the cast's needs—your understanding of the characters' motivations and of the story. Then, on the set, you have to be the leader and set the tone and the pace of the shoot with both the crew and the cast.

In addition to all of that, you have to be an artist yourself. Besides interpreting, inspiring, directing, and controlling the artistry of others, a director must also contribute his or her own artistic talent to the film. Everyone speaks about a director's vision, but just how does that vision manifest in a film, and what are the elements that go into a style of directing? I'll explore several areas of the director's artistic palette in this chapter.

Creating Movement

Films are, after all, moving pictures, and one of the tools of a director in making a film is movement. If there are lots of shots in your film made with a static camera shooting actors who aren't moving, it will be a visually boring film. On the other hand, well-designed movement that is inspired by the dramatic content of the script will capture an audience's attention.

As the director, you can infuse scenes with movement in a variety of ways. You can choose to move the actors around in a scene, move the camera, move the background, or create a sense of movement through the editing of shots.

There are many ways to move actors in a scene. The actor can move from a full shot in the background, for example, to a close-up in the foreground. Or she can move across the stage or scene in front of the camera, maintaining the same relative size of the shot.

Most scenes combine the movement of actors with the movement of the camera. The actor who is walking across the set, for example, can be followed by the camera in a pan shot. Or the actor can be walking toward the camera and the camera can dolly back, as in a shot of two friends walking and talking on the beach. The camera moves backward, capturing the movement and dialogue of the actors, and the beach and the ocean waves in the background.

Many scenes are shot with a complex series of movements being made by both the actors and the camera at different points in the scene. For example, back to our film, *Something Is Rotten*, there might be a scene where our heroine is arguing with the detective. It might start with a two-shot in which she approaches the detective and attempts to get him to change his mind about something. The detective, troubled by the request, might move away from her, and the camera follows him to a medium close-up. Then our heroine continues her argument and moves into the shot, which widens to a two-shot. The troubled detective again moves away, leaving our heroine in a close-up, showing her frustration with him. As she again moves toward him, trying a new argument, the camera dollies back to a medium shot of her. As the end of the scene approaches, the camera pans to the detective—who has now moved to the door—and widens to a full shot as our heroine follows him to the door, where the scene ends.

Another way of getting movement in a scene is by moving the background or by having movement in the background. A dialogue scene may be shot at an outdoor cafe, for example. As the two actors say their lines, people and cars move along the street in the background. Or a scene may be shot in a moving vehicle, such as a car or a train, giving the scene movement by the fact that the actors, even though they are sitting, are going someplace.

Script Notes

There are ways to create the illusion of movement on film more cheaply than actually having movement. For example, a shot of a nineteenth-century train pulling out of a station can be very expensive. A way to shoot a stationary train that seems to be moving, however, is to move both the camera and a background set behind the train in tandem alongside the train. The train will appear to move but you never have to start the engine.

Finally, movement can be created by using a variety of camera angles that change the point of view in a scene. This is a good way to enliven an otherwise slow or static scene such as that of a woman putting flowers on a gravesite. You can first shoot her placing the flowers on the grave. Then you can do an overhead of the woman as she stands looking at the grave, a lonely figure among hundreds of marble headstones. Then you can do a close-up on her as tears fall from her eyes.

Finding the Right Pace

The rate of movement in a scene or film is called its *pacing*. Pacing is the inherent rhythm or tempo of the picture. It can be reflected visually, emotionally, in the soundtrack, or in the editing. The script itself contributes to the pace as well. A script that has a lot of short, action-filled scenes will have a faster pace than one with long dialogue scenes. Pacing is particularly important to comedy because the timing of reactions is critical to comedy.

Don't be lulled into thinking that action scenes automatically speed up the pace of a film. Even a car chase or battle will seem slow and boring if it is dragged out too long. Particularly boring are action scenes that lack interesting details. It is the details of a scene that get the audience's attention and involvement, and without interesting details, numerous explosions or screeching turns will only seem mundane.

Pacing is sometimes reflective of the director's own energy and enthusiasm. It's often difficult to maintain energy and enthusiasm during a long and tiring shooting schedule. But as a director, you have to keep your own energy high so that you can inspire the cast and crew. Otherwise, the lethargy on the set will be reflected in what is on the screen.

Counterpoint

Even if you are planning your shots very carefully, be sure to get extra coverage in case something goes wrong with your plan. It is much cheaper to do a few extra takes and cutaways during production than to have to reshoot a critical scene later. You and your editor will be grateful you have some "insurance" shots if you run into trouble in the editing room.

Time Expansion

A scene can often be made more interesting when it is expanded in time by adding extra detail. This is particularly true of action scenes, but not only action scenes., For example, let's say that in *Something Is Rotten*, our heroine has finally come face to face with the perfumed robber. He pulls his gun on her and threatens to kill her because she has discovered who he is. She tells him that before he pulls the trigger, she wants him to smell the incredible new perfume she has developed. She knows he will appreciate it. His curiosity piqued, he agrees to smell it. The script then describes the rest of the scene as follows: "She gets a large flask of perfume and opens it. She brings the bottle to him and holds it near his nose. As he smells it, she suddenly thrusts the perfume into his eyes. He drops the gun and grabs his stinging eyes in pain."

As the director, you could shoot this scene in a simple full shot and get some coverage of each character. Your shot list would be:

- Full shot of heroine bringing the perfume to the robber's nose, robber smelling it, heroine throwing perfume into his eyes, robber dropping gun and grabbing his eyes, heroine grabbing gun and running from the scene.
- Close-up of the robber grabbing his eyes.
- Medium shot of heroine running from the room.

Or you could expand the scene and your shot list would look something like the following:

- Full shot of robber and heroine.
- Pan with the heroine as she picks up the flask of perfume and brings it to the robber.
- Tilt up to the robber's expectant nose.
- Close-up on the robber's ecstasy as he smells the perfume.
- Close-up on the heroine as she waits for the right moment.
- Move out to a medium two-shot as the smiling robber opens his eyes and the heroine jerks the flask violently, splashing perfume into his eyes.
- Tilt down to the gun on the floor as the heroine grabs it.
- Dolly back to a full shot as she runs to the door and he gropes around looking for water, his eyes stinging.

It obviously takes more screen time (and shooting time) to film the scene the second way, but it will increase the tension and the pace of the scene because of the added detail.

Time Compression

Time compression can also increase the pace of the film and is a valuable tool if you need to cut the screen time, such as for a television movie. Let's say the script calls for the heroine in *Something Is Rotten* to get out of her car, walk up to the perfume company's offices, and walk in. You may have shot three set-ups—a full shot of her getting out of the car, a medium pan of her walking up to the building, and a medium shot of her opening the door and walking in. If the scene seems too slow, you can eliminate the pan of her walking up to the building to compress time and speed up the pace.

Montages are devices, sometimes written into the script, sometimes conceived of with the director in developing a shooting script, that use a series of short, expressive visual images to tell a portion of the story. A montage is another frequently used way to compress time, because in a short period of screen time—usually only about a minute—you see time pass or learn a lot of information about the characters very quickly. In the film *Up Close and Personal* (Jon Avnet, 1996), for example, there is a montage accompanied by music that shows the couple played by Robert Redford and Michelle Pfeiffer falling in love, compressing many months of time in the story.

Communicating Through Composition

We have talked about the importance of movement and pacing in a director's visual style. The *composition* of the shot or the "framing" of the shot is another aspect of a director's visual contribution to the film, although the DP will generally also be involved in the framing of the shot.

In general, in composing a shot, the main subject of the picture should be placed near the center of the frame, with other items in the frame balancing the subject. The idea is to make the viewer's eye go to the portion of the frame on which you want him or her to focus.

For a shot to aid in the storytelling effort, it must be composed in a way that reinforces the idea or meaning you want to communicate in the scene. For example, if you want to communicate that the heroine is vulnerable and frightened by the perfumed robber, you can place her seated, looking up at him, to show the power he has over her in that moment.

Technically, a shot that is well-composed will have accurate details, will fill the screen, will usually have a stable horizon, and will be balanced by what is often referred to as the "rule of thirds."

Accurate Detail

In composing a shot, you always have to make sure that the shot you have planned will be close enough to the subject of the shot to be recognized easily by the viewer. Sometimes long shots are just too long. For example, a house in the woods that you are supposed to be establishing might be shot from so far away that it is barely recognizable as a house. If you move the camera in a little closer, you will still have the beautiful panorama of the woods that you were going for, but you will also be able to see the house.

If you are shooting in video, most video formats provide less detail than film, so you should be particularly careful that you are getting the detail you want in the shot.

Filling the Screen and Stable Horizon

Another consideration in deciding the composition of your shot is whether the subject or image you are focusing on fills the screen. Novice cinematographers often shoot too loosely, with a lot of uninteresting extra space in the shot. Don't be afraid to ask the DP to go in more tightly on a subject. It often makes the shot more interesting.

A shot that is well-composed will also generally have a stable horizon. For example, if the shot contains some ground and then a bank of trees, the horizon or the line where the trees start shouldn't be tilted to the left or the right but should be parallel to the bottom of the shot. If, however, you want to create a particular effect, such as the point of view of a person with Alzheimer's disease who feels disoriented because she is losing the ability to distinguish depth of field, you might tilt the camera so that the horizon isn't stable, reflecting how the person sees a staircase or floor.

Verbal Action

pacing   The rhythm, tempo, or rate of movement of the shots in a film.

montage   A stylized form of editing short, expressive shots together to provide a lot of information in a short period of time.

composition   The arrangement of various objects in a picture so that the whole will be balanced and pleasing to the viewer, and will direct the viewer to the main subject of the picture.

The Rule of Thirds

A well-composed shot should also be aesthetically balanced. One rule of thumb for finding that balance is that the important details in the frame should usually appear on lines that trisect the frame. This is called the rule of thirds. The human eye often finds a picture uninteresting when the main elements in the frame are located on a center horizontal line, for example. Head shots are often framed with the subject's eyes about a third of the way down from the top. Two-shots are often framed with the subjects aligned to vertically trisecting lines.

Of course, the rule of thirds isn't applicable for every shot. In art—and composing a shot is an artistic endeavor—rules are often made to be broken. You should first know the rules, however, and know why you are breaking a rule. The late Stanley Kubrick often broke the rules of shot framing in his films, placing the actors "too" far away or "too" close. His films are very effective, however, because he used the odd framing to create a feeling and better communicate the film's story.

Sometimes, even well-balanced shots don't work well in a film. For example, when two actors are standing facing one another in a two-shot, there is the tendency for the viewer to look back and forth from one character to the other, which can be distracting. Therefore, many directors use over-the-shoulder or reversal shots in putting together lengthy dialogue scenes, rather than staying with a two-shot.

Introducing Sound Effects and Music

Sound is an integral part of any film, and as the director, you also must be aware of what sound can help you bring to the feeling and reality of the scene you are filming. Each action in life and on the screen has a distinctive sound associated with it. The roar of a car's engine or the howling of the wind communicate information about what is happening or what is going to happen soon.

Sometimes, using a sound effect might be as effective as seeing the actual shot of some portion of the action in your scene. For example, we have a shot where a young baseball player is practicing her pitching. Suddenly we hear the shattering of a window and see the startled and upset look on the young pitcher's face. The sound of the glass shattering may be just as effective or more effective in terms of the story than seeing a shot of the broken window.

Sound will do much to express the atmosphere and mood of a scene. Wolfgang Petersen's *Das Boot* (1981) used the creaking sounds of the submarine in very effective ways to build tension in the film. In other films, sound—such as soft rain on the roof or a crackling fireplace—can be used to set a tranquil mood.

In addition to setting the mood for a scene, sound can be used to express a character's feelings. If, for example, you want to show the character feeling calm and peaceful, you might have her sitting in the garden listening to the trickling of a pond's waterfall and chirping birds. If you want to show her anxious, have her in the kitchen as the phone rings incessantly and the television blares in the background.

Sound can also heighten emotion when it is used as a counterpoint to the visual image on the screen. For example, your character may be in her apartment grieving the death of her loved one. She hears from the hallway outside her door the laughter of the couple responsible for her partner's death.

Cutaway

Directors use the look of their locations to make a statement about the characters and the story. For example, a messy room of one character versus the perfectly arranged drawers and shelves of another gives us visually the information that there may be conflict ahead between these two very different characters. In working with your production designer to prepare the settings for your shots, consider a variety of design approaches to see what will best create a world on screen that reflects the characters and story depicted in the script.

If music is an important part of your film, which in many films it is, you should have already hired a music supervisor and/or composer who will be working with the director and the producer to plan the music for the film. In certain scenes, such as the memorable scene in *Top Gun* where the jet planes seem to be flying to the beat of the hit song from that film, the scene was cut to the music. Even though a different track of the music will be created and edited into the film later, playing music during the shooting of certain scenes will help give the actors and director a sense of the tempo of the scene, and the scene will work better in the final film.

Sound and music are two more important tools of the director's artistic palette, and the sound of a scene should be carefully considered when planning each shot.

Focusing on the Narrative

Perhaps the most important consideration for the director in planning and executing a shot is whether the shot moves the story forward and gives the audience new information about the story. You don't need to see a full shot of a house and then a medium shot of the same house just so the audience can see it better. But if the medium shot focuses on a "For Sale" sign, it gives the audience narrative information they didn't have before and moves the story forward.

One way to learn how film stories can be told visually rather than simply through dialogue is to watch silent films. Many of the early silent film directors, as well as subsequent great directors such as Alfred Hitchcock, Federico Fellini, and Ingmar Bergman, display a masterful understanding of how to select specific camera angles and point-of-view shots to tell the story rather than relying on dialogue or conventional techniques. For example, in George Stevens's classic western *Shane*, in a critical barroom scene, rather than simply panning or doing a full shot to establish the scene, Stevens sets the mood of a lazy, relaxed day by having the camera follow a dog as it walks across the barroom floor.

If you go back to your script and analyze each scene, you will often find clues that spark ideas for visually telling the story. For example, the writer might describe an object in the scene, such as a photograph that the character is holding. You can simply show the character holding the picture. Or, to emphasize her grief, you can show a close-up of her finger stroking her loved one's face in the picture, using that image to express the character's grief more potently than simply showing her holding or looking at the picture.

Maintaining Consistency of Style

One of the marks of a novice or student filmmaker is that her film is often inconsistent. Because the filmmaker wants to show off all the techniques she has learned, the audience will see on the screen a lot of different kinds of shots, angles, and effects, and all of them will not necessarily fit together very well or serve the story equally well. A more experienced director won't be interested in proving how much she knows but only in finding the best way to tell the story.

There are many approaches directors can take in telling a story. One thriller might be shot in a very realistic style, while another thriller might be shot in a dark, noirish style. For example, in the film *Arlington Road* (1999), the people and the neighborhood are shot in an almost hyper-realistic style. The film is about right-wing terrorists who are living across the street from a professor who is an expert on terrorism. As the film progresses, realistic images of the normal-seeming neighbors make the lead character and everyone around him think he is crazy for being suspicious of them. Another thriller, *Along Came a Spider* (2001), was shot using a darker, film-noir tone. That style better fit the story of an older detective who has just lost a partner and is reluctantly brought into the investigation of a kidnapping. In each case, the director chose a style that seemed right for the story and stuck to it, bringing consistency in his or her approach.

The Least You Need to Know

- Motion pictures require movement to be interesting, and there are a number of ways directors can bring movement to a shot.
- Showing details helps keep a scene interesting and helps quicken the pace of a film.
- Good composition of shots is the responsibility of both the director and the cinematographer, but the director should know the basic principles of shot composition.
- The most important consideration for the director in deciding on each shot is whether the shot helps tell the story and moves the story forward.

Dealing with Production Problems

In This Chapter

◆ Coping with delays caused by cast and crew members

◆ Anticipating equipment breakdowns and weather delays

◆ Dealing with schedule and budget problems promptly

◆ Safety considerations during film production

So many things can go wrong on a film set that it's amazing good movies are ever made. I was once working on an independent film that was in pre-production and everything seemed to be going quite well. The crew and cast were assembled on location and everyone was busy doing his or her job. The location sites and sets looked great. The team had a great spirit and everyone was excited about the upcoming shoot, which was going to start in less than a week. Then we got a call from the lawyers and executive producer—one of the investors had pulled out, and the other investor was not willing to finance the entire production. Because a completion bond hadn't yet been secured, we had to close down the production and go home.

Losing the entire financing for your film is certainly one of the worst things that can go wrong, but other setbacks can and will also happen. Some problems will affect your schedule and budget, others will affect the quality of the film, and some will affect both. Good producers and directors learn to expect the unexpected and develop flexible strategies to deal with breakdowns, break-ups, divas, performances that aren't working, cash shortages, and a host of other problems.

Dailies Can Save Your Film

One way to uncover potential problems before they become huge disasters is to screen dailies every night during production. Dailies are safeguards that can help you avoid shooting scenes that will present major problems once you get into the editing room. If you are shooting on film and in close proximity to your film lab and sound transfer house, you should be able to see the first day's dailies on the second night of production and a new set of dailies each night thereafter. If you are on a distant location, it may take a little longer to get dailies, although it's possible to transfer dailies to video, digitize them, and transmit them to the location. If you choose the latter method, you won't see the dailies on film but rather on video.

Dailies are tremendously valuable to a production. They give the director an opportunity to evaluate the performances of the cast, which sometimes seem different on film than they do when watching them on the set. Also, the director can see whether she is communicating well with the DP, the sound mixer, and others on the crew to get the kinds of shots she wants on film. After viewing dailies, the director will know whether a critical scene has worked and will ideally still have time to reshoot it if it didn't work. The sooner everyone knows there is a problem, the more opportunities there will be to solve it. Don't try to save the expense of developing, syncing, and screening dailies (and shipping or transmitting them if you are on location). It is worth it and may save you money in the long run.

If you are shooting in any video format, you can see what you have shot without having to send it to a lab, so you should watch dailies the same evening they are shot.

Some film directors like to use what is called a "video assist," which is a video camera that is attached to the film camera. The video camera shoots the same shot that the film camera shoots. After the shot, the videotape can be reviewed on a monitor right on the set. Most film directors, even those who used this system, don't use it to replace dailies but rather as an extra tool to get a sense of how the shot is working and to see whether additional takes are needed. The frame of the video shot won't be exactly the same as the film shot, and the detail, depth, and even the performances may all look a little different on video. Still, for those productions that can afford it, it can be a helpful tool.

Script Notes

For the crew, dailies are evidence of their hard work and are morale boosters. Members of the cast, however, may be thrown off by dailies. It is hard to watch one-self and be objective. A cast member may not like a performance in a scene, even though the director is satisfied with it. She may then change the character in subsequent scenes, throwing off the film. Therefore, directors sometimes prefer that actors don't see the dailies.

Solving People Problems

Although filmmakers often fear that equipment problems will delay a schedule, films are labor-intensive endeavors and productions get behind schedule because of human breakdowns more often than because of equipment breakdowns. Both cast and crew members know that word will get around if a person walks off a shoot or causes a lot of trouble on a shoot, and that person will have difficulty getting work in the future. Because of that, there are probably fewer ego and personality clashes on film productions than there might otherwise be or than rumor has it.

In fact, however, most cast and crew members are thoroughly professional and will keep their commitments and do their best on the job even when they are unhappy about some aspect of the shoot. Still, there are people who will cause problems that might either delay the shoot or make it harder to get good work done. And there are conflicts that naturally arise as they might when any group of people are working together intensely.

Personality Clashes

Despite everyone's professionalism, there are people who simply don't get along with each other—whose personalities seem to clash. Occasionally, two such people will end up on the same shoot together. You, as the producer or director, should try to discover such problems in pre-production. If a particular member of the team, such as a key department head, is too difficult for the director or producer to work with, she may have to be replaced. There is not enough time on a film shoot to have group therapy sessions to help everyone get along.

In cases when both parties are very valuable to the production and it is not practical to replace either one, the producer will have to find ways to get both people to get along for the sake of the production.

Creative Differences

Lengthy and stubborn arguments over creative issues can occur between any two or more of the major creative participants on a film. Directors, producers, writers, or actors can clash with each other. DPs and production managers can also join the fray. If you find that you are a participant in one of these creative clashes, try to keep your ego out of it. Really think about the issues that are at stake. Are there compromises that can be made? Can you take the first step by showing that you are willing to be reasonable so that the other person might also try to compromise? Is there a better way to communicate your position to the person you disagree with so that she can see your point of view? Is the problem a serious creative difference or difference in vision for the film, or are people just posturing or being egotistical and blowing the issue out of proportion?

When the problem really is a creative difference, is there a creative compromise that will work for both parties? Will the two parties agree to a third party deciding the issue? Creative differences have been known to shut down entire productions and have been responsible for numerous projects never getting into production in the first place, so it's wise to learn how to be flexible and to keep your own ego out of the discussions as much as possible.

Unskilled Crew Members

If it becomes apparent that any member of the crew cannot do his or her job competently, do not be afraid to fire and replace the person even once the production has started. Some crew members get in over their heads on a shoot. They may have experience on small productions but aren't prepared for the stress and rigors of a feature film. They should be replaced as soon as you notice there is a problem.

Also, don't be afraid to fire a volunteer or intern, even the investor's nephew. Everyone has to pull his or her weight on a set. It's bad for the morale of the entire crew if anyone, even an intern, isn't working hard to get the job done.

Sometimes, people such as the producer and director need to talk to each other to confirm that there is a problem with a crew member. I was directing a documentary once and the producer and I both had problems with a particular crew member. He was not doing the job the producer hired him to do and was an enormous distraction to those of us who were doing our jobs. When I finally told the producer my feelings, he was relieved. He had only been keeping this particular fellow on because he thought he was helpful to me. The next day he fired him.

> **Cutaway**
>
> Working with untrained actors requires ingenuity. For the movie *Cold Turkey* (1971), Norman Lear was directing a crowd scene in a small town and was using untrained extras from the town to portray the crowd. He wasn't getting the kinds of reactions he wanted from the crowd so he staged a verbal fight with his star, Dick Van Dyke. The crowd reacted in astonishment as Lear started screaming at Van Dyke, calling him stupid and incompetent for the way he was doing the scene. Van Dyke hurled insults back at Lear as the camera rolled and got the stunned reactions of the crowd, watching these crazy Hollywood types. When Lear had gotten the shots he wanted, he and Van Dyke stopped fighting and smiled. Lear then explained to the crowd that the fight had just been a director's device to get them to react the way he wanted them to.

Untrained or Unskilled Actors

Actors who are not good film actors, even those with relatively minor parts, can delay a production by blowing their lines and not hitting their marks. You may have to do many takes of a simple scene and the scene still will not be good enough. Sometimes you can do tricks like shooting reaction and listening shots of other actors and extras and having the inexperienced cast member read his or her lines as a wild track. The best precaution, however, is being careful not to hire performers without training and experience.

Sexual Harassment

Another potential area for trouble and therefore delays on a set is the sexual harassment of one employee by one or more other employees. Sexual harassment can be verbal behavior such as unwanted sexual comments, or nonverbal behavior such as looks and leering, or physical behavior such as pats or squeezes. It is not only sexual harassment when a supervisor harasses an employee, but can also be sexual harassment if the behavior of co-workers create an intimidating, hostile, or offensive working environment for an employee.

To prevent sexual harassment on your production, inform the entire cast and crew that it will not be tolerated and encourage anyone who experiences it to first ask the harasser to stop and, if the behavior does not stop immediately, inform the line producer, production manager, or producer as soon as possible.

Going in New Directions

Another cause for a delay on a film set is when members of the cast or the director decide to rewrite the script on the set. Someone may have a brilliant idea but, in the long run, it will usually cost time and money to implement and may turn out to be worse for the film than sticking to the script as written. By going in a new direction in the scene, you may end up throwing off your whole film and regretting it in the editing room, and you will waste precious time on the set discussing the change. The whole production's schedule is based on knowing what you are going to shoot at the time you plan to shoot it. Everyone is prepped for a particular shot. A newly written scene and set of shots will take longer to set up and often longer to shoot, probably causing you to get behind.

Is it ever worth it to go with that brilliant idea that your lead actor had or that you had in the middle of the night before the day's shoot? It might be, but only on rare occasions, and usually only when you have the writer on the set to make sure that the change works with the rest of the script. As I'll cover later, there are sometimes shooting problems that must be solved by rewriting a scene, but it is not a good thing to do regularly on a production. Generally, if a suggestion for a change is really that brilliant, someone would have thought of it in the months of getting the script ready for production or even in pre-production. Production is not a time to continue to experiment. It's a time to commit to the script you have and film it.

Script Notes _____

One of the simplest but often forgotten methods to deal with conflict on the set is to simply compliment the cast and crew on their work. All involved like to know that they are appreciated, but sometimes, with so much else to do, the director and producer forget to express their appreciation to the cast and crew. A crew member or actor who feels appreciated is less likely to cause trouble, so be sure to tell people when they have done a good job.

Dealing with Equipment Breakdowns

Murphy's Law—that anything that can go wrong probably will—is proven every day on film shoots, especially those on distant locations. As I mentioned previously, to remain on schedule, a film shoot requires a large group of people to work together cooperatively. In addition, many of those people are operating complex equipment that could be misplaced or forgotten, or could break down. The breakdown of an essential piece of equipment, such as the camera, sound recorder, or a key light, would not be so terrible if it wasn't that the resulting delay can be very costly. A large number of delays can even be fatal to a production. Production managers and other crew members need to do all they can to prepare in advance for an equipment problem in order to minimize the time that is lost.

Some of the steps that should be taken to prevent possible delays as a result of equipment breakdown or loss include the following:

◆ Prepare a thorough equipment checklist prior to the shoot.

◆ Prior to moving to any new location, make sure that everything is accounted for.

◆ Make sure all equipment has been tested by the crew member responsible for using it.

◆ Double-check all rechargeable batteries and make sure you have extra batteries of all types.

◆ Make sure you have backup items for all parts that wear out such as lamp elements, belts, or plugs.

◆ Make sure to have the necessary tools and items needed to make electrical and mechanical repairs on the set.

◆ When on location, in advance of the shoot, make an emergency list of the closest places to get replacement equipment.

Anticipating Weather Problems

Another troublemaker for location shoots is the weather, especially for those films that include many exterior shots. Start by scheduling your shoot, if at all possible, during the months when there won't be rain or snow, unless you want rain or snow in every scene. Even then, it is always easier to make fake rain or snow and keep your crew dry than it is to shoot in the real thing. Not only can wet weather cause delays but so can uncomfortably hot or cold weather, such as working in the desert in one hundred degree heat.

As I suggested in Chapter 7, "The Set-Up: Script Breakdown and Shooting Schedule," you should anticipate weather problems by having interior cover sets available for the days when there is bad weather. What if, however, it rains for several days and you have exhausted all of your cover sets? You may have to either juggle your schedule, figure out how to shoot in the rain, or rewrite your scene for an interior location.

One of the reasons Southern California has become the movie production capital of the world is that it rarely rains there except during the winter months, and even those months have a fair number of sunny days. To avoid costly weather problems, plan in advance by studying the weather patterns for the area in which you are going to be shooting. Be realistic. You may have to sacrifice a prettier location for one that has better weather. In any case, have a flexible enough schedule to accommodate stormy weather.

Dealing with Scheduling Problems

Last-minute scheduling problems can cause real headaches for productions, particularly those filming on location. In addition to the causes for delays I have discussed, scheduling problems can be caused by cast members getting sick or by locations needing to be changed for some reason external to the production. (If you want to see a movie about movie-making where everything goes wrong that could possibly go wrong, including location, budget, and cast problems, watch David Mamet's very funny *State and Main* [2000].)

Whatever the cause, you have to solve the problem. Either you have to find another suitable location at the last minute, replace a cast member, or, if many of her scenes have already been shot, try to juggle the schedule so that her scenes can be shot later. If it is a serious illness of a lead actor, the situation may be covered by your cast insurance. In that case, you may have to reshoot scenes or even shut down production until the actor recovers or you hire someone else, which is a huge headache.

Facing Budget Problems

Almost all films, particularly independent films, will have a Completion Bond or Completion Guarantee Insurance. This coverage protects the film's investors, providing that the film will be finished even if it goes over budget. If the film begins to get behind schedule or go over budget, the completion bond company may step in, fire the current director, and use a director of its own choosing to finish the film. Or the bond company may require the producer to reduce her fees if it must take over the film. It's important to have a Completion Bond, and you usually can't get financing without it; but it's painful for you as a filmmaker—producer or director—when things get so bad that the bond company has to step in.

To prevent that, watch your budget and schedule carefully at all times for signs that you are going over budget. Take action yourself before it gets to the point at which the bond company will be forced to act. Sometimes delays are caused by problems for which you have other insurance coverage, such as equipment breakdowns. If you have extensive coverage, be sure to contact your broker at the first sign of a problem.

If the cause of the delay is a number of human errors that simply aren't covered by insurance, what do you do? You can either try to explain the problem to whomever is financing the film and see if you can get more money for the budget, or you can try to see how you can cut back and save money on the rest of the shoot to make up for the overages and delays.

Realistically, it isn't wise to count on getting more money from your investors if you are an independent filmmaker, even if it seems like a small amount compared to what they have already invested. Many investors would rather cut their losses and get out than—as they might fear—throw good money after bad. Or they would be just as content to see the completion bond company take over the shoot and finish the film.

If you are doing a studio film, the studio will probably come up with the money needed to finish the film, but they won't be happy about it and they, too, might send in someone to watch things on the set or even replace the director. If you go over budget and cause headaches for the studio, don't expect to work for that studio again unless the movie ultimately makes them a lot of money or wins them awards. And Hollywood is a small town. Word will get around to other studios that you couldn't control the budget on this film.

That leaves the option of going back to the script and schedule to see where you might be able to shorten scenes, cut them altogether, or tighten the schedule by, for example, re-dressing a location for several scenes to save the time of a move. Often the writer can be helpful in trimming the script or coming up with alternative locations or ways of doing a scene or sequence that might be cheaper.

> **CAUTION**
>
> **Counterpoint**
>
> The Industry-Wide Labor-Management Safety Committee has developed a complete set of safety bulletins. These bulletins cover a variety of potential hazards such as firearms, helicopter, explosives, open flames, artificially created smoke, venomous reptiles and more. Copies of these bulletins should be attached to the call sheets when appropriate. Anyone who works directly with such hazards should be fully aware of the guidelines and experienced in their work.

Preventing Accidents and Injuries

Film sets can be dangerous places. By far the worst thing that can happen on a production is the serious injury or death of a member of the cast or crew in the course of doing his or her job. Particularly dangerous are scenes involving stunts, special effects, aircraft, wild animals, water, fire, and guns.

Most states where you might be filming have safety guidelines, and so do the various guilds, unions, television networks, studios, and the Association of Motion Picture and Television Producers. Some of the safety issues you will be concerned with are safety considerations that are common to any workplace where there is a lot of construction, heavy equipment, and physical activity going on. You need to inform your crew of safety guidelines for such activities as lifting and moving equipment, preventing falls, handling chemicals and flammable materials (such as paints), and electrical safety.

In addition, on film sets, there are special safety issues surrounding activities like the performance of stunts and action scenes and the filming of certain special effects. These activities require special training and it is important that you hire experienced people to do your effects and stunts, people who are as concerned about the safety of the cast and crew as they are about getting the most incredible shot.

The Least You Need to Know

- ◆ View dailies each night to prevent problems in the editing room or costly reshoots.
- ◆ Don't be afraid to fire and replace people who are causing problems on the set.
- ◆ Don't do any serious rewriting of the script on the set unless you want to go over budget.
- ◆ Anticipate equipment and weather problems by having equipment replacements and cover sets close at hand.
- ◆ Don't go over budget unless you want to have the completion bond company take over your film.
- ◆ Take all safety precautions necessary, especially for stunts and special effects.

Producing and Directing Non-Fiction Films

In This Chapter

◆ Developing a non-fiction shooting script

◆ Doing research and pre-interviews

◆ Creating action sequences for non-fiction films

◆ Listening intently and keeping the interviewee relaxed

Let's say that you haven't yet been able to sell your perfume-industry caper script, *Something Is Rotten*, to a major studio or independent producer but, in the course of researching and writing it, you became fascinated by the world of perfume. You want to do a documentary about the perfume industry and the process of developing new scents for perfumes. How do you go about writing a script and shooting the documentary? How will this non-fiction film be different from the fictional film you had been developing?

Non-fiction films have many things in common with fiction or narrative films. But there are also different kinds of problems and different kinds of techniques that you should know about before attempting to write, produce, or direct a documentary or other non-fiction film. Perhaps the most obvious difference is that on a fiction film shoot you have to know how to work with actors. On a non-fiction film, although you may have an actor as a narrator or actors doing reenactments, you will primarily be filming "real people," and that requires very different skills than working with trained actors.

The term "non-fiction film" is frequently used in this chapter rather than documentary because non-fiction films can include many types of productions, such as educational films, industrial films, and even home movies, in addition to documentary segments for television shows or longer documentaries for television or theatrical release. Most of the information included in this chapter applies to all types of non-fiction films.

Cutaway

Commercials are really in a class by themselves. Many commercials, particularly slick-looking national television commercials, have more in common with feature films than most non-fiction films. They use skilled, sometimes famous actors, are tightly scripted, and are shot on 35mm film, with high budgets and the highest production values. Other commercials, however, might be shot more like very low-budget, non-fiction films, such as the typical commercial showing a car dealer standing in front of his lot talking about what good deals he gives. And, as far as the content of commercials, although sales pitches are technically non-fiction, despite truth in advertising laws, one could argue that in many commercials, the content is more fiction than non-fiction.

Developing a Non-Fiction Film

The funding to do a documentary, educational, or other non-fiction film may be based on a script, but it is more likely to be based on a shorter proposal that describes the subject—the point of view of the film—and gives the length of the proposed show. A budget can be estimated from the number of shooting days and other factors, and a final budget can be prepared as soon as the script is written. Once funding for the project is secured, you can begin to research and interview the people you plan to film in order to write the script.

The Script

Although a scene in a non-fiction script will not be as close to what is ultimately filmed as a scene in a shooting script of a fictional movie, it is still important to write a script before you shoot. Contrary to what many people think, the best documentaries, and even good educational or industrial films, tell stories and have a narrative logic like fiction films. The difference is that instead of deriving the characters and stories from her imagination, the writer of a non-fiction film must construct the story from the facts discovered through researching the subject and interviewing people who have information about the subject.

As with fiction films, which we discussed in Chapter 6, "Act I: Developing the Script," a non-fiction film should have a major point or theme and a dramatic structure. It should include interesting characters who are trying to do or get something, tension and conflict between opposing forces, and a climax and resolution.

For example, in your documentary about the perfume industry, begin by finding your characters and deciding what you want to say about that industry. Is there someone in that world you find particularly interesting who has a strong point of view about perfume and how to develop new perfumes or market them? Are there other people who have other methods or who are the competitors of your interesting person? What is the biggest controversy or conflict in the industry? Who do you agree with on that issue? As you research your subject more and talk to more people, your research will begin to give you the shape of your story—its beginning, middle, and end.

Preparing Pre-Interviews

A very valuable part of your research will be to do pre-interviews with people who will be filmed. Not only will you learn more about the subject of the film, but if you tape-record the interviews, you will be able to write a script that in some scenes at least may closely resemble what you will film. Most people when asked a question will respond in a similar way when asked the same question again.

Pre-interviews are also a time to get to know the people you will be filming and to develop trusting relationships with them. If the subjects of your film are comfortable with you as a person, they will answer your questions more honestly and openly and will be easier to direct when the cameras are rolling.

It is usually important not to ask your subject all of the questions you plan to ask on film in the pre-interview. Save some of the most probing questions for the actual on-camera interview. If you do that, you will get more interesting, spontaneous reactions than you would if the person knew everything you planned to ask.

Script Notes _____

You can use the same format for a non-fiction script as for a dramatic script, although, for dialogue, you will have to summarize or paraphrase what you expect an interviewee to say. Non-fiction scripts can also be written using the "A-V style" script format. In this format, the page divides into two vertical columns. The audio—including dialogue, narration, music, or other sound—is written in the left-hand column, and the right-hand column contains a description of the corresponding action or visual information.

Planning Action Sequences

Your non-fiction script will be visually boring if it is all "talking heads." Even if every subject has fascinating things to say, films and videos are moving pictures and it is important to have movement in your film—and not simply the movement you can get from cutting back and forth from one talking head to another.

While researching your script, get to know the visual world of your subject. What are the normal activities of the person you want to film? Can you film the person in her environment doing something interesting and use the interview material as voice-over? Is the person comfortable doing things while talking? Are there action sequences or activities you can film that will help the audience get background information about the subject?

In my example of the documentary about the world of perfume, an interview subject could provide some background information on how perfume is developed while you show visuals of beautiful fields of flowers with workers carefully picking flowers.

Spend time thinking of ways to use interesting visuals to tell your story and to bring movement to the film. Even in television magazine shows like *60 Minutes*, where a lot of film time is stationary talking heads, we often see the interviewer walking and talking with the subject or see other visuals while the subject is talking that brings movement to the show. Try to come up with activities that will give your audience a unique look into the subject or the world you are filming rather than just stereotypical shots.

Choosing the Narration and Interviewing Style

There are several decisions you must make early on in the actual writing of your script. One is whether you will be using narration and whether the narration will be done by filming an on-camera narrator or by recording an off-camera narrator doing *voice-over*.

An on-camera narrator will be a character in your film. She will not only give information and provide transitions for your film, but will also be able to express the point of view of the filmmaker and weigh in on the conflict presented in the film. An off-camera narrator, on the other hand, will be more useful in simply providing transitions and giving information over visual sequences. The point of view of the film is usually better expressed by people who are on-camera.

You may also decide not to have any narration at all but simply let the story tell itself through the interviews and action you are filming. If that is the case, you need to plan to shoot enough film so that everything you want to say about the subject and the story you are telling is clear to the viewer and so that the transitions from one sequence or segment of the film to another are not awkward.

A second important decision you must make as you are preparing to write your script is the interviewing style you will use. Do you want the person doing the interviews to be on-camera as in the *60 Minutes* style of television news documentary? This style has also been used effectively in theatrically released documentaries such as Michael Moore's *Roger and Me* (1989). In that film, Moore appeared to be a naive reporter who, in fact, often confronted his subjects with difficult questions. He became the main character in the film, and the evasive "Roger" of the title, the CEO of General Motors, was the antagonist.

The other frequently used style of filming interviews is to keep the interviewer off-camera and to cut her questions out of the film. If you do that, you will be able to use your footage more effectively if the people you interview state the question in some way in their answer. Neither of these two styles is right or wrong, but one style may fit your subject better than the other.

Using Stock Footage, Stills, and Reenactments

In some non-fiction films, particularly historical documentaries, you may be using *stock footage*, as well as still photos or *reenactments*. Stock footage, such as film from the Vietnam War, for example, is footage that you can buy from stock footage companies or film libraries. It can bring alive a historical period or bring more movement to your film. You may have to research what is available from many sources to find footage that is appropriate for your film.

Still photos also will require research and are often available in library collections about historical subjects. If you are filming a particular person, she may have family photos that will be interesting to film. You will have to schedule a time to shoot the photos. They should be mounted so that they are easy to film. You can make these shots more interesting by having the cinematographer pan a photo, or move closely in on it, focusing on some specific part of the photo.

Reenactments are scripted scenes performed by actors. They are either factually accurate scenes of situations from the past that cannot be filmed or they are hypothetical situations that are used to illustrate a point or part of the story. Reenactments are used frequently in "reality" television shows, such as *Unsolved Mysteries*.

Any or all of the above elements may help you tell your non-fiction story. Consider what will work best for you as you research and write your script.

CAUTION

Counterpoint

The presence of an on-camera personality asking questions should only be used if that character is important to the story of the film. For every rule, however, there are exceptions. In *Start-up.com* (2001), produced by documentary filmmaker D. A. Pennebaker, one of the film's co-directors occasionally asked the main subject of the film a question on-camera, but she was not a major presence in the film. It worked because there was a good story with interesting characters and conflict to keep the audience involved.

Going into Pre-Production

Pre-production on a non-fiction film involves many of the same steps you have already read about in Chapters 7 through 10. You need to plan your shooting schedule, find locations, get permits and permissions, hire your crew and cast (if you have a cast), and order your equipment and film or tape stock. Only a few things will be different for non-fiction films.

Locations

Unlike in a fiction film, where you will be creating sets at locations or building sets on a sound stage for your actors to work on, in a non-fiction film you may be shooting the normal activity that goes on at a location, without altering the location. You often will have to go through bureaucratic hoops to get permission to film at workplaces, schools, hospitals, or other public or private venues. Some places may charge your production for filming at the location or request a donation. If you can't afford it or are doing the film for a good cause or non-profit organization, you may be able to get the fee waived.

In addition to getting permission to shoot at the locations where you want to shoot, you will have to schedule the people you will be filming and estimate how long it will take to film each scene they are in, whether that is an interview or some specific activity. In planning the scenes and shots, always keep in mind that the people you are filming are not actors, so the more familiar their environment, the easier it will be for them when the cameras are rolling.

Finally, you will have to assemble the crew. Unless you are filming a major documentary for a television network, you will probably want to work with a relatively small crew. A small crew can be less obtrusive when filming on real locations and can be less intimidating to the real people who will be filmed. Also, most documentaries are not funded well enough to have a very large crew. Be sure that the people you hire have experience on documentaries. They will need to move fast, be ready for spontaneous takes, and be willing to sacrifice perfect lighting in order to not lose a spontaneous moment.

Verbal Action _____

voice-over   The voice of the narrator or of another character when she is not seen on film. The device is used in both fiction and non-fiction films.

stock footage   Archive material from film libraries, such as World War II shots or sequences, that are recycled from other films and are available for a fee.

reenactments   Scenes acted out by actors that re-create either factual or hypothetical situations in non-fiction film.

Interviewing Non-Actors

Even if you don't want your documentary to consist of a lot of talking heads, to get interesting information out of people, whether you use it over other visuals or on-camera, you will generally have to do a number of interviews. The key to getting a good interview is to be prepared and to keep the interviewee relaxed.

Preparation

Before you interview someone on camera, you should know exactly what you want to get out of the interview. You should write out your interview questions in advance of the interview and keep the written questions on your lap. During the interview, don't read from the questions, but keep eye contact with the interviewee. Before you finish the interview, you can check your written questions to make sure you haven't missed something important.

The reason it is important not to look at your questions during the interview is because it will take you away from listening to the answer. If you really listen, you may find valuable areas for follow-up questions that are not on your original list of questions. Also, by intently listening to the interviewee, you will help keep him or her relaxed.

The kinds of questions you should ask are focused, specific questions rather than open-ended ones such as "What do you think about the world of perfume?" A question like that will either lead to a long, rambling answer or something too brief to use, like "It's great." A question like "Tell me about how you created your newest perfume," on the other hand, gives the interviewee a specific story to tell in her answer.

Also, don't ask complicated two- or three-part questions. For most people it's better to stick with one issue at a time. Finally, it should be obvious that asking a question that only requires a simple "yes" or "no" for an answer will not get you a very interesting response.

Relaxing the Interviewee

Before starting to shoot, talk to the person you are interviewing off camera. Go over the general areas you will be covering. Explain that if she makes a mistake it's nothing to worry about. You have plenty of film (or tape) and can reshoot the answer to the question again.

Be relaxed yourself and you will set the tone for the person you are interviewing. Get her mind off the upcoming interview by chatting about something else. Make sure the person is offered something to drink or eat so that she won't be thirsty or have low blood sugar during the interview.

Adjusting Your Interview Position

Interviews in which your questions will be cut out of the film are conducted with the interviewee looking at you. You should be seated as close as possible to the camera, with your head level with or below the camera. If you then maintain eye contact with the person throughout the interview, it will appear as though the person being filmed is looking directly into the camera.

If you are going to be on-camera, such as in the TV magazine-show style, you will be seated off to the side of the camera so that the interviewee will appear to be talking to you. After the interview, you can get a reversal shot to film your questions and reactions.

Conducting the Interview

Start the interview with easy, factual questions to get the interviewee comfortable and more relaxed. Save any delicate, intimate, or emotional questions for later in the interview.

When it's time for more sensitive questions, sometimes it's better to ask them in an indirect way at first, depending on the person you are interviewing and your relationship with him or her. For example, you may know that a perfume executive has had cancer and is hesitant or uncomfortable talking about his own experience. You might ask him to talk about why his company supports cancer research. He may talk about his personal experience in his answer, or you may have to probe further by asking him to talk about any personal experience that led him to get his company involved in cancer research.

It's important to try to push through people's boundaries to get the most memorable interview. To get people to open up, your first job is to really concentrate on what they are saying. Many people rarely have people listen to them intently. Your sincere and complete interest in them is flattering and will encourage them to talk about things they may have rarely discussed before. Also, you should encourage them gently by saying something like "Yes, go on," or just by remaining silent. Your silence, combined with eye contact and a curious and interested expression, will signal to the interviewee that you know she has more to say and you are interested in hearing it.

Directing Action in Non-Fiction Films

You may have conducted some great interviews, but you don't want your film to be all talking heads. You have therefore lined up some shots of your subjects working or playing in their familiar environment, but can you get them to go about their tasks naturally rather than being stiff or self-conscious in front of the camera?

Again, it's important that you be relaxed. If you are stressed or worried about being behind schedule, your subject will pick up your anxiety and it will be harder for him or her to be natural. If you are relaxed and the crew is cheerful, everything will be easier.

Keeping the Participants Busy

When the camera starts to roll, it's important that the action you have set up occupies the person's body and mind so that she will become engrossed in the activity and oblivious to the camera. Her attention should be totally on the activity. The crew should not make eye contact with the person or any other kind of contact that might distract him or her from the activity or make him or her more aware of the camera.

Keeping the Camera Unobtrusive

When filming various activities carried out by real people rather than actors, you have to figure out how to best film that activity without changing it too much because of the presence of the crew and camera. Often you may be filming people in natural locations who you haven't interviewed or worked with at all.

In a film I did about AIDS, for example, we used the AIDS anthem, "That's What Friends Are For," as music over both the opening and closing of the film. I wanted to shoot high school kids being affectionate with each other—holding hands, flirting, hugging, or standing arm in arm—and put together a montage to that song. My dilemma was how to get the students to be themselves and not either mug for the camera or be too self-conscious to engage in the behaviors I wanted to film. The solution was actually easy enough. We got permission to film on the grounds of a public high school campus during the lunch hour. There was a large outdoor area at this campus where kids hung out before and after lunch as they were waiting for class to start. At our request, the principal made an announcement that a small film crew was filming an educational film and needed a shot of the high school. He said the crew would be outside the school in the courtyard and students should simply ignore us and go about their business at lunch.

We set up the camera in a corner out of the way of the area where the kids hung out. At first a few students came over and made faces in the camera, but after a few minutes most of them lost interest in us. They couldn't really tell when we were shooting and when we weren't and, because we were using a zoom lens, they couldn't really tell what part of the area we were focusing on. As I noticed couples or groups who were interesting, the cinematographer shot them. Later, after we got the shots we needed, the production manager went to each of the people we shot and asked them to sign a release form. Most of them were surprised that they had been filmed. The resulting montage was a poignant look at friends showing each other affection to the lyrics to the song.

Capturing Spontaneous Takes

Much more so than in feature films, one of the great pleasures of shooting non-fiction films is the opportunity to film things that happen spontaneously. These events can often be some of the most memorable moments in a film. All you have to do is to be in the right place at the right time and allow your camera to roll.

That happened in a film I directed about Norman Cousins and his belief in the power of the mind to affect physical healing. Norman was a golfer and we had spent a somewhat uneventful day on the golf course filming him and his buddies. When we arrived at the last hole, a ball suddenly came over from the driving range and hit one of Norman's buddies in the chest, knocking the six-foot-tall man flat on his back. Norman immediately got on the ground and talked to him reassuringly and soothingly as a member of the crew brought some ice for his chest. Soon, the man, calmed by Norman, was breathing normally again and was able to slowly get up. Our cinematographer had reacted fast and caught it all on film. Although it was an unfortunate and painful experience for the man who was hit by the golf ball, it gave us a perfect scene of Norman's philosophy in action—something we never could have conjured up or scripted.

Writing and Directing Narration

Good narration must be simple, clear, conversational, and fresh. It isn't easy to write and often requires several rewrites. Narration is usually written and shot or recorded after you have done a rough assembly of your film. If you are using an on-camera narrator, you may have to film her segments during the shoot rather than reassembling your crew and equipment at a later date. If that's the case, try to schedule it for the end of the shoot so you can make any adjustments to the script based on what you actually filmed.

The narrator will probably be a professional actor, but saying narration to a camera is harder than doing a scene with another professional actor. As the director, you have to provide the listening for your actor behind the camera in the same way you actively listened to your interviewees.

If you are recording voice-over narration, you will usually do that in a professional sound studio with no distracting background noise. As you listen, usually on headphones in another room, watch for the narrator's voice trailing off at the ends of sentences and for the kind of emotion you want in the reading. If the narrator has trouble with the phrasing on a particular line, it's okay to have her or him reword it as long as the meaning doesn't change.

The Least You Need to Know

- Like a fictional film, a non-fiction film must have a storyline and dramatic structure to be effective.
- Your crew should have experience in doing documentary films.
- By being relaxed yourself, you will help to relax the person you are interviewing.
- Start an interview with simple, factual questions and move later into more sensitive material.
- Keep on-screen non-actors busy and focused on what they are doing so they will be less aware of the camera.

Part 4

It's a Wrap:
Post-Production

It's a great feeling to have finished a successful film shoot, but you still don't have a movie. You have a lot of little pieces of a film or video that now have to be put together in the third phase of filmmaking—post-production.

This part of the book covers what you need to know to edit your film and finish it either on film or on video. It will also provide a sample post-production schedule and give you guidance on clearing copyrighted material and preparing your credits.

Chapter 16

Preparing to Edit

In This Chapter

- ◆ Assessing the different editing options
- ◆ Editing on film vs. on non-linear computer systems
- ◆ Establishing a working relationship with your editor

Post-production is the time to put your film together—to edit it and add effects, titles, music, and credits. As post-production starts, you can feel relief that the shooting is over and your movie is "in the can," but you still have a long way to go before your film will be ready to show to an audience. The quality of work you do in post-production can still mean the difference between a good film and a bad one or a good film and a great one.

As new formats for shooting movies have evolved in the last few years, nothing less than a revolution has taken place in film editing. In the not-so-distant past, films were only edited by physically cutting and splicing film. Today, however, perhaps as many as 80 percent of feature films, particularly studio films, are no longer edited on film. Instead, they are transferred to video and edited on computer-based digital *non-linear editing* systems. (Non-linear simply means that you can edit out of sequence, which you can do on film, too.) I'll look at the differences between the methods and cover what you need to do to be ready to edit your film by either method.

Editing History and Current Options

From the early days of filmmaking, feature films have been edited on film and some productions, particularly low-budget features, still choose that option. Basically, to edit on film, a *workprint*, which is a positive print of the dailies of a film, is made from the negative and a soundtrack is dubbed from the production sound recordings onto *mag stock*. The picture and sound are synced and the editor then watches the footage on an upright Moviola or on a flatbed table, marks cut points with a grease pencil, and makes the actual cuts with a splicer and tape.

 Verbal Action

non-linear editing   Editing a film or video out of sequence. The term is often used to refer to computer-based digital editing systems.

workprint   Also called cutting print, is the positive print used in editing that is printed directly from the original camera negative.

mag stock   Magnetic sound recording stock which has edge perforations that match those perforations on the picture stock, thereby allowing it to be pulled along with the picture at the same speed and relative position.

The first video editing systems were "linear" systems and were used to edit movies shot on video or films that were ultimately going to be shown on television or sold as videos. For film, the dailies were first transferred to videotape (as explained later in this chapter). The videotape was then laboriously assembled by rerecording selected shots from tape deck to tape deck in the order desired for the final film. This type of video editing was very time-consuming and frustrating: because the videotape was not being physically cut and spliced as film was, the editor was required, upon trimming, extending, or adding a shot anywhere but at the end of the cut material, to rerecord all the cut work that followed the change. Film editing, by contrast, gave the editor the option to work non-linearly—he or she could add or extract material anywhere in the cut without affecting the footage that followed it.

Just as computers have changed so much about the rest of our lives, they were introduced into motion picture editing and have changed the process dramatically. Avid, Lightworks, and other companies ushered in the age of digital non-linear editing by both using computers to digitize footage and creating software that allows editors to move around pieces of digitized film out of sequence and to edit non-linearly, like cutting on film. With these systems, rather than physically cutting film or rerecording videotape, the editor merely creates files that tell the computer in what sequence to play back pieces of digitized material representing the images that have been shot. The editor can make changes at any point to any part of the sequence without affecting what follows.

These computer systems are very popular for editing all kinds of films and videos. Still, if you did your shoot on film, you may prefer to edit on film in the traditional way rather than using a computer system. I'll look at the advantages and disadvantages of both options.

Editing on Film

There are two basic types of editing equipment that are used when editing on film—an upright editing machine, often called a Moviola after the most popular brand name, and a flatbed editing machine, such as the Kem or Steenbeck.

The upright machine basically pulls separate rolls of developed film and soundtrack from reels on the bottom of the machine to the top, either independently or in synchronization. Film is fed into the Moviola and can be viewed on a little viewer that is part of the machine. The editor uses foot pedals to start and stop the machine, reverse the film, or play it at a slow speed. After marking the film at the place where a cut is desired, the editor then pulls the film from the machine, puts it on a splicing block, and cuts the film between frames. The unused portions of the dailies are then labeled and hung on small hooks in a "trim bin" in case they are needed later.

The other type of editing machine, the flatbed, basically works the same way but pulls the film and sound track reels from left to right across a table, rather than up and down. The advantage of a flatbed machine is that it has a larger viewing screen, is gentle on the film, and has several fast-forward speeds.

On a feature film, an editor and one or more assistants may work for months to cut and assemble the scenes in a script manually. It is a very physical process and many skilled, veteran editors lament the loss of contact with the film in the newer digital systems in the same way that some writers still feel attached to the typewriter or—God forbid—pen and paper!

Editing Digitally

If a project originates on film but is going to be edited digitally on a non-linear system, then either the film negative or the workprint dailies must be transferred to videotape to be input into the editing equipment. The two most popular non-linear editing systems used now are Lightworks and Avid, but there are many other systems. These machines look more like computers than traditional film-editing equipment—because they are computers. In most systems, the computer and the hard drives where the digital footage is stored are in towers that are placed under a table that has two or more monitors for viewing the footage and a keyboard and a mouse for telling the computer how to move around the footage.

In addition, the digital editing room will have videotape input machines which convert images into a series of bits saved on the system's hard drives. Once film is converted to video, digitized, and stored on the hard drive, the computer can then play back the images by rapidly reading the data that is stored in it and converting it into the information or images displayed on the monitor.

The editing room will also have a VHS machine to which edited tapes can be output and various sound machines such as a CD player and an audiotape machine for inputting sound during the edit.

Script Notes

If you have shot on film but plan to edit digitally, you need to decide whether to make a workprint from your negative. It is possible to edit a film without doing so, but it can cause problems. Even the best digital editing systems will not show everything on the film. A good rule of thumb is if the movie is eventually going to be shown in theaters, rather than on television or video, make a workprint of the dailies.

Advantages of Digital Editing

The major advantage of digital editing is how much faster it is to edit a film digitally rather than manually cutting film. The editor no longer has to look through reels of film to find a shot—the computer can instantly access and display any part of any shot at any time. Shots can be organized and re-organized by simply dragging shots into a new "bin" or digital file folder. Also, cuts are made instantly rather than by the tedious cutting and splicing that an editor must do manually. The same applies to extending or trimming a scene.

A second major advantage of digital editing is that it makes it easier for an editor to try out different ways of assembling a scene. In film, if an editor wishes to recut a scene while retaining the option of returning to the previous version, she must have the lab make a dupe of the old scene, reconstitute the footage back into the dailies and recut. This is time-consuming and expensive, and requires another reconstitution and reassembly if the original version is opted for. Digitally, however, the editor simply creates a new file for the alternate cut. Both the original and one or more recut scenes can then be viewed to see which one works best.

Finally, digital systems give the editor the ability to instantly create and view optical effects (such as fades, dissolves, wipes, titles, superimpositions, and so on). In film editing, the editor marks the place on the workprint where an optical is desired, but the filmmakers will only know how well the effect works when an optical house actually creates it. If the editor or director doesn't like the optical, it must be discarded or re-ordered and the time and expense of producing the first optical has been wasted. With a digital system, an optical house will still have to create an optical negative with which to strike release prints when finishing the film (see Chapter 19, "Finishing the Film or Video"), but the editor can first experiment with the effect on the computer until she's certain that the effect is what she and the director want.

Disadvantages of Digital Editing

Despite these significant advantages, digital editing systems also have some disadvantages over editing on film. First, the cost of renting digital non-linear editing equipment is, at this time, much more expensive than renting film-editing equipment. Some of that cost may be saved, however, because a film can be edited so much faster. You won't have to hire an editor for as many weeks or one or more assistant editors for as long.

Another disadvantage of the computer systems is the low resolution of the digitized images you will probably be working with. Some non-linear systems will digitize at "broadcast quality," but systems which have to digitize large amounts of footage from a feature film will generally only digitize the film at fairly low resolutions. At these resolutions, detail is lost, which can make it difficult for an editor to determine the visual quality of a shot. If you want higher resolutions during editing, you may be able to get them—but at an extra expense.

As far as viewing the assembled film at different stages of the editing process, with digital editing you can only look at an assembly on the monitor. When editing on film, however, you can view your edited reels in a screening room at any time. With digital editing, it's only possible to screen your assembly on film if an assistant editor manually assembles a film workprint from the output cut lists provided by the digital editing system.

Computer-based systems also have the disadvantage of more frequent downtime than traditional editing equipment. Avid's or other editing systems

Counterpoint

In his book, *In the Blink of an Eye*, Walter Murch—the editor of Francis Ford Coppola's *Apocalypse Now* (1981) and *The Conversation* (1974)—discusses an unexpected downside of computer-based editing systems. In film and linear video editing, editors are forced to wait and watch while fast-forwarding or rewinding to find a shot. Computers save this wasted time but may prevent the editor from discovering some interesting and useful shots that wouldn't have been discovered otherwise.

experience a variety of technical problems such as software conflicts, hardware incompatibilities, corrupted files, or defective cards. As with personal computers, any one of a number of problems can crash the system and stop the editing process. Problems may take days to fix, causing editors many headaches and much frustration (and ultimately adding to your post-production costs).

Finally, digital systems allow filmmakers to edit faster than ever before, but because of their high rental costs, producers tend to allow for fewer weeks of editing than with traditional editing equipment. Many editors are concerned that the shorter editing time can lead to a less creative or interesting cut. Traditional film editing's slow, deliberate pace can foster creativity by giving the editor and director time to walk away from a cut and then come back to it again with a fresh eye. Reflection over a period of a few months can be good for a film. By allowing producers to shorten the editing process, digital systems may be causing films to be rushed to completion, whether they're really ready or not.

Getting Ready to Edit

Once you've decided how you are going to edit your film or video, you have to prepare for the edit. The process of preparing for editing is different depending on whether you are planning to edit on film, video, or on a computer-based system. What all of the processes have in common, however, is the need to carefully log and keep track of all the film or video you have shot.

Preparing for a Traditional Film Edit

If you are editing on film, the lab will have made a workprint of your camera negative and a sound house will have made a mag track of your production sound tapes. The workprint for each take is then lined up and synced to the corresponding sound track and these are the dailies that the director views each evening. Along with the dailies, the editor will have the notes from the script supervisor and any additional comments from the director made during the screening of dailies.

Both the workprint and soundtrack will then be coded or *edge coded*. This means that numbers will be printed on the edge of each track, allowing the editor and her assistant to log in and keep track of which soundtrack goes with which picture.

The workprint itself will then have two sets of numbers on it—the original key numbers printed on the negative film by the manufacturer that are also viewable on the workprint (and will be necessary later in cutting the negative) and the new edge code number. These different sets of numbers have to be entered in logbooks that refer key numbers to code numbers and code numbers to scene numbers. In addition, labels have to be made for every scene.

It's clearly important to have a very organized assistant editor to create the logs and keep track of every piece of film and its corresponding soundtrack.

Preparing for Editing Video

Videotapes are coded differently than film, with electronic code numbers call SMPTE (the Society of Motion Picture and Television Engineers) time code. The time code is burned into the picture areas of a videotape so that it is visible, creating a "window dub." The code is normally placed in a little rectangular black box somewhere near the bottom of the screen. The numbers are standardized to include a lot of information that can be used to identify the particular tape and frame with which the code number is associated.

If you shot on video and are editing on video (either on a linear or non-linear system), you should log in your shots the same way you would for film, but you will use the time code rather than edge numbers to keep track of your footage.

As you prepare to edit on the complex non-linear systems, be sure to test all the equipment before beginning to edit your footage. Also, because the computers allow the editor to create certain special settings and to have information set up in different ways, at this stage, configure the system the way you want it. Next, digitize the video so that it is loaded into the system, and you will be ready to work.

 Verbal Action _____

edge code   (a.k.a. edge number) A number printed on the edge of the film to keep the film and soundtrack in sync.

telecine   A device that takes a film image and converts it into a video image.

3:2 pulldown   (a.k.a. 2:3 pulldown) The method for telecining 24-frames-per-second film to 30-frames-per-second videotape.

field   One half of a video frame, with each field containing either the odd scan lines or the even scan lines.

Telecine for Editing Film on Video

Telecine is the process whereby film is transferred to video. The machine commonly used for this process is called a Rank Cintel, so the telecine process is sometimes called "ranking" the film.

Because film is shot at 24 frames per second and video at 30 frames per second, a special formula is needed to add the frames necessary to properly convert film images to video images during telecine. The *3:2 pulldown* is the formula used to do this. With this formula, every other film frame is held for three video *fields* (a field is half of a video frame) rather than the normal two. The first video frame is two fields, the next is three, the next is two, and so on. Some people call this a 2:3 pulldown, since the first frame is made up of two fields. This "pulldown" process assures that when you watch the video version of the film, it's in real time, or very close.

During telecine, you need to monitor the transfer. Make sure that the Rank is playing at exactly 24 frames per second, not slightly slower or faster, which would result in sound drifting out of sync over an extended period of time. If the machine varies speed, it can be even worse. It is important that the telecine is very precise because you will be editing your film's sound and picture to it. If it doesn't accurately represent the timing of the original film, when you go back at the end of the edit to cut on film, you will be in trouble.

Cutaway

There is one other slight problem in the film to video conversion—video isn't really exactly 30 fps but is 29.975 fps. So when you're doing the 2:3 pulldown, you're slowing down the actual program length. When you play the videotape back, it will play slightly slower than the speed for which the pulldown was calculated. Unless you make an adjustment, it will slowly drift out of sync if transferred back to film. To avoid this problem, make sure that the computer-editing system you use can make the needed adjustment. An Avid, for example, will pull out the extra frames that were added in the telecine process so that the master "clip" is an exact copy of the film roll, giving you a 1:1 correspondence between a frame on the computer and a film frame on the negative.

Working with Your Editor

The most important thing to do before cutting begins is for the director and editor to establish clear communication about both the process of editing and the director's vision for the film. The director and editor have to work as a team, so they should have mutual respect and an ability to communicate well with each other.

Directors have different ways of working with editors. Many directors want the editor to do a first cut before the director gets involved in the process. Some like to sit in the editing room and comment on every cut from the start. Still other directors may drop into the editing room on occasion to see how the first cut is progressing. Whatever your style as a director, make sure you tell your editor what your expectations and plans are so she can adjust.

The other thing you should agree on is a basic timeline for the editing process. On many productions, the editor will begin cutting the film during production. She will attend dailies screenings and take notes on which takes the director prefers, and if the director has any particular scheme in mind for how a scene should be put together. As the shoot continues, the editor will work to assemble a first cut and will usually have it ready shortly after the last day of production. Other times, only an assistant editor may be handling the dailies and organizing and logging the film. The editor may not start until near the end of production so that she can work more closely with the director even on the first cut.

In any case, the editor should develop a plan and a schedule for the entire post-production process, including picture editing, music and sound design, titles and negative cutting, or an on-line video editing session.

The Least You Need to Know

♦ Editing on film is more time-consuming, but the equipment is more reliable and the process gives you more time to think about your cut.

♦ Editing digitally enables you to try out different assemblies and compare them without having to make dupes and reconstitute already-cut dailies.

♦ Telecine is the first step in the process of preparing film for digital editing by transferring it to videotape.

♦ Directors have different styles of working with editors, but the important thing is that communication and expectations are clear and that a schedule is set in advance.

Chapter 17

Editing the Rough Cut

In This Chapter

◆ Making cuts appear seamless

◆ Understanding the principles of editing

◆ Getting started with the rough cut

◆ Editing dialogue

◆ Editing non-fiction films

Editing, like writing, is a creative, story-telling process. Also like writing, where a writer usually does a first draft and then rewrites and polishes her work, the editing process can be divided into stages. First, a *rough cut* or first assembly is made and then the editor and director fine-tune the rough cut, turning it into a film that is clear, concise, and dramatically effective.

Like a writer, the editor's focus throughout the entire process of editing a film should be on how to best tell the story. Even though I will be covering many editing techniques in this chapter and in Chapter 18, "Fine-Tuning the Film," in considering each cut, you and your editor should be concerned about the story first and technique second. What matters to the audience is a strong, well-told story, not flawless techniques.

The best thing that a director can give an editor is enough footage to be able to tell the story well. No editor will be able to save a film that, either for budgetary reasons or because of the lack of skill of the director, doesn't have enough coverage—such as different angles, cutaways, or reversal shots—for the editor to put together a story that is visually interesting and smoothly edited.

Knowing Basic Editing Principles

Before actually beginning to assemble the rough cut, the editor should prepare by reading the script and viewing all the footage that has been shot. The actual editing process then starts with choosing an individual shot and a second shot to cut with it. There are certain principles editors use to choose shots, decide on how to arrange and juxtapose shots, and determine when to trim or extend shots. Some of the things an editor must keep in mind as she chooses shots and strings them together are the best acting performances and the best technical values (camera motion, lighting, and so on). She must make each individual cut as fluid and seamless as possible (unless a deliberately rough effect is desired) and cut to new and appropriate angles at dramatically proper points in the scene. And, most important, the editor must cut the film to tell the story in as involving and emotionally charged way as possible.

Matching Cuts

Good editors seek to achieve seamless, smooth, invisible *matching cuts* whenever possible. These are cuts that don't draw attention to themselves and that come at a logical point in the shot. It's not always easy to determine where that logical point is, but it usually is obvious when a cut isn't made at the right point. When a cut is good, it seems to be continuous; when it isn't good, it makes the viewer notice it and brings him or her out of the story.

There are various techniques editors use to achieve seamless cutting and make the action seem continuous. When the viewer's eye is distracted, a cut is less noticeable; so one frequently used editing technique to disguise a cut is to cut on action. A movement like the slamming of a door, the raising of a glass for a toast, or any other gesture or actual physical movement of an actor in the shot are natural points to cut. It's important that the movement in the shot is not too subtle or faint or the cut will be noticeable.

> **Script Notes**
>
> There are times when it works to cut on a static shot rather than movement. If a scene shows a woman walking into a room and then stopping in her tracks at the sight of a dead body, the cut goes from the woman standing still to the unmoving dead body. Both the stillness of the body and the shocked, frozen state of the woman are what you want to communicate, not movement; so it's appropriate to cut those static shots together.

To make matching cuts or cuts that are seamless, the editor must not only find movement in the shot on which to cut whenever possible but also consider such issues as:

- Do the shots have a similar visual tone or do they vary in light and color?
- Is the dialogue continuous?
- Is there a similarity in angle or screen direction?
- Is there a significant dramatic change from one shot to the next?

Understanding the Purpose of the Scene

The purpose of a scene is another critical consideration in determining how to cut and assemble it. For example, in *Something Is Rotten*, we may have a scene in the script of our heroine eating breakfast at home. What is the purpose of the scene? Is it to show something about her character, such as whether she is an organized, fastidious person or the opposite—a disorganized or messy person? Or is the scene there to show how rushed and busy she is and how quickly she must leave home each morning?

If the purpose of the scene is the latter, the editor would need to find ways to cut the scene so that it takes up very little screen time. The unedited or "raw" footage might have a shot of our heroine entering the kitchen, another of her walking across it, another of her opening the refrigerator, yet another of her taking out the milk and orange juice, and finally a shot of her putting the milk on the counter, dropping the orange juice bottle on the floor, and crying out in total frustration. By focusing on the purpose of the scene, which is to show how rushed she is, the editor can cut each shot to a fraction of its actual length to give the sense that the character is hurried. Instead of seeing her walk across the kitchen, we will see her start across and then will cut to the refrigerator door for a second before her hand enters the frame to open the door. We then can collapse the time further by just showing her putting the milk on the counter and dropping the juice, rather than including the shot of her taking the milk and juice out of the refrigerator.

On the other hand, if the purpose of the scene is to show how fastidious she is, the shot inside the refrigerator as she takes out the milk and orange juice might be important because it will also show how all of her refrigerator shelves have neatly stacked containers with labels on them. An editor who does not understand the purpose of each scene could cut the footage in a way that is completely wrong for the film.

Deciding How Little to Show

Editors are generally focused on how little they need to show to impart the necessary information in a scene, rather than how much. Each cut promises the viewer more information to move the story forward, but if the next shot is uninteresting or unimportant to the story, it will slow the film down.

For example, when our heroine leaves the house after this rushed, disastrous breakfast, she is going to the perfume factory. We don't need to show her driving from her house to the office. It's usually enough to see her leaving the house in one shot and pulling up to the factory in her car in the next. We might show an establishing shot of the factory first and then her car entering the frame, if the factory hasn't been seen in the film before.

Even on the first assembly, it's wise for the editor not to include more of the scene than is needed to tell the story.

Using Shorter or Longer Cuts

When you know the purpose of a scene, you can use the length of the shots in the scene to communicate that purpose. Whether you use shots of long duration or short duration or a combination of long and short shots communicates different things about the scene you are editing.

In general, shorter cuts build the action, excitement, energy, and tension of a scene. They also can give the audience an overview of a scene, through showing them a series of snap-shots of the scene, in effect. Short cuts tell the viewer that things are happening quickly in the story and can indicate that something significant is about to happen.

Longer shots expand time. They can be useful when you want to focus attention on something in the shot, such as a new location or an important person or object in the context of the story. If, for example, a character in the film has to endure an uncomfortable moment, such as our heroine in *Something Is Rotten* while waiting for her boss to decide her fate at the company, then longer shots will reinforce the anxiety she is feeling.

 Verbal Action

rough cut First assembly of a film that the editor prepares from selected takes, in script order, leaving the finer points of timing and editing to a later stage.

matching cut (a.k.a. match cut) A cut in which the two shots cut together are linked logically and visually, often by action or movement within the shots.

jump cut A cut which breaks the continuity of time by jumping forward from one part of an action to another.

Jump Cuts

The opposite of a matching cut is a disconcerting mismatch between shots called a *jump cut*. For example, if you cut from a shot of a person sitting to a shot of the same person standing in the same spot, it creates a jump in time that will be disturbing to the audience. The same thing will happen if the image size and angle don't change very much from one shot to the next, such as two close-ups of the same person placed next to each other. The cut seems to jump in those cases, but if there is a change to a medium shot in the second shot, for example, then the cut will seem natural and will not be noticed as much. If the director doesn't get enough coverage of a scene, then the editor will sometimes be forced to use jump cuts if there is no opportunity to reshoot the scene.

In the 1960s, some filmmakers began to use jump cuts to express the disconcerting nature of life, or for comic effect. Unless you intentionally want to create a jumpy or disturbing feeling in your film, however, don't use them. They will call attention to the editing and take the viewer out of the story.

Relational Cutting

Scenes or shots that have been filmed that have no direct connection in reality are given an implied relationship in a film when the editor cuts them together. For example, when we see someone walking up to a house and we cut to a woman in a room in a house, we assume that she has entered the house even though we have not actually seen her enter the house. In reality, she may not have entered that exact house, but is doing that interior scene at a totally different location or set. The director may have even used a stand-in as the woman walking up to the house if it was a long shot and you couldn't see her face. But the audience will still think it's the same person because of the adjacent relationship of the shots.

In the same way, *parallel action* or parallel cutting, which may be called for in the script, creates a relationship between scenes or shots. In parallel cutting, shots from two different locations or two different characters or groups of characters are repeatedly inter-cut to develop the different story lines dramatically and inform the audience that something is going to happen when these two parallel characters or groups of characters meet. This is a common technique used to build tension in action and suspense films where there is fast inter-cutting between the good guys and the bad guys. In romantic films, parallel cutting is often used to develop the two characters who will ultimately meet and become romantically involved.

The term cross-cutting is sometimes used interchangeably with parallel cutting or it may also mean cutting which gives the viewer different points of view of one subject or group of characters in the same scene. Both types of cutting give the viewer story information through the relationships between shots.

Cutaway

In the early 1920s, Lev Kuleshov, a Russian cameraman and experimental filmmaker, demonstrated how the same shot juxtaposed with different following shots could yield different reactions in the audience. In a famous experiment, he showed three different audiences the same shot of an actor with three different follow-up shots. The first showed the man followed by a plate of soup on a table. The second showed him followed by a dead woman in a coffin, and the third by a little girl playing with a toy. Despite the fact that the shot of the man was exactly the same in all three sequences, audiences described him in the first instance as hungry, in the second as a sad husband who had lost his wife, and in the third as a happy father.

Scene Changes

Many of the same techniques for achieving seamless cuts or good continuity in assembling the individual shots in a scene will also work to provide continuity between scenes. It's important to provide either a visual or audio link between the last shot of one scene and the first shot of the next to alert the audience to the change in scene and make that change seem natural.

There are several things the editor can look for in the footage to make those scene transitions. First, a similarity in movement from one shot to another makes a good transition. For example, in a shot of our heroine leaving her house, she is moving from right to left. If the editor cuts as she reaches about the middle of the frame and, in the next scene, as she enters her office, there is also a tracking shot of her moving from right to left, the editor can pick up her movement in that shot at about the same point in the middle of the frame. As the motion is completed, it becomes clear that she is in a new place and a new scene is beginning.

Other visual clues can also make good scene transitions. If a scene ends with a close-up of a flask of a new perfume that our heroine has on her desk, and the next scene begins with a close-up of another, similar flask of perfume and it pulls back to reveal a storage area where there are many similar flasks of perfumes, the transition to the new scene will be smooth.

Scene changes are also clear if there is some other aspect of the character, such as her attire, that has changed from one scene to the next. If our heroine is in her bathrobe in one scene and in her business suit in the next, it is clear that it is a new scene and therefore it is a smooth transition.

When the footage isn't there to provide visual links between scenes to make them appear continuous, then editors can cover a scene transition with a shift in sound or by running the sound or dialogue for the new scene over the end of the earlier scene. Visual transitions are usually smoother, but some editors and directors like to use sound or dialogue to bridge scenes.

Editing Dialogue

Dialogue is critical to the storyline, and the way in which dialogue is edited in a film will have a big impact on how the story moves. Although dialogue is important, nothing is more boring than a movie that is too talky and filled with long dialogue scenes.

In the editing room, there may be places where unnecessary dialogue can be removed to speed up a scene. A simple look by one of the characters may say all that is necessary.

In order to condense speeches, editors often use cutaway shots. In a shot where one character is speaking, for example, the editor can cut to a shot of a person listening or another relevant shot. During this cutaway, as the speaker completes a thought, the sound cuts to another sentence later in the scene. If the cut makes logical sense, to the audience it will sound like the normal flow of speech. Before the shot returns to the original speaker, a pause, a few words, or even whole sections of dialogue can be removed. The same technique works if the editor needs to add a section of dialogue to the scene.

In a dramatic film, where the dialogue is often quite consistent from one take to the next, it is often possible to use the sound from one take and the picture from another. If there are slight variations, the editor can trim or expand pauses between words to keep the footage in sync.

Creating the First Assembly

Now that you are familiar with many of the techniques editors use in selecting shots and putting them together during the editing process, it's time to discuss exactly what the editor does to create the first rough cut of the film.

As I mentioned earlier, the editor should spend time looking at the footage and getting to know it as well as possible. Each time an editor views footage, she will see different things. During the first look at a take, it may seem good, but on a subsequent viewing the editor may notice, for example, an extra in the background with a look on her face that is inappropriate for the shot, making the take unusable.

CAUTION

Counterpoint

If at all possible, if the editor is working on a computer-based non-linear system, she should always view the footage either on film, if a workprint has been made, or on the editing videocassette that has come from the telecine house rather than the digitized image in the editing machine. The editing machine will have a much lower resolution and may obscure important details in the shot.

Sometimes the editor will only use the takes that have been selected by the director in putting together the rough cut. Other times, editors and directors feel that it's best to let the editor bring a fresh eye to the project and form her own opinions about the best take or what works and what doesn't.

After the editor has chosen sections of one take or another that she wants to use, she will begin to cut the selected pieces of film together. There will be many false starts along the way, as the editor looks at the scene coming together and decides whether it seems to be working. If she is unsure about a scene, she may ask the opinion of an assistant editor or of another trusted associate. Eventually, she will move on to the next scene until she has put the entire film together.

Editors often edit scenes out of order or non-linearly and then cut them together later. Other times, when it's possible, and because of the need to find good transitions between scenes, editors may edit scenes in order.

Most editors put together a rough cut fairly quickly. During this initial assembly, editors usually don't worry too much about getting everything to work perfectly. Because it is easier to cut footage out than it is to add material, most rough cuts are quite a bit longer than the finished film will be, sometimes as much as twice as long or longer.

The purpose of doing the rough cut first is so the editor and director will have a sense of the overall story and direction of the film. Editing decisions can have a far-reaching effect on the story—on the viewer's interpretation of the story and emotional reactions. By making changes in the way she assembles material, the editor has the possibility of ...

◆ Shifting the center of interest in a scene.

◆ Emphasizing some information or limiting other information in a scene.

◆ Changing the significance of an action to create more tension, humor, or another emotion.

◆ Changing the duration or order of shots to affect the emotion of a scene.

◆ Creating relationships that may or may not exist in reality.

To create these types of effects, film editors use all of the basic techniques or principles of editing that we have covered.

Editing Documentary Films

Although the basic principles of editing are the same, the process of editing a documentary or non-fiction film can be somewhat different than editing a dramatic film. Since the non-fiction film is not as tightly scripted as a dramatic film, the writer or director (often the same person in documentaries) will have to give the editor more guidance before the rough cut than with a dramatic film.

Preparing the Paper Edit

If possible, it's a good idea to audiotape the interviews in a documentary and have those tapes transcribed prior to editing. The transcriptions allow the writer or director to see where there is repetition or how the interview material might be best used or arranged. From the transcriptions and videocassettes of the dailies with time code on them, the writer or director can make a *paper edit*, which is a list of selected shots in their proper order. The shots will have an in and out time from the time code on the videocassettes. The editor can then take the paper edit and assemble a rough cut.

A paper edit is necessary so that the writer/director can begin to shape the story from the interviews and actual material shot. What the real people are presumed to say in a script prepared before production may not be what they actually say on camera. As is often the case, good, unexpected material that was not in the script may be present in an interview or an action sequence. If the editor simply uses the script as a guide to assemble a rough cut rather than using a paper edit, she might leave out that good material.

 Verbal Action _____

parallel action   (a.k.a. parallel cutting) A device of story construction in which the development of two pieces of action are presented simultaneously.

cross-cutting   Often used interchangeably with parallel cutting, it is the inter-cutting of shots from two or more scenes so the fragments of each scene will be presented to the viewer's attention alternately; also cutting between different points of view of one subject.

paper edit   A list of shots in their selected order, usually prepared prior to editing non-fiction films.

A good paper edit will begin to clarify and narrow the focus of the documentary footage by picking material that is about one theme. Sidebars and subplots may work in the print media, but film and video are more linear mediums so the paper edit gives the writer/director and ultimately the editor the chance to build a theme and stick to it, telling one story with a beginning, middle, and end, rather than several stories. In documentaries a lot of material will have to end up on the cutting-room floor, perhaps even more than in features, in order to make the narrative flow of the story make sense.

Adding Narration

Although narration is used in both fiction and non-fiction films, it is used more frequently in documentaries and may not be written and recorded until after the film is edited. If the voice-over narration has not yet been recorded by the time the editor and director are putting together an assembly of the film, the editor or director can record in their own voice a "scratch" track that can be used in editing. The track will then be replaced by the actual narrator's recording after the picture editing has been completed.

The Least You Need to Know

- ◆ An editor should reread the script and view all of the footage before beginning to edit a film.
- ◆ The goal of good film editing is to be invisible or seamless rather than to have cuts that are noticeable.
- ◆ The purpose of a scene is an important factor in how it is edited.
- ◆ The editor has the ability to greatly affect the interpretation of the story and the emotional reactions it will cause by how she cuts the film.
- ◆ In editing documentaries, most writer/directors prepare a paper edit before the editor begins to assemble the rough cut.

Chapter 18

Fine-Tuning the Film

In This Chapter

◆ Starting the fine-tuning process
◆ Finding the right pace and rhythm for your film
◆ Using optical effects for transitions or emphasis
◆ Being sensitive to the film's dramatic structure
◆ Using test screenings during editing to gain feedback

It is both exciting and disappointing to view the rough cut of your film. You won't have seen your entire film together before this and it will be exciting to see the story or narrative continuity for the first time. You'll get a first glimpse of how the story is working. At the same time, it will be disappointing because the film will be too long, will have clunky, awkward sections that don't seem to flow, and will lack any sort of rhythm or pace. When you view the rough cut, you will know that you still have a lot of work to do.

You and your editor will then begin the second critical stage of editing, which is to prepare the final cut of your film. This stage of editing is all about refinement and then more refinement. It is about making something work a little better here and there and then here again. In this chapter, I'll cover what you need to know about fine-tuning your film.

Starting the Fine-Cut Process

During the rough assembly, your editor has been focusing on the narrative flow of the story. He or she has been putting together the footage—both picture and sound—so that the narrative is clear and complete. The basic story that the writer intended to tell is there in the cut for the director (and sometimes the producer) to see. In putting together that first assembly, the editor has been resisting trying to make each scene "perfect" at this early stage because it will be a waste of time. He or she knows that what is perfect for a particular scene at one moment will necessarily change as other scenes change and a fine cut progresses.

Like rewriting or editing a book or script, when a change is made in one place it may affect the story in other places. Even during the fine cut, editing does not involve simply making a scene perfect and then moving to the next scene and never revisiting the first. After certain changes later in the film, for example, dialogue in an earlier scene might become superfluous and the editor will have to figure out how to cut it out. A take of an actor's performance that was outstanding in dailies might seem over-the-top when watched in context of the whole film and a different take might have to be substituted. A 30-second speech in the script may work better as one off-camera line of dialogue, and the editor will need to recut the scene accordingly. Or, sometimes, entire sequences may have to be dumped.

Cutaway
In *The Touch of Evil* (1958), Orson Welles uses a three-minute tracking shot to open the film. It follows a car—from a scene in which a bomb is planted in its trunk—as it drives across the border. Soon after Charlton Heston's character enters the foreground of the shot, the car passes him and explodes. Welles could have filmed the scene with many shots to increase the pace, but instead relied on story, composition, and performances to build tension.

Changes like the above examples and new changes that need to be made as a result of the first changes aren't apparent in a single pass through the film. The process of fine-tuning a cut involves going through the film, making a series of cuts, then viewing the film again and repeating the process until you feel the final cut is as good as you can make it. During this fine-tuning stage, you and the editor need to plan your time so that you can go through the entire film a number of times before "locking the picture" or making the final cut.

Finding the Pace and Rhythm

One of the aspects of a film that is fine-tuned in this second editing stage is the pace of the film. The role of pace differs in different film genres, but it is always important in heightening the drama (or in comedy, the comedic moments) of a film.

Variations in the pace will affect the viewer's emotional response to the film. As a general rule, if you want the tension, intensity, energy, or excitement of a film to increase in a sequence, the shot duration is progressively shortened. Or long and short durations might be contrasted to show the leisurely pace of one character in contrast to the hectic pace of another character.

In editing, pace involves both the timing of shots or their duration and the rhythm of shots that are strung together. A cutting rhythm can be set up by controlling the duration of successive shots. The editor should know the relative lengths of shots within a sequence. The shots should not be all the same length, or the scene will have no rhythm. The lack of rhythm will then lessen the emotional impact of a scene or sequence.

Feeling the rhythm of a film is somewhat of an intuitive process. You can tell when a film does not have a rhythm, but it's difficult to tell someone how to make it have rhythm. The editor simply must be able to feel it and have the skill to create a rhythm that works for the particular story.

In finding the rhythm of a scene, the editor must also respect the performances. If the editor notices a pause between two lines of dialogue, it may be part of the performance and not something to be tampered with to shorten a shot. The editor must be able to distinguish between an error in a performance and a deliberate pause for effect by the performer. If the editor understands the purpose of the scene, she will know whether subtle nuances in the delivery of dialogue are part of the performer's intentional rhythm in playing the scene or are errors in timing.

There are several intrinsic rhythms within a scene or sequence in a film that the editor must be sensitive to, including …

- The movement of the subject of the scene.
- The movement of the background of a scene.
- Superimposed movement in a part of a scene, such as a flashing light.
- The rhythm of the voice of the subject in dialogue scenes.
- The rhythm of the background noise or music.

As the editor edits, she will be taking two shots, each of which has its own internal rhythm, and will be inter-cutting them to create a new rhythm. Rhythm is also affected by the type of transitions used between sequences, which I'll cover later in this chapter.

Cutaway

Director Oliver Stone and his Oscar-winning editors in *JFK* (1991) use juxtaposition and pace to effectively dramatize the film's story. Stone describes his technique as "vertical editing," in which you cut abruptly to what a character is thinking, feeling, or describing. This allows the filmmaker to quickly enhance or undercut what a character is saying as well as open up a conventional dialogue scene. The film also employs almost every style of editing ever devised, including documentary re-enactment, film-within-film, cuts that are almost subliminal, classical continuity editing, unmotivated foreshadowings, rapid alternative versions of the same action, parallel cutting, multiple point of view, and many opticals such as freeze frames, zoom-ins, whip pans, and color desaturation. The film was originally criticized for its "MTV" style, but Stone and his editors understood that sophisticated film audiences, who can read images and absorb emotional and narrative information rapidly, would respond to the film.

Using Optical Transitions

One traditional method of editing that was used more frequently in the first several decades of filmmaking connects shots in a scene or sequence with straight cuts and then uses fades or dissolves to connect the sequences. These optical effects convey to the viewer the passage of time, whether it is short time gaps or long periods of time.

Today, filmmakers are just as likely to join two sequences together with a straight cut, using such cues as lighting, dress, locale, color, or sound to tell the audience that it is a new scene. Dissolves may be reserved for signaling a long gap in time, and it is not unusual to see a movie with no effects other than a fade-out at the end.

In Chapter 3, "Mise-en-scène: Basic Elements of Films and Videos," I introduced the basic types of opticals that are available to filmmakers. During the fine cut, the editor and director will decide whether to use any opticals as transitions or for any kind of emphasis. When editing on a computer-based non-linear system, the editor and director can visually try out the optical to see how it will look before making a decision to use it. When using traditional film-editing equipment, however, the filmmakers will have to imagine what the optical will look like at this stage. The following list covers the basic optical options:

- ◆ **Fade:** The fade is used rarely in films today unless the filmmaker wants the viewer to take a very noticeable pause between two sections of a film or wants to emphasize some important change in time, place, or feeling. Even in opening a film, many filmmakers do not use the traditional fade-in but prefer to open with the impact of a full sharp image. Most films, however, still end with the fade out.

- ◆ **Dissolve:** Although the dissolve is not used as often today as it has been in the past, it is still an effective transition. In contrast to a fade-in/fade-out in which the screen goes momentarily to black (or white) the dissolve is a gradual blending of two adjacent shots. The dissolve is not only used as a temporal transition—to bridge time gaps—but can be equally effective in creating the mood and rhythm of a scene. Dissolves are often used effectively in montages. When in a jam, filmmakers also use dissolves to cover a jump cut.

◆ **Freeze frame:** After the dissolve, the freeze frame is probably one of the most commonly used optical effects. In it, a single frame is repeated, which makes the action appear to have stopped. Freeze frames are sometimes used to end a film since they suggest holding still a moment in time.

◆ **Wipe:** The wipe was an extremely common transitional device used in American films of the 1930s and 1940s. In a wipe, the incoming image wipes across the outgoing image. There are many varieties of wipes including horizontal, vertical, and diagonal wipes. Because they call such attention to the device itself, they are not used often today, but there may be times when a wipe can provide an effective transition in your film.

◆ **Sound opticals:** Sound can be used to help bridge an abrupt transition and make a moment more dramatic. Instead of blending picture images as in a dissolve, a sound dissolve blends a sound from an outgoing shot with the sound from the incoming shot.

For example, in *In Cold Blood* (1967), Richard Brooks uses a fade-out after the murderers approach the house of their intended victims. The following morning the house seems calm—we don't know what has happened. A family of friends enters and as two girls go upstairs, the father goes into the kitchen. At the same instant he sees the severed phone wire, the audience hears a girl's scream off-screen. Then, in a sound dissolve, her scream becomes a police siren, moving the audience to the next stage of the action.

◆ **Other opticals:** There are many other opticals that have been used throughout film history. Some of them are too attention-getting or gimmicky to be used very much today. You should still know them because they are part of the film language that has evolved and can occasionally still be used effectively today, depending on the film. They include the following:

  ◆ **Ripple dissolve** is a wavy blending of the adjacent images as if oil were pouring over the screen.

  ◆ **Turnaround or flip wipe** is a flipping of the on-screen image to reveal the incoming image on its reverse side.

  ◆ **Iris** is a progressively circular narrowing or expanding out of the image, like the iris of an eye, usually against a black background.

  ◆ **Mask** is like an iris, only it doesn't expand or narrow and may have the shape of a keyhole or other viewing device.

- **Impact dissolve** is a dissolve using a series of flash cuts (very short cuts) of two different shots in which the images will appear to be simultaneously present.

- **Fast motion** is an optical that increases the apparent speed of the action by printing every other frame to double the speed or every third frame to triple the speed.

- **Slow motion** is an optical that slows down the action by printing every frame more than once. (Slow motion produced by an optical effect will appear jerkier than slow motion achieved by running the camera at a high frame rate.)

- **Reverse action** is printing the last frame first to show the movement in a shot in reverse.

- **Split screen** is used to divide the scene into multiple images or to show two different scenes simultaneously.

- **Superimposition** (a.k.a. multiple exposure) is an image printed over another one or several images printed over each other.

Focusing on Structure

In Chapter 6, "Act I: Developing the Script," I discussed the need for good structure in writing a script. In the editing process, the filmmakers must also be sensitive to good dramatic structure or, despite a good script, the film may turn out to be slow to start, boring in the middle, or saddled with an ending that doesn't work. When editing is good, it can heighten the impact of a well-structured script. When it isn't good, it can weaken the dramatic structure of a good script.

The editor and director, like the writer in writing the script, must keep in mind the three-act dramatic structure and be sensitive to the needs of each act when fine-tuning the film.

The Opening

The beginning of a film must establish the characters and the problem or question of the film that will be resolved as the story progresses. It must move fast enough into establishing that question to "hook" the audience, and yet it must not move so fast that it hasn't given the audience enough information about the characters to make the viewers care about them.

When editing the opening sequences of the film or the first act, the editor must know the purpose of that act to know how fast or how slow to pace the film—what to tighten and what to leave at a more leisurely pace.

The Middle

Many times, viewers will come out of a movie and say that they were bored in the middle of the film. Even if the writer has provided a reasonable number of dramatic moments or "twists and turns" in the second act of a film, editors must find ways to keep that act moving at a brisk pace. The middle act is the longest act and will have the greatest number of scenes and sequences in the film. The editor must ask if every scene is really necessary or whether a scene can be cut—or at least cut back to its essence.

The Ending

We've all heard the Hollywood phrase, "the ending isn't testing well." The reason an ending isn't working might be in the editing rather than the writing. If the ending is too slow, the audience will be impatient. Once they know what happens and have the answer to the question posed in the first act, the filmmakers shouldn't keep them in the theater very long. Or, the ending may be edited too abruptly and may not give the audience a chance to have the emotional catharsis that the story promises. Again, the editor has to understand dramatic structure to give the audience what it is expecting at the end of the film.

> **CAUTION**
>
> **Counterpoint** _____
>
> Film, like other art forms, must have unity and structure. Each shot must set up an expectation, which must be fulfilled in the next shot and the next. In the same way, each scene must set up an expectation for the next scene and each sequence for the next. The opening act must set up the middle and the middle must lead to the end. In focusing on the shot, the editor must not lose sight of the larger segments of the film.

Getting Feedback from Test Screenings

While fine-tuning a cut, the editor and director, whether editing on a non-linear computer-based system or on a traditional film- or video-editing system, will be sitting for hours intensely focused on a small screen and deeply involved in both large story problems and tiny details of a shot. That environment is not really conducive to judging whether a movie is working. The filmmakers are literally and figuratively "too close to it."

For film projects that will ultimately be shown in theaters, it is essential that the editor and director screen the movie on a large screen during the editing process. The transition from a small screen to a large one can change the pace of a movie—parts of it may seem to speed up and other parts may seem to slow down. For example, a wide shot that might have seemed boring on the small monitor and was therefore shortened may reveal fascinating details on the large screen, so you may want to lengthen the shot.

If for budgetary reasons it's impossible to view the project on film prior to the negative cut (see Chapter 19, "Finishing the Film or Video"), then you should at least make a videotape of the cut that you can take out of the editing room and view in a different setting, perhaps on a large-screen television.

Another way to get more objectivity on the film is by watching it with an audience—even if that is only one other person who is not part of the editing team. When unbiased audience members view the film with you, you will have a chance to see the film through the eyes of the people in that audience.

Although studio films are almost always tested on audiences composed of the studio's "target audience" for the film, filmmakers have varying opinions about the value of test screenings with large audiences. Some love to get the feedback and others resent the idea of leaving creative decisions to what amounts to a vote. Also, there is the problem of conflicting feedback coming from audiences that disagree with each other. One audience may laugh at what is supposed to be a funny moment and another may be silent. Do you tamper with the scene that the first audience liked or keep it?

Another drawback to test screenings is the fact that it is often hard for audiences of people who are not filmmakers to compensate in their minds for the fact that they are seeing a picture that is not yet polished—that doesn't have titles, opticals, and a fully mixed soundtrack. The absence of those items may influence the audience's reactions.

Despite their limitations, however, test screenings with large audiences can bring valuable insight as to whether all or part of your movie is playing well. The audience comments may tell you something isn't right with the movie, but the audience won't know why the scene or sequence doesn't work. It will be up to you to go back into the editing room to see if you can discover why the audience reacted the way it did.

Some films that are edited on digital non-linear editing systems may be test screened on video rather than on film. The advantage of doing that is that you can eliminate the cost of cutting a workprint if editing on video, and also because digital editing systems will allow you to output a tape that has opticals and a temporary mixed soundtrack (see Chapter 19), making the tape seem more like a finished film to the audience.

Script Notes

Documentaries generally run either feature-length or shorter. You may want to cut more than one version of a documentary if it is to be distributed in different venues. In the film I did on sexual harassment on the job, for example, we cut one version that was one-hour broadcast length for television and another version that was approximately 30 minutes that was used in corporate training programs on sexual harassment.

Finding the Right Length

Some film projects, particularly those that are produced to be aired on television, will have to be cut to a very precise length. Feature films, on the other hand, can vary in length from 90 minutes or less to over 3 hours. Theater owners generally are nervous about films over two hours because it means that they can have fewer shows per day and thus bring in less money in a day. Therefore, usually only big studio-produced potential blockbusters run three hours or longer. Recent examples include *Pearl Harbor* (Michael Bay, 2001) at 183 minutes and *The Lord of the Rings: The Fellowship of the Ring* (Peter Jackson, 2001), running 178 minutes.

Ideally, you will want to find a length that makes your movie as tight as it can be. Your goal should be a well-edited, taut film that keeps the audience interested and involved, but still allows the themes and dramatic moments in the film to emerge clearly. You have to be willing to be hard on yourself and not hold on to a sequence that slows the movie down just because you love it or because it was such a hard scene to get right in production. Also, only keep scenes that work in the context of the entire film. If two sequences repeat the same idea or emotion, drop one of them.

The Least You Need to Know

- A fine cut involves several passes through the film, making cuts and viewing the film until it is what you want.
- The pace of the film is affected by both the duration of the shots used and the rhythm of the shots as they are strung together.
- Certain optical effects that were used frequently in the past, such as wipes and irises, are only rarely used today.
- Test screenings have drawbacks but can give filmmakers valuable insight into whether a film is working.

Chapter 19

Finishing the Film or Video

In This Chapter

◆ Editing your film's sound

◆ Creating music for your film

◆ Adding opticals and titles to your film

◆ Finishing on film and on video

At the point that the picture editing is finished—either because everyone involved is satisfied that they've created the best possible cut or because the producers or the studio won't spend more money on the picture edit—the fine-tuning of the picture stops and the next stage of finishing the film begins.

During this phase of post-production, a lot will happen. The sound, including music and sound effects, will be designed, cut, and mixed. The opticals and titles will be made. If you are finishing on film, the negative will be cut and release prints will be struck after an answer print has been color-corrected. If you are finishing on video, you will do an on-line edit to add the effects and titles and clean up the original tape. In this chapter, I'll cover what needs to be done in each of these important areas.

Planning the Sound Edit

Some filmmakers treat sound editing as simply something that has to be "cleaned up" as you finish the film. In fact, however, the sound of a film is tremendously important to the mood and emotion of a film. A movie that is poorly shot but has a clear and easily understood soundtrack will seem better to audiences than a film that has nicely lit, well-composed images but a muddy or hard-to-understand track.

In the sound edit, your film's sound will be refined, balanced, and enhanced. If you are doing a low-budget or independent film, the same editor who did the picture edit may do the sound edit. On large studio features, however, sound editing is done by specialized sound editors and usually a sound designer to plan the overall sound and create unique textures or effects with sound.

The sound edit begins like every successive edit in a fine cut with a screening of the last (in this case the final) picture edit of the film. Every scene should be examined for sound problems, for where effects might be needed, or for where sound might enhance the feeling of a scene. This process of deciding where to place sound effects (and music, which I'll discuss later in this chapter) is called *spotting*.

The next step is for the sound editor (or editor if there is no separate sound editor) to divide the sound into several different tracks, a process called splitting tracks. You will have a minimum of three tracks—one for dialogue, one for sound effects, and one for music. On documentaries or films where there is narration, you will also have a separate track for the narration. Tracks are often split many more times and on a complex large-budget feature there may be a hundred or more tracks. On larger pictures, there may be a dialogue editor who is responsible for the dialogue tracks, a sound-effects editor responsible for the sound-effects tracks, and a music editor who is responsible for the music tracks. In video, building up the layers of sound on these tracks and mixing them is called *sweetening* the tracks.

Aesthetically, the important thing to remember about sound is that the emotion you are seeking in the film should guide you as to what sound is most appropriate in a scene. Also, only one type of sound—either dialogue, effects, or music—should dominate at any one time. Of course there are exceptions, just as there are with the rules for editing picture. The famous French director Jean-Luc Godard, known for his use of the jump cut, also experimented with sound, allowing various sounds to compete with each other in some scenes.

Verbal Action _____

spotting   The process of going through the final picture edit of a film and deciding where to place sound effects and music.

sweetening   In videotape and digital editing, the process of building up tracks and mixing sound, and all audio post-production sound work.

room tone   The ambient sound on a location site, which is generally recorded during production and is used to replace any silences on dialogue or effects tracks.

The Dialogue Edit

The goal of the dialogue edit is to construct tracks so that they are as "clean" as possible—without distracting noises. The *room tone* that was recorded during production on each location will be used in the dialogue edit to replace any silence in the edited dialogue sequences, or unwanted sound—such as rustling paper—between sections of dialogue. Even a very quiet location has an ambient sound or tone and it should be inserted anywhere there is silence on the dialogue track.

It's often difficult to find room tone that exactly matches the dialogue. Sometimes, when the recorded room tone doesn't match well, the dialogue editor might find room tone in pauses between words on the takes of the same scene that weren't used.

Next, sound effects that were recorded during production should be cut out of the dialogue track and put on another track for the sound-effects edit.

Once the full dialogue track has been cleaned and constructed, the editor will then usually split each character's voice into separate tracks. The reason for doing this is that later in the sound mix, the mixer will be able to adjust the levels for one character without affecting the level of another.

Looping

As I first mentioned in Chapter 9, "Collaborators: Hiring the Cast and Crew," looping—or as it is also called, ADR, for automatic dialogue recording—is the process of re-recording dialogue during post-production when the original dialogue recorded during production is unacceptable for some reason. Sometimes there may be too much background noise on the track, and other times it may be that the director wants another reading of the actor's line to change the performance or delivery in some way.

Some directors rely more heavily on looping than others. Recording dialogue in post-production allows a filmmaker the freedom to concentrate on the visuals during production—particularly in scenes where there is a lot of action and it is difficult to get good sound or on locations where there is a lot of background noise.

There are, however, drawbacks to using ADR. They include the fact that re-recorded sound tends to lack the same realistic feeling or authenticity of production sound, that ADR is expensive, and that it is often difficult for an actor to match his or her performance during production or to make the performance as good as when working on the set.

The Sound-Effects Edit

Sound effects include the sound of everything that you see in a shot—such as footsteps, rain, cars, crumpling paper—as well as sounds that are heard from off-screen such as a doorbell, a phone ringing, or a distant gunshot. Good sound-effects editing in films goes beyond the obvious. Sound effects can create moods and reactions, including suspense, joy, loneliness, or terror. The same picture of a man walking down a country road may have a very different meaning depending on the sound effects. If there is a howling wind sound, the mood might seem ominous. If there are birds chirping, however, the mood will seem happy.

The sound-effects editor (or the editor on smaller shoots) will not only clean and split the sound-effects tracks, he or she will also embellish those effects and create new sound effects.

Sound effects are available from a number of sources. You can buy sound effects on discs, and most mixing facilities have a sound-effects library with a range of sound effects such as crowd scene sounds, different species of birds, dog barks, footsteps on different surfaces, and, of course, the Hollywood staple—gun shots and screams.

Sound effects can also be created on a *foley* stage, which is a special sound-proofed studio with a variety of walking surfaces and props where skilled foley artists can create sound effects that work in perfect sync with the picture. The art of foley was invented by a film director, Jack Foley, who started out in silent films and worked through the transition into the sound era. Many of the tricks for creating sound effects that he invented are still used today.

Cutaway

Foley recordings are an efficient way to create a number of sound effects on a single track without editing. A foley-created track will be in sync with the picture, which will save time in editing and in the sound mix. The disadvantage of doing foley recording for sound effects is that renting a foley stage and paying foley artists is expensive. Small, easily controlled sounds such as walking, breathing, writing, hitting, brushing teeth, or turning pages lend themselves to foley recordings. Outdoor sound effects such as traffic noise, thunder, wind, and airplanes are generally acquired either through production recording or sound-effects libraries.

Adding Music

Music is a powerful and important part of any film. It can enhance a scene, but if used wrong it can be terribly distracting and ruin a scene. Sometimes the music in a movie may be composed of catchy, well-known songs and other times a movie score may be quite subtle, barely noticeable. Whatever type of music is used, it will make some impact on the scene and will affect the audience's reaction to the scene. If you want to see how important music is to a film, try watching a horror film with the sound off and play sweet, calming music over it. Suddenly, a scary scene will seem silly.

It's important to think about the music in the film as early as possible. Many directors and producers begin imagining the type of music for the film while working with the writer on the script. Others play music they hope to use or music similar to what they hope to use in a scene while on the set, between or during takes, to help communicate a mood to the actors or influence their movement. Sometimes directors listen to music during dailies to help them get a sense of the rhythm of the scene.

Generally speaking, the sooner music is thought about before and during the editing process, the better the final music and film will be. If a composer is brought in at the last minute, after the picture editing has been completed, and she only has enough time to take one pass at writing the score, the music may be completely wrong for the movie—and it's probably too late to change it. To prevent this, some directors used pre-recorded music as "temp" or temporary music score during the picture edit. Trying out temp music in various scenes allows the filmmaker to generate a dialogue with the composer about what she is looking for. The composer may have a completely different take on the score, but at least there is a point of reference to begin a conversation about the type of score desired.

In addition to a composer, who will actually write the music score for your film, many films also have a music supervisor. The music supervisor will find the right composer for you and also find existing music for your film, which you may be able to license (see Chapter 20, "Completing Other Post-Production Tasks"). A music supervisor's ideas, either for specific music or for a particular composer or genre to help provide stylistic or structural clues to a scene or to the entire film, can be very important to a film's success.

Smaller-budget films may only have one or the other, but most larger-budget studio films have both a music supervisor and a composer. Both of these members of your creative team should be chosen using the same criteria you used to hire others. Do their styles complement the project? Do you communicate well with them? Can your budget accommodate both their rates?

In addition, studio films will also have a music editor. On smaller-budget films, the picture editor or sound editor will also edit the music track.

Although the amount of music will vary greatly from film to film, most feature-length films will have thirty to forty minutes of music. The various types of music used in a film include:

- **Underscoring:** The basic background music in a film, which may be the dominant sound in some scenes and subordinate sound in others.
- **Visual vocal (or visual music):** The music of an on-camera singer, band, or orchestra.
- **Background vocal (or background music):** The music of an off-camera singer, band, or orchestra.
- **Source music:** Music coming from a specific source in the picture such as a radio, television, or jukebox.

The composer and/or music supervisor should screen the final picture cut of the film uninterrupted to get a sense of the overall pace, themes, and feel of the picture. Then the composer and/or music supervisor (and music editor if there is one) should have a music *spotting* session with the director and the producer. At this session, the group will decide on specific spots in the film in which music will be used. It may take more than one spotting session to complete this task. Once it's completed, the exact music cues will be timed to the second and the composer can then write the music for each cue.

 Verbal Action

foley   The creation of sound effects that are synced to the picture on a sound stage by a foley artist.

optical printer   A camera that re-photographs images to make optical effects.

legal effects   The lengths for fades and dissolves which can be executed by most printers (16, 24, 32, 48, 64, and 96 frames).

optical sound master   The mixed soundtrack of a film that is printed on a piece of film and used for striking release prints of films.

Mixing the Sound

Now that you have created all the parts of your film's sound on multiple tracks—the dialogue, sound effects, and music—it's time to blend all those tracks into one track in the sound mix. Everything you have been doing so far has been geared toward your mix. The better you have prepared for the mix, the better your movie will sound.

Depending on the size of your project and whether you are editing film or video, sound mixing will be done on different types of equipment. In all mixes, however, the basic principle is the same. One machine will play back the audio tracks in sync with each other and with the picture. A console will make it possible for the sound mixer to adjust the levels of each of those tracks and record them onto a single track. On large-budget features with a hundred or more tracks, there may be more than one sound mixer doing the mixing. In addition to the sound mixer(s), the director and editor or sound editor if there is one should be present at the mix.

Throughout the sound mix, the mixer is making a constant series of decisions about the relative volume of sounds, their equalization, and the pacing of sound fades and dissolves. A good mixer will be able to make many of those decisions alone, but for more subjective decisions the editor and director should give the mixer guidance.

The mixing session is exciting because you will finally be able to see and hear your film with all the parts coming together. Mixing sessions, however, are also time-consuming and expensive. Ten minutes of screen time may take from thirty minutes to two hours to mix.

Adding Opticals, Titles, and Photographic Effects

In finishing your film on film, you will usually have several opticals made by a laboratory or optical house, such as dissolves or a fade-out or any of the other types of opticals that we discussed in the last chapter. Opticals are made on film by an *optical printer*, which is a specialized camera that is designed to re-photograph images on film in such a way as to incorporate the desired effect.

Making optical effects is a complicated and delicate process. There are many opportunities for error and for damaging your negative. Therefore, it is critical that you make sure you use an optical-effects house that has a good reputation, high-quality equipment, and experienced staff.

When editing on video but finishing your film on film, you may be tempted to add dazzling video effects. Many non-linear editing systems allow you to do titles generation, dissolves, wipes, 3D, and other custom effects as you edit. Remember, however, that most video effects are not cheap in film. So, if you are finishing on film, watch out or your costs will skyrocket.

Also, if you want to do an effect such as a dissolve or fade to black, which can be done on film through an optical effect, remember to consult your lab or optical house to determine if the effects have to be of a particular length, called their *legal effects*. For example, the printer used to create your final print may be limited to dissolves of only 24 or 48 frames.

Script Notes _____

It's important to choose a good sound mixer and mixing facility. Both should be experienced in doing the kind of film you are doing, whether it's a feature, documentary, or other project. Check the reputation of the facility and make sure the equipment is well-maintained and able to accommodate your mix. Meet with the mixer to determine his or her attitude. And be sure to bring coffee and treats for the mixing session to put everyone in a good mood.

Optical Track

Besides the opticals for the picture, your final sound will also be transferred to an optical track by a laboratory. The optical track or *optical sound master* is made from either the ¼-inch tape, DAT tape (digital audiotape), or mag stock from your sound mix. The optical sound master is a separate piece of film that has no picture image on it but has a photographic image of your sound along its edge. This track will eventually be contact-printed with each release print of your film. Generally, the same lab that will be doing your release prints should do the optical sound master.

Titles

At this point it's finally time to add your titles, including the name of the movie and the opening and/or end credits for your cast and crew. (For more on credits see Chapter 20.) Will your film open with simple, white titles on black (like most Woody Allen films), with titles over picture, or with a separate title sequence? If it's titles over picture, make sure you choose shots where the titles won't obscure important faces or objects or distract the audience from some piece of essential dialogue. Titles can be very expensive when they are superimposed over action and they can be ineffective unless there is a high contrast between the title and the shot's background on which the title will appear. If you plan to use a separate title sequence involving graphic effects, you need to determine as soon as possible if your software can handle it, if you are editing on a computer system, or if you need to go to an outside title designer.

In many films, the original idea for the titles may change during post-production. For example, let's say you had originally intended to have the titles play over the first scene, but when the scene is cut it plays so well that you don't want to clutter it up with titles. So you try titles in black after the first scene, but that slows down the pace too much. Then you try titles in black at the head of the movie, but that seems too plain. Graphics would help, though, so you consider bringing in a title designer. Is there money in the budget? No? So you go back to titles over the first scene or keep looking for another solution.

Once you have decided how you want your titles to look, a special titles house—or sometimes the same optical house that you used for your other opticals—can make your titles for you. Titles can also be generated on video and then transferred to film. If titles are made on film, the first step will be to have title cards made that will then be filmed.

Whatever process you use, to save yourself money and headaches later, be sure to double-check the titles carefully at an early stage to make sure there are no errors.

Photographic Effects

Special photographic effects are different from opticals. Instead of being created by filming two already-filmed images as with an optical, effects are created by making original film images of such items as landscapes, miniatures (models of buildings, boats, spaceships, and so on), matte paintings (often used to simulate a background in a live-action scene), and animation. A photographic effects or special-effects house may specialize in a certain kind of effect, such as front-screen projection, rear-screen projection, or matte paintings.

If you are using special photographic effects in your film, you should have been planning them in pre-production and usually in consultation with a special-effects artist who will help the director plan shots with the effects in mind.

Special effects are used frequently in studio films but less so in lower-budget independent films because of their expense and because it is a very technical field that requires the use of a special effects consultant and a company that specializes in creating effects. A whole book could be written on special effects, and they are more complicated than we can get into here.

Verbal Action

original camera negative (OCN)   The negative film that originally passed through the camera.

timing   The process of adjusting the color balance for the printing of each scene once the negative has been conformed (also called grading).

conform   To cut the original camera negative (OCN) to match the final cut of a film.

answer print   The first color-timed print from the cut negative of a film.

Finishing on Film

Whether you have edited on film or on a computer-based non-linear editing system, at this point you will be finishing everything on film if you plan to release or distribute your film in theaters. The process of finishing the film will be different for films that will only be shown on television or on videotape.

Negative Cutting

After the picture edit is final, the next step in finishing the film will be for your negative cutter to exactly *conform* or match the negative to your workprint or, if you didn't make a workprint, to the negative cut list supplied by the editor from the digital editing system. This cut list is usually accompanied by a videotape that contains both picture and sound and can be used as a guide by the negative cutter.

Something to watch for in editing film on computer systems is that the computer allows you to cut a shot into your project many different times, but on film you can use each piece of negative only once. Therefore, you must keep track of when you are "duping" your film frames on the computer. Using the same footage more than once will become an expensive disaster when the negative cutter tries to conform your video back to film.

As with every member of your team, it's important that your negative cutter has experience and a good reputation. He or she will be working with the most precious part of your film—the *original camera negative*. If any part of it is damaged or destroyed in any way, it can be disastrous to your final film.

Counterpoint _____

Labs and negative cutters have to be extremely meticulous and careful when handling the original camera negative. If problems occur, it will affect the subsequent reputation of the editor or lab and, of course, will affect the quality of the film that is partially destroyed. When a negative is damaged, the solution is sometimes to use alternate takes of the portion of the film that is damaged. That is why it is always important to have more than one take of a shot.

Answer Print and Color Correction

After the negative is cut, the film reels are sent to the lab where a lab employee called a color timer will, with the help of the director of photography, director, and editor, correct the color balance on each shot. Correcting the color balance ensures that each scene has the appropriate color and all shots are matched to other shots in the same scene. This color-correcting process is called *timing* the film.

After all the color adjustments are made, the lab strikes a color-balanced print from the cut negative. This print is called the *answer print* or sometimes the first trial print. The filmmakers will check the answer print and continue to request changes in the color balance until a satisfactory timed print is struck. Only the reels of a film that aren't correct will be reprinted. On most feature films, the timing is usually correct by the fourth or fifth answer print. It's best when there are fewer prints since the negative degrades each time it is used.

When the answer print is approved, a timed inter-positive is made of the film and from this an inter-negative is made, which is sometimes called the *dupe negative*. It's from this last negative that most of the release prints are made. A very few prints, sometimes called EK prints, will be struck from the original timed cut negative because they will be at least one generation closer to the original and thus will have less contrast and be in sharper focus. These prints are often used at premiere screenings in major cities.

Finishing on Video

If you have shot your film on film or video and will only be needing a videotape output of your final film, such as for television broadcast or for direct-to-video films, then you will most likely be finishing your film on video. To do that, you will create an edit decision list (EDL) and use it in an *on-line editing session* to finish your project.

An on-line session is essentially the video version of negative cutting, only more automated. During an on-line session, you will re-create every edit using the original tapes shot in production (or original telecine tapes if shot on film). The final product of the on-line session is the *edited master*. The on-line session, which can take as long as 10 hours for a 2-hour movie, will also re-create dissolves and other opticals. Unless they are being done elsewhere and dropped in later, titles can be created during the on-line edit with the on-line facility's titling machine.

Verbal Action

dupe negative   (a.k.a. inter-negative) A negative printed from a positive print (an inter-positive) from which release prints are printed.

inter-positive print (IP)   A fine-grain print made from the conformed original negative which is used to produce subsequent dupe negatives.

on-line editing   The process of editing the original videotapes into the final broadcast-quality viewing tape, including adding opticals.

edited master   The final edited videotape created at the on-line editing session.

When the on-line session is finished, dubs are made of the edited master for use by the sound editor and composer. The edited master itself will then be color-corrected. In much the same way as a color timer goes through the answer print of a film to adjust the color, the edited master will be color-corrected to create a final color-corrected master. If the process is done using digital equipment, there will be almost no generational loss.

When the sound mix is finished, the final soundtrack will then be laid on top of the temporary audio tracks and the project will be finished, giving you a master to either broadcast or from which to make tapes to rent or sell.

The Least You Need to Know

- ◆ Prepare for the sound mix by dividing the sound into at least three tracks—dialogue, sound effects, and music, and cleaning and building up those tracks.
- ◆ Music can greatly enhance or ruin a film, so it is best to start thinking about music early in the filmmaking process.
- ◆ The sound mix will balance and equalize the sound and blend all the soundtracks into one.
- ◆ If you are finishing on film, a negative cutter will cut the negative to match the workprint or will cut according to a negative cut list from the digital non-linear editing system.
- ◆ If you are finishing your film on video, you will create an edited master at an on-line editing session where you will also be able to add opticals and titles.

Chapter 20

Completing Other Post-Production Tasks

In This Chapter

◆ Setting up a post-production schedule

◆ Clearing copyrighted material, including music

◆ Using public domain or material covered by fair use

◆ Guidelines for making your credit list

Film editing and post-production can be a confusing, often maddening, ordeal. Too often, the process ends not when the filmmakers are completely satisfied with what they've created, but when time or money (or both) run out. And post-production has grown even more complex as special effects have become more widely used and new and developing technology offers more choices of how to finish your film.

Still, what will make the post-production period go smoothly is a good schedule that everyone feels is practical, a basic understanding of all elements of the process, and a focus on creating the standard delivery requirements—what must be turned over to your distributor (if you have one) when the film is completed. Fortunately, filmmakers can learn from the experience of many similar films to make the most of post-production.

Making a Post-Production Schedule

Post-production schedules can vary a great deal depending on the budget, the kind of film you are doing, and the way in which you are editing and finishing your film or video project. Half-hour television shows are usually completed in 2 weeks. One-hour shows usually require 4 to 6 weeks of post-production. Two-hour movies for television may take 12 weeks, and theatrical features may spend anywhere from 12 weeks to 8 or more months in post-production.

Script Notes

Post-production actually begins during pre-production with the preparations of a post-production budget and schedule, the lining up of crew and facilities for post, and the planning of arrangements that must be made for any special processes such as visual effects and opticals. Although changes and delays are not uncommon, the more thorough the planning, the better the chance that the film will remain on schedule and on budget.

Many productions hire a post-production supervisor to create a schedule and supervise all the activities that must go on in post. An experienced post-production supervisor will have worked on films with budgets similar to yours. He or she will be able to create a practical, efficient schedule and keep everyone moving and on schedule.

Generally, the editor will begin assembling the film during principal photography as soon as one scene or sequence has been completed. Let's imagine that *Something Is Rotten*, our perfume caper, was made as a medium-budget film. Twenty weeks might be a reasonable schedule for post-production on that film if we edit it on film, and perhaps three or four weeks less if we edit it digitally. Although you must estimate the time for your own production's particular needs, the hypothetical schedule for *Something Is Rotten* that follows can be used as a guide.

Weeks 1–2

The editor will receive the last batch of dailies from the shoot during this week, along with the script supervisor's final notes. He will continue the assembly of the rough cut of the film, either editing traditionally on film or on a digital non-linear editing system. While the editor is working, the exhausted director is taking the week off to recover from production.

Meanwhile, the producer should begin assembling the list of tentative screen credits for *Something Is Rotten* during this week. It's important to start early on preparing the credits. There were several writers on the script, and one of the writers may protest the writing credit. If so, it will have to be resolved by a Writers Guild arbitration (see the section "Writers" later in this chapter).

In addition, the producer needs to make sure all the clearances and releases have been secured for any copyrighted material, including music and any film clips that have been used. In *Something Is Rotten*, we have planned to use clips from some perfume commercials and also have used some popular dance music at a scene shot in a bar. The producer began the process of getting clearances in pre-production, but she must check with the attorneys to make sure that all the licenses are secured now (see later section "Getting Clearances: Legal and Copyright Issues" in this chapter). Without the proper clearances, the distributor will not distribute the film.

By the end of week 2, since the editor has been working all through production, he should have completed the first rough cut of *Something Is Rotten*. The director, who worked 20-hour days, seven days a week for the entire shoot, will return from her trip to Kauai and get back to work.

Weeks 3–6

The DGA contract gives a director of a feature film budgeted over $1.5 million a minimum of ten weeks or one day of editing for each two days of shooting, whichever is greater, to complete his or her cut of the film following the editor's first rough assembly. (On large studio films, experienced directors may negotiate for more than one cut, each one followed by a test screening. If that is the case, the schedule may go much longer than the one outlined here.) On television movies, the director has a minimum of twenty days to complete his or her cut on a two-hour television movie. If the TV movie runs more than two hours, the director has five hours for each hour in excess of two hours.

On lower-budget films, most directors are sensitive to the budgetary and delivery date requirements of the production and will generally waive the full time allowed to complete their cut if necessary. Let's say that is the case with the director on *Something Is Rotten*. During this period, the director and editor will re-edit and screen the film several times, cutting each successive version of *Something Is Rotten* tighter than the last.

The producer or the post-production supervisor, meanwhile, will be checking the availability of sound mix stages, as well as foley and ADR stages, throughout this editing period, aiming to hit a target date on which the sound mix will begin.

If we had decided to edit the film digitally, the director's cut would be going much faster. Unfortunately, the digital equipment was just too expensive for our budget.

Weeks 7–8

At this point, the director's cut is finished and is screened for the producer of *Something Is Rotten*. During week 7, the producer will add her changes to the picture, if she has any. Also during this week, the director and producer will spot the picture with the sound effects editor for sound effects and with the composer for the music cues.

We are kicking ourselves—all of this would have been completed by week 4 if we had been editing digitally!

If any cutaways or retakes are necessary, they must be shot by week 8. Fortunately for us, the director got good coverage and we don't need anything else. Also, any photographic effects should be completed and cut into the picture during this week. We didn't have any so we are off the hook on this one, too.

By the end of week 8, the producer should be finished with any changes he or she requires in the cut, and the picture edit should be locked.

The final picture cut of *Something Is Rotten* will then be transferred to video with time code. Copies of the VHS will be given to the sound editors (dialogue, sound effects, and music, when there are all three) and to the composer.

Cutaway

The popularity of editing sound effects and music digitally is also on the rise. Most films are being done with a combination of both traditional and digital sound. More than 50 percent of the work done at sound effects houses is now done digitally. Sound editing equipment and software that is compatible with digital editing systems is often used. Files from a digitally edited show are loaded onto the sound editing system's computer with the help of an edit decision list. The cost of using digital equipment is more expensive than conventional equipment, but the quality it produces is better. Digital equipment also allows filmmakers to listen to several tracks simultaneously while in the process of building their sound effects tracks. A well-informed post-production supervisor should be able to make the best choices for each picture.

Week 9

By this week, the negative cutter can begin cutting the negative. (This step won't be necessary if the film is only for television or video release, but *Something Is Rotten* has a theatrical distributor so the negative will be cut.)

The main titles and screen credits should also be finalized this week. At the same time, any opticals that will be done at an optical house should be ordered. We only have a few dissolves and a fade out for the end. We haven't got a television sale yet, but we are being optimistic that we will so the editor is beginning to trim the picture for the television version during this week.

If only we were editing digitally—most of the above work would have begun by week six!

Weeks 10–13

During these weeks, work will be progressing on both the sound tracks and the picture. For sound, we will begin looping, or ADR, of actors in a few scenes where the dialogue wasn't clear. We have had to work around the schedule of one of the actors who is shooting another movie. Any foley recording will take place—we have a few sequences where foley will work well so it will be worth the expense—and the dialogue and sound effects tracks will be edited.

Meanwhile, our composer is working away on a great score for *Something Is Rotten*.

On the picture side, the opticals and titles are scheduled to be finalized and cut into the picture during this period. Also, the negative cut will be completed sometime during this period and the answer print and color correction process can begin soon afterward.

Weeks 14–16

It may take up to five weeks to mix *Something Is Rotten*. Since there are many sound tracks on the film, we are going to *pre-dub* during this period, which means we will mix several tracks together prior to the final mix. For us, as with most films, the dialogue tracks are the first to be pre-dubbed. Since we have a large number of sound-effects tracks, we are also going to pre-mix some of those tracks during this period.

Weeks 17–20

This is it—we are in the home stretch! During these final weeks of post-production, we will be doing our final sound mix and the final color-correction of the picture. (If we were making a television movie, we'd be on-lining and making a video master, but we're not.)

The distributor decided we didn't need any test screenings for *Something Is Rotten*, which is good because that would have added at least a week to our schedule for each test screening. We would have had to pre-dub before each screening and then go back into the editing room to re-edit the picture to incorporate any changes after the screening. Fortunately, the executives at the distribution company like the film so much that we do not have to go through that process.

We're done and ready to make release prints. *Something Is Rotten* will soon be coming to a theater near you.

Getting Clearances: Legal and Copyright Issues

If you have planned to use any copyrighted material in your film—such as songs, film clips, or quotes from books—you need to obtain permission to do so—which is called getting a *clearance*. In order to get a clearance, you will have to get a signed permission or *license* from the owner of the copyright and pay a fee.

Verbal Action

pre-dub   Mixing several sound tracks together prior to the final mix.

clearance   In film, obtaining the rights to use copyrighted material.

license   The proof of legal permission to use copyrighted material in a film or video, usually in the form of a contract.

public domain   Material that was never copyrighted or for which the copyright has lapsed.

fair use   A provision of the copyright law that authorizes use of a limited amount of copyrighted material.

Ideally, the process of getting clearances and licenses for material you want to use in your film will have begun in pre-production and will have been taking place throughout production. In post-production, it's time to make sure everything is properly licensed or else you will have to cut it out of the film.

Getting clearances for everything you want to use in the film can be time-consuming and expensive. There will no doubt be legal fees involved as well as the costs of tracking down the rights holders. If you are doing a studio film, the studio will be very careful to obtain all necessary—and even some unnecessary—clearances to protect itself from lawsuits.

It's unlikely that anyone will file a lawsuit against you if you put a copyrighted song over your home video that will only be shown to friends, but as soon as a movie is shown publicly, you will risk a lawsuit if you haven't obtained clearances for all the copyrighted material in the film. Distributors, including television broadcasters and even film festivals, will not accept your movie if the required clearances haven't been obtained.

To protect yourself, consult an entertainment attorney before you lock your picture and do your mix to make sure you have gotten all the necessary clearances and releases.

Using Public Domain and Fair Use Material

You won't need to obtain clearances on material in the *public domain*, which is work that either was never copyrighted or work in which the copyright has lapsed. In the United States, works that were created more than seventy-five years ago are likely to be in the public domain, but not necessarily. You should always have a copyright search done either by your attorney, a copyright service (most are located in Washington, D.C.), or through the Library of Congress before you assume something is in the public domain.

Copyright law provides for a very limited amount of copyrighted material to be used through the *fair use* doctrine. If you are doing a non-profit educational film, the chances that a short excerpt from a copyrighted work might be considered fair use is much greater than if you use the same material in a commercial feature or TV movie. Again, it's best to consult an experienced entertainment attorney before assuming you can use copyrighted material under the fair use provision.

Clearing Music

Clearing music for your film can be a difficult and frustrating task. If you want to use a song by a popular artist, for example, you will have to get permission to use the musical composition, as well as permission to use the particular recording of the song. If the recording is by a well-known singer, the license fee for the recording may be prohibitively expensive. Many times, filmmakers only get permission to use the song itself and then hire another singer to perform it.

Getting music cleared is usually such a hassle that many producers use music clearing services to do it. These companies are able to accomplish the process faster and more easily because they do it all the time and have contacts at record companies and with music publishers.

If you are going to get the music cleared yourself, you should start by contacting the publisher of the music. Usually, the publisher is a member of ASCAP (American Society of Composers, Authors and Publishers) or BMI (Broadcast Music, Inc.), and you can call their offices in New York or Los Angeles to find out how to contact the publisher of the music you want.

To include a musical composition in your film, you will need what is called *synchronization* or *sync rights*. This term came into being because the music is synchronized to the picture. To perform music in public, you also need *public performance rights*. In the United States, public performance rights for theatrical films are generally included in the deal you make for sync rights. For movies that are broadcast on television, the broadcaster usually obtains the public performance rights also. If you want to put out a soundtrack album from the movie on CD, tape, or another format, you will need *mechanical rights*. If you plan to make significant changes to a song such as altering the lyrics, you may need to negotiate *adaptation rights*. Many composers and publishers, however, will not allow any changes to be made to their songs.

Counterpoint

Acquiring rights is a negotiation, so don't simply accept the price you are quoted. If you're working on a worthy project, a record company or publisher may make a special exception for you. One advantage of using a music clearing service is that they know with whom to negotiate and the going rates for licenses. You may not be able to bargain for a better deal on your own.

That's just getting the song. Next, in order to use even just a few bars of a pre-existing recording of the song, contact the owner of the recording, which is usually the record company. From them, you will need a master use license to use the actual recording in your movie. You should also ask the record company if any re-use fees are due the performers on the record.

To get both of these clearances, you will generally need to submit a written request that outlines the nature of your movie, how you plan to distribute it, and the way the music will be used in the film. You will usually have to pay more for a song if it is used under the movie's titles or featured in some way than if the song is only background music in a scene.

How the movie will be distributed will include in which territories and for how long you will be licensing the music. Big-budget feature films generally clear music rights for all media (theatrical, broadcast and free cable TV, pay cable TV, home video, and all formats not yet invented) in all territories (domestic and foreign) in perpetuity (forever). If you can't afford such all-inclusive rights, then just try to get the rights you really need for your film. For example, students often make deals to acquire just film festival rights. Or you might just get non-theatrical rights if you are making an educational video.

Even if the music licensing process goes well, it can take months. To avoid all the rights issues mentioned above, you can use pre-recorded music from a production music library. This music is packaged specifically for re-use. You pay an affordable fee, usually for each "needle-drop"—each continuous section of a recording used once.

If you have an original score written for your movie, you will avoid most of these hassles. Usually, the producer will own the rights to the music written for a film because it is considered a "work made for hire." Sometimes the composer will lower his fee in exchange for retaining the music rights, in which case the producer must obtain from the composer a license to use the music.

Clearing Film Clips

If you want to use a scene from an existing movie in your film (whether it is a full-screen excerpt or something visible on a TV in one of your scenes), you need to get written permission. Clearing film clips is much like clearing music. You should start by identifying who owns the copyright to the movie you want to use. Sometimes this is the production company, and other times it is the distributor or television network. For older films, it can get confusing because the film may have been bought and sold several times since it was made. Some companies have a clip licensing department and are eager to license their material, and others may refuse your request.

Even after you track down, negotiate a fee, and license the right to use a film clip, you may still have to get permission to use various elements in the clip. For example, if there is music in the clip, you generally need to obtain a separate license for it.

Verbal Action _____

synchronization rights   (a.k.a. sync rights) The right to include a musical composition in a film.

public performance rights   The right to have a musical composition performed in public.

mechanical rights   The right to include a musical composition in a film's soundtrack album or CD.

adaptation   The right to change or "adapt" a musical composition.

billboard   To visually or verbally name the title of a film from which a clip originated when it is shown in a film.

If there are actors in the film clip, the Screen Actors Guild (SAG) and the American Federation of Television and Radio Artists (AFTRA) have regulations governing the "re-use" of actors' performances in union productions. The SAG contract governing films made before 1960 may allow you to use some clips for certain uses without paying actors or getting permissions if you *billboard* the clip by putting the name of the film on screen or having it said verbally each time the clip is shown. You can avoid billboarding by clearing and paying the talent or their estates. Contact SAG for details. The WGA and DGA also have regulations governing the re-use of material created by their members and should be contacted as well.

You also may be using stock footage in your film, obtained from a stock footage library or archive. Usually, the fee is determined by the length of the clip and how you plan to distribute your movie. Generally, you pay a small fee to get a selection of possible clips, and after you edit your show, you pay a higher rate based on the exact number of seconds you use.

Even though a library supplies a film clip, you may still need to clear separately what's in the clip, including music, actors, news anchors, and so on. Sometimes libraries supply pirated footage for which even the clip is not cleared, and you may risk a lawsuit if you use it without the owner's permission, so make sure you use a reputable film archive or library.

Preparing Credits

Another task that must be completed in post-production is the preparation of the final credits for your film, which you will need in order to make both the main or opening titles and the end credits. Screen credits vary greatly from picture to picture, but there are basic guidelines that apply to all productions.

Union and guild requirements govern the placement of some credits, others are placed based on tradition in the industry, still others are negotiated before the shoot begins, and some are given at the discretion of the producer after principal photography. It's important to start making your credit list early because some credits will require approval by the union of the crew member involved.

Following are some of the various union requirements for film credits, but it's always wise to ask the unions or guilds for copies of their latest credit requirements just in case there have been any changes.

Directors

The Directors Guild of America (DGA) requires that the director of your film, assuming he or she is a member of the guild, be given credit on a separate title card that is the last title card appearing before the first scene of the film, or the first card following the last scene of the movie if the credits don't run until the end of the movie. The DGA also requires that the size and type of the director's credit be no less than 50 percent of the size in which the title of the film is displayed, or the largest-size title given to any other person, whichever is greater.

In television, the DGA has basically the same rules, except that the director's name only has to be no less than 40 percent of the episode or series title, whichever is larger.

> ## Script Notes
>
> If your film is for television, check the network's delivery requirements for the format of the credits to find out the amount of time you have to run them, which is often very short. The number of screen credits you can give other than those that are required contractually or by the guilds is often limited on television. Also, it's a good idea to have your credits checked by your attorney and the distributor's production executive before finalizing them.

Writers

The writer's credit is governed by the Writers Guild of America (WGA), assuming the writer of your film is a member. On a feature film, the writer's credit must be on a separate card that has to appear immediately preceding the card for the director and must be in the same style and size type as that used for the producer or director, whichever is larger.

The WGA is very specific about what words must be used in the credit. If the same writer or writers wrote both the story and screenplay, then the contract says that the screen credit should simply read "written by." The writer's credit should read "screenplay by" when the screenplay is based on original material written by someone else. The story credit in that case should read "story by." When the screenplay is based on source material other than an original story written for the film, the credit should read "From a story by," "Based on a story by," "Based on a novel by," and so on. You also need to give the title of the source material if it is different from the film's title.

In television, the credit is "written by" if the screen credit is for both the story and teleplay, or "teleplay by" and "story by" if the story is based on other source material.

Also, even if you have had 29 writers doing drafts of your script, the WGA will only allow 2 of them to get screen credit (or 2 teams of more than 1 writer). The producer will first decide which writers he or she feels should get the credit and submit a Notice of Tentative Credits and a copy of the final shooting script of the film to the Writers Guild and to each writer. If a writer protests the proposed credits to the Guild, the Guild may first try to see if the writers themselves can agree on the credit. If not, the producer must submit three copies of the different drafts of the script to the Guild's credit arbitration committee, as well as any source material. A committee of volunteer WGA members will then read the drafts and determine which 2 of the writers will get screen credit.

Cast Credits

The credits for the leading actors in your movie will usually be negotiated by each actor's agent or manager prior to the actor's signing on to the film. Major film stars often require that their names be placed above or before the title of the film. Whether the actor's credit is in "first position" or "second position" and so on is also negotiated.

The only thing the Screen Actors Guild requires is that a cast of characters is placed on at least one card or scroll at the end of a theatrical film, naming each performer and the role he or she portrayed. All credits on this list should be the same style, size, and type.

The same is true for television, except that if a cast member is credited elsewhere (in the opening credits), he or she does not need to be credited again in the cast list at the end.

Other Credits

Other unions may mandate certain other credits. Some of the crew credits that are regulated by unions include the following:

- **Director of photography** credit on a separate card adjacent to the writer, producer, or director.

- **Art director** on a separate card adjacent to the director of photography credit. If there is to be a production designer credit, prior permission must be obtained from the union.

- **Editor** on a separate card in a prominent place (usually next to the art director).

- **Unit production manager** credit, according to DGA rules, has to be in a prominent place on a card shared by no more than three names, and the only technical credits that may receive a more prominent place are those of the director of photography, art director, and editor. If you wish to give the UPM a "production manager" credit, it must be approved by the DGA.

- **First and second assistant directors** are the same as the unit production manager, except that these credits must follow the UPM credit.

- **Costume designer** credit may be given only to a member of the Costume Designers Guild.

- **Set decorator** credit has to be in a prominent place. It usually appears after the second assistant director credit.

- **Makeup artist/Hair stylist** credit has to be given; the placement is at the producer's discretion.

The credits for the writer, director, producer, major cast members, director of photography, art director, and editor are often in the opening titles, but most of the other crew credits are in the end titles. The opening titles also generally have a presentation credit for the company (or companies) that financed the film and a release credit for the distributor. Sometimes in Hollywood films, the producer, director, and major cast members all negotiate credits above the title. After the distributor's logo, the opening credits may have three cards reading something like "Makeshift Pictures Present / A Patty Smith Production / A Judy Jones Film" where Makeshift is the financing company, Smith is the producer, and Jones is the director. Then the lead actors are each listed on a separate card and finally there is a card with the title of the film. Both the producer and director would get a credit a second time in the opening credits that follow.

At last you have finished your film, but there is still more to do. The next and final part of this book covers the distribution process—getting your film to the audience for which it is intended.

The Least You Need to Know

♦ To ensure a smooth post-production period, plan and stick to a practical schedule for finishing the film.

♦ Make sure that you have obtained clearances for all copyrighted material you are using in your film.

♦ Clearing music is often an expensive hassle, so most producers hire a composer to write an original score for a film.

♦ You should begin preparing your credit list as soon as you finish production and should check with all unions and guilds for their credit requirements.

Part 5

Now Playing at ...?
Distribution

The initial desire that inspired you to become a filmmaker included, most likely, wanting people to see your film. You've now made the movie, but how will it gain an audience? The last thing you want is for your film to sit on a shelf somewhere, unseen by anyone.

This part of the book covers all forms of connecting films with audiences: the traditional studio theatrical distribution, the challenges of independent film distribution, television sales, non-theatrical distribution, and the new avenues for film distribution on the Internet.

WHEN YOU SAID YOU WERE "SCREENING YOUR NEW MOVIE", I THOUGHT YOU MEANT AT A *THEATER*, NOT ON A COMPUTER IN YOUR *MOTHER'S BASEMENT.*

Chapter 21

The Hollywood Distribution System

In This Chapter

- ◆ The basic studio distribution deal
- ◆ Home entertainment and foreign distribution
- ◆ Elements of studio marketing campaigns
- ◆ Saturation and platform releasing strategies

In the United States, the major Hollywood studios distribute the majority of films that we see in local theaters each year. In deciding what films to make and distribute, the studios aim for those that have the potential to become major blockbusters or at least to reach a mass market rather than a specialized market. They also seek to distribute a few pictures each year that they hope will win them a slew of awards and give the studio prestige and goodwill with actors, writers, directors, and producers that they might want to work with in the future. These prestige films are usually released at the end of the year during the holiday season, just in time for "Academy Consideration."

As discussed in Chapters 4 and 5, studios will have financed the development of some of the films they distribute and will distribute other films that have been financed independently. Whether a film has been financed by the studio or independently, the studio's marketing and distribution departments will handle the release of the film. In this chapter, for those with a studio distribution deal, or those hoping to have one, we'll cover how the studios tackle the task of selling and distributing a film.

Script Notes

If you have produced a low-budget film, don't expect the major studios to be interested in it. A low-budget film that is likely to earn back the cost of its negative and make a little profit for its investors might seem great to you, but it won't be worth the time of a major studio. Because of their large overhead, studios generally want films that they feel will earn a substantial profit. For a small film, look for an independent distributor.

Signing the Distribution Deal

If the studio that developed your film decides to distribute it or if you have developed and produced your film and a studio has agreed to pick up your film for distribution, you will have to sign a distribution agreement with that studio. If the studio developed the film, it will be a Production-Distribution Agreement, otherwise it will simply be a Distribution Agreement.

Studio distribution deals are exceedingly complex and Byzantine. You should not even begin talking about any terms of an agreement with a studio yourself. You will need an experienced entertainment attorney to negotiate the deal and look out for your interests.

The basic elements that will be covered in a studio distribution deal include the following:

◆ The territories covered by the agreement (for example, the United States and Canada for domestic distribution).

◆ In some cases, a minimum box office guarantee for those territories.

◆ The minimum amount the distributor will spend on prints and advertising.

◆ The breakdown of how the box-office proceeds will be disbursed, including the percentage of gross receipts or adjusted gross receipts that the producer will receive after the studio has recouped a certain amount. This will also include a definition of profits.

◆ In some cases, the amount of an advance paid to the producer by the distributor in exchange for the right to distribute the film. Not all producers receive advances and, for those that do, the amount of the advance will usually be deducted from the producer's ultimate profit participation.

Those are the basic elements that will be covered in a distribution deal, but the actual terms can vary enormously. If you are lucky enough to have one studio or several studios very interested in distributing your film, your attorney will be in a position to negotiate for you the best terms—a large advance, strong guarantees, a substantial commitment to spending on prints and advertising, and a decent profit participation.

When the distributor gives you a substantial advance and commits to spending a lot of money on prints and ads, then the studio has a greater investment in seeing the film succeed than if it is only paying you a low advance and not committing to spending much money distributing and marketing the film. With little invested in the picture up front by the studio, it may only give it minimal advertising support. And, in the crowded theatrical market, even a good film can die quickly without a reasonable advertising and publicity campaign. A distribution deal where the studio has made only a minimal commitment to the film may be almost as bad as no distribution deal at all. (See Chapter 24, "Alternative and New Media Distribution," for alternatives.) That's the reason it's critically important that you have an experienced attorney who knows the film industry and its practices advising and negotiating for you.

When the distribution agreement is drawn up, however, don't just sign it on the advice of your attorney. Read it first and ask your attorney to explain the parts you don't understand. Don't accept the explanation that something is just "standard or boilerplate language." Everything in a contract can be negotiated and you have a right to understand and disagree with any part of the agreement. You are handing over the film that you have nurtured and developed to the studio to release to the world. You have a right to know exactly what you are agreeing to.

Home Entertainment Distribution

Each major studio has a home entertainment division that markets and distributes videotapes and DVDs to the home entertainment market. This is a source of revenue for your film, whether or not your domestic theatrical release is very successful. Almost always, your domestic distribution deal for the theatrical release of the film will include a deal for the home entertainment release of your film on video and DVD.

The video and DVD release will be coordinated with the theatrical release. It will generally come after the film is no longer in theaters but soon enough after so that the advertising from the theatrical release is still in the public's recent memory. The success of the theatrical release will certainly help the home video and DVD release, but some films that were only moderately successful in their theatrical release will do very well on video.

A DVD release often includes extras on the DVD, such as funny outtakes from the film or interviews with the stars. Sometimes these clips are hidden in various places on the DVD and thus have gotten the name "Easter Eggs" because you have to hunt for them.

Foreign Distribution

I have been talking about the domestic distribution by a studio, which refers to the release of the film in the United States and Canada. Foreign distribution is the distribution of the film in the rest of the world. If your film has been picked up by a studio for domestic distribution, the same studio or distributor may not be handling the foreign distribution of your film. You may have to (or want to) find another distributor to handle it, but you shouldn't try to sell your film in foreign territories yourself, without some kind of help.

If a studio is handling the foreign distribution of your movie, the studio will work with a network of contacts or sub-distributors in each different territory in the world to sell both the theatrical and foreign television rights to your film. A territory might be a single country or it might be several countries. The studios have a marketing and distribution staff who know the regulations, import taxes, and customs of the various countries or territories and who will develop appropriate marketing materials for each foreign territory by modifying the original marketing campaign to fit the special needs and attitudes of the people in the territory. The studio will also have to make prints and videos that will fit the distribution requirements of each territory.

> **Counterpoint**
>
> If a film is not commercially successful, it does not mean that it is a bad film. Commercial success can be greatly affected by many things, including the public's mood or interest in the subject at the time of the release of the film or a misleading ad campaign that targets the wrong initial audience. If your film does not open strong, try to get the distributor to try a different ad campaign.

Marketing Your Film

Let's say you've been lucky enough to get a decent distribution deal from a major studio for your film. Be prepared to lose control of your film at this point, if you haven't lost control already. The studio's marketing department, not you, will devise the strategy for selling your film, including where to open the film and when. Some distributors may listen to your marketing ideas, but it is the studio's money that will be paying for the marketing campaign so the studio's people will generally have the final say. Also, it's very possible that the studio's marketing team may have a better idea of how to sell your film than you do, because that's their specialty.

What will the studio do to market your film? The marketing strategy will differ depending on the genre of the film, the target audience, the marketable elements of the film (stars, director, subject matter, source material such as a best-selling book, or even a well-known writer or producer), and any other marketing "hook" the clever studio marketing team can come up with.

The first target of a distributor's marketing campaign are sub-distributors and the exhibitors (theater chains) that will be exhibiting the film. Theaters range from those that are part of large first-run theater chains, which generally only show the films of the major Hollywood studios, to smaller independent theaters or art houses, which run a variety of films including foreign films and independent films distributed by smaller distributors.

The advertising campaign that the distributor is going to use to sell the film to the public is usually a very key factor in an exhibitor's decision as to whether to show the film in its theaters. To some exhibitors, the effectiveness of the ad campaign may be even more important than the movie itself. Exhibitors are savvy about advertising campaigns and know that the ad campaign is critically important in determining whether the theater will make money on the film.

When a movie first opens, most of the tickets will be sold because of the advertising campaign and not because of the quality of the film itself. Only after a film has been open for a week or more will a film generate good "word of mouth" that will keep ticket sales strong. The initial audience, however, is brought into the theater largely through the advertising campaign.

The advertising and promotional campaign for a studio film is generally in full swing for only about two weeks. After that, it may be cut back and, if the film survives, it will be because people tell their friends to see the film. When a film maintains a strong box office over several weeks or months, largely through word-of-mouth promotion, then it is considered in marketing jargon to have "legs."

Most effective studio marketing campaigns are targeted toward one or more specific audiences or "demographics" rather than toward everyone. One of the advantages of test screenings is that they can help the studio's marketing department learn what type of people are responding well to the film. If, for example, a sophisticated suspense thriller that also has a few car chases in it is marketed to young males 18–25 years old, the ad campaign may pull them into theaters, but it won't get a good word-of-mouth from these guys who probably want more action than this film delivers. If the film had been tested with a cross-section of the population, however, the marketing department would have discovered that older adults, both male and female, were responding well to the sophisticated dramatic themes in the film and the marketing campaign would be aimed at that core audience instead.

You can expect a good studio overall marketing campaign to contain a number of different elements, including most of the following items.

Press Packet and Stills

The press packet or press book is a folder that contains copies of the newspaper ads for the film, a synopsis of the story, the film's running time, and a complete credit list of both cast and crew. The press packet is given to potential exhibitors and sub-distributors, and is also given to film critics at pre-release screenings.

Carefully chosen production still photographs will also be part of the press packet and may be a separate aspect of the marketing campaign. Production stills can be put up outside theaters or used to accompany print reviews and stories about the film.

One Sheet

The film's *one-sheet* is also an important marketing tool. It is the color poster that is displayed in the front of theaters while the movie is playing, inside along their walls announcing "coming attractions," or in bus stops, subway stations, and so on. The one-sheet consists of some sort of graphic such as a photo or drawing, the title of the film, a catchy descriptive or intriguing ad line accompanying it, the credits for the principal cast and crew, and any good quotes from reviews of the film. The one-sheet design is usually replicated in the newspaper ads for the film.

For example, on *Something Is Rotten*, our comedy perfume caper, the one-sheet might have a photo of our heroine sniffing a bank vault as a dog would while the male co-star who plays the detective character looks on, embarrassed and confused. The tag line (we're still working on a better one) is "A thief never smelled better."

The Trailer

The marketing tool that will probably reach most of the likely customers for the film is the trailer that is run in theaters or on television prior to the film's release. Trailers usually run less than three minutes and generally contain highlights from the film that hint at the story line and show dramatic or comedic moments.

The trailer also will generally be rated by the Motion Picture Association of America (MPAA), as will your film. No one is forced to submit a film to the MPAA for a rating, but the vast majority of producers do and all major studios do. The basic mission of the rating system is to give parents (and others) advance information about movies so that they can decide what movies they will allow their children to see or what movies they want to see themselves.

Many distributors make more than one trailer, each with a different rating. If the film the trailer is promoting is an "R" rated film, the distributor may make a "G" rated trailer that can be shown before any film and an "R" rated trailer to show in advance of another "R" or "NC-17" rated film.

Television and Radio Ads

Films, particularly those that open in many theaters at the same time, are often heavily marketed on national television. Television ads are similar to trailers, only shorter— usually no longer than 30 seconds. In fact, sometimes trailers are constructed so that one or more parts of a trailer can be lifted and used as a television ad.

Television ads are most effective when they are placed near programs that are likely to attract the same target or core audience as the audience to which you expect your film to appeal.

Radio ads for a film often use the same audio clips as the television spot. Sometimes, however, it's better to construct an entirely new radio campaign since, without the visuals, different audio clips from the film may be more effective. Radio spots may vary in length from 10 seconds to 30 or 60 seconds. As with television ads, the radio ads are most effective when played on programs that have listeners who are the same type of people likely to be interested in your film.

Electronic Press Kit

Studios often make an electronic press kit, especially for very big-budget movies. It usually consists of video footage showing the filmmakers in action on the set of the movie. This footage is used for television promotion on shows like *Entertainment Tonight* or *Extra*.

Script Notes

In a film's marketing campaign, attention has to be paid to the lead time needed by print, television, and radio media, respectively, to do reviews and stories about your film. Studios know the schedules of newspapers, magazines, television shows, and radio shows and contact them well in advance of their deadlines so that any publicity will hit on or before the release date of the film.

Another part of an electronic press kit might be the film itself on video. Some newspaper or magazine reviewers might prefer to watch the film alone rather than at a screening with an audience or with other critics.

Internet Promotion

All the major studios have websites to promote their films, but besides their own websites studios also use the Internet in other ways to market films. A potential blockbuster is likely to be promoted on both Internet Service Providers like AOL and search engines like Netscape or Yahoo!, either through ads, links to stories about the film or stars, contests to win tickets, or other types of promotion.

Release Strategies

Distributors may take six months to a year to plan and execute the marketing and develop a launch or release strategy for a film. There are several typical release strategies that studios use for their films.

Saturation

On films with major stars that a studio hopes will become a hit or blockbuster, the studio will open the film "wide," which is also called *saturation* or saturating the market. The film will open simultaneously in several thousand theaters across the country. Movies that open in this way are always supported by a very expensive national and local ad campaign. And, of course, the studio will have to make thousands of release prints of the film, another huge expense involved in using this release strategy.

The thinking behind this kind of release is that a blockbuster is made by making the opening of the movie a national event. The opening of the first *Harry Potter* movie, for example, was promoted to kids for months before the film opened. When the movie opened everywhere across the country on the same date, it was supported by every conceivable type of advertising and promotion. Kids everywhere dragged their parents to the movie on opening weekend, not wanting to be the only kid in school who didn't see the film. The movie broke all previous box-office records for a film's opening.

Platform Release

In addition to saturation, a studio may use several types of *platform release* strategies. All of these strategies are less expensive than a saturation strategy. The studio may open a film simultaneously in a few theaters in New York, Los Angeles, and other major cities. The film will be supported by less expensive local newspaper, radio, and television ads, rather than expensive national ads. After a week or more, the studio will roll out the film to secondary markets in smaller towns or smaller theaters, if the film is doing a reasonable business. If not, the film may go back on the shelf while an alternate marketing campaign is prepared, or may stay on the shelf indefinitely or until released on video and/or DVD. It may never reach smaller theaters.

The platform release strategy is used for small- to medium-sized studio films that are expected to do well but not expected to be huge blockbusters—usually thrillers, dramas, and comedies that don't have really huge stars and lots of glitzy special effects. Studios also use this strategy on most independently financed films that they have picked up for distribution.

Limited Engagement

A limited engagement release is when a film only opens in one or two cities, usually Los Angeles and/or New York. It is generally for films that the studio has even less confidence in, perhaps because the film lacks major stars or is expected to draw a narrow or more sophisticated, limited audience. The advertising and promotion of these types of films is targeted to the more limited audience. If the response to the film is good during the first one or two weeks, the studio will then make more prints and eventually release it in other cities. If it isn't good, it will go on a shelf or head straight to the video market.

Release Date

Studio marketing and distribution executives agonize over what weekend to release a film. They find out when the other studios are releasing films and try not to release films that will compete for the same audience—for example, two big action films—on the same weekend.

Also, studios tend to release certain kinds of films at certain times of the year, but no rules are set in stone. Big action-adventure, science fiction or horror potential blockbusters are usually released in early summer. The idea is that teenagers, who often make these films blockbusters by seeing them several times, are free to hang out at the mall and see a movie over and over because they are not in school in the summer.

Major studio films for adults, often with socially conscious themes and artistic merit, are frequently released at the end of the year during the holiday season, from Thanksgiving to New Year's Day. Some films only open for a week in New York or Los Angeles during this period to qualify for the Academy Awards and then open again later in January or February.

If the film gets good reviews and there is the hoped-for "Oscar buzz" about the film itself or the performances, the studio will promote it heavily in the trade papers for Academy Awards and other awards. If the film then wins some awards, the studio can re-release it later in more markets, using the awards in a new advertising campaign for the film.

> ### Cutaway
>
> Today, the studios are not only focused on winning for their films prestigious Oscars or Academy Awards from the Academy of Motion Picture Arts and Sciences. They also promote their films with the members of the Hollywood Foreign Press Association, which gives out the Golden Globe awards, as well as the Writers Guild, the Directors Guild, and the Screen Actors Guild, all of which give yearly awards to their members. Also, the New York and Los Angeles film critics each have an association that gives out awards. Studios heavily promote their films to all of these groups with free videocassettes, free screenings, letters, ads, copies of the script, and any other methods they can come up with. When they get a coveted award, it is then listed in the newspaper and other ads for the film.

Certain months, such as April and May or August through early November, are considered the off-season, and not as many new films are released during these periods. Many films, however, have a better chance of breaking out and finding their audiences if they are released in one of the not-so-crowded periods.

Merchandising and Commercial Tie-Ins

Although it is rare for low-budget films to make money in this way, Hollywood studio marketers are masters at finding ways both to promote their films and to make money through merchandising and commercial tie-ins, particularly on big "event" films. Games, dolls, toys, T-shirts, posters, jewelry, and other items can be sold or given away to promote and advertise the movie and/or to make money on the product being sold.

Studios often set up deals with retail outlets where items are sold as a tie-in to the movie, such as a doll based on a movie character or a game based on the movie's plot or action. Or the studios may make a deal with a company like a fast-food chain to give away plastic mugs that display the name of the movie and some sort of graphic art promoting the movie.

At premieres, the studios often give away caps, T-shirts, mugs, or other promotional items with the movie's name and perhaps a catchy ad line on it. These gimmicks get the name of the movie out into the culture, but they are usually too expensive for movies other than the big-budget potential blockbusters.

Verbal Action

one-sheet A poster-sized advertisement for a film that is graphically eye-catching and usually displayed outside of or on the inside walls of theaters.

saturation A major studio film distribution strategy that involves opening a movie in thousands of theaters nationwide on the same date.

platform release To open a film in a few major cities and gradually expand the release to other markets if the movie is successful.

Publicity Junkets and Premieres

Studios are also famous for creating elaborate publicity junkets to sell their films. They have been known to shuttle critics and journalists around in private jets, put them up in expensive hotels, feed them lavish banquets, and give them access to the stars of the film in the hope of getting a good review or story about the film.

The stars themselves often go on press junkets to publicize the film. Each star, if he or she is willing to cooperate and is available, will be booked on television talk shows or radio shows, or set for interviews by magazine or newspaper journalists. Some stars do this task willingly. Others refuse or aren't available.

Studios also frequently throw great bashes for the film's premiere—usually either in Los Angeles or New York, although sometimes the premiere is held somewhere else, depending on the film. To promote a Mel Gibson movie, a good deal of which took place in a jungle, I was invited to a premiere that re-created an entire outdoor jungle, similar to the one seen in the film, on the roof of a hotel in Hollywood. The film wasn't very memorable but the party sure was. And this particular premiere party was a relatively low-end one compared to many more expensive and elaborate shindigs.

The Least You Need to Know

- ◆ Studio distribution deals are complicated and need to be negotiated by an experienced entertainment attorney.

- ◆ Home entertainment distribution (video and DVD) is almost always handled by the same studio that handles domestic theatrical distribution, but foreign distribution may be handled by another studio or foreign sales entity.

- ◆ Studio marketing divisions will plan a multi-faceted marketing campaign for a film geared at mass audiences and particularly at the target or core audience they expect to respond to the film.

- ◆ Studios often use merchandising or commercial tie-ins with food and retail outlets to promote big-budget films.

Chapter 22

Independent Feature Distribution

In This Chapter

- ◆ Getting assistance: the Independent Feature Project
- ◆ Developing a strategy for applying to festivals
- ◆ Identifying the major film festivals
- ◆ Knowing the independent distributors

Somehow, you have managed to make an independent film without a distribution deal. You loved making your first feature and you've got the filmmaking bug—you want to make more. You may not want to raise all the money again—either your relatives are all tapped out or you discovered that it's much harder to find money than it is to make the film. You may be hoping that someone who sees your film will become your champion and a company will actually pay you to make your next film. If that's your dream, then it's time to realize that your years of hard work in getting the film made must be followed by an equal commitment to getting it seen and promoted to independent distributors.

For most filmmakers, the quickest and best route to getting a distribution deal for an independent feature film is through a film festival, where distributors and agents will be attending and looking for products to buy or represent. With so much depending on attracting a buyer at a film festival, you should know all you can about the different festivals and have a well-thought-out strategy for both getting accepted at a festival and attracting attention to your film once it's there.

In this chapter, I'll cover where to find help getting a distributor how to devise a film festival strategy, as well as give you an overview of the independent distributors who will be prowling around the festivals looking for films like yours to distribute. I'll also provide some tips for making your film stand out from the hundreds of other films the distributor will be considering.

Getting Help from the Independent Feature Project

An important ally for independent filmmakers and an organization that might be able to help you get your film seen by buyers is the non-profit Independent Feature Project (IFP), which began in 1979. The organization's mission is to encourage and facilitate the development and exhibition of new films from diverse American filmmakers. Championing the cause of independent filmmaking, the IFP supports filmmakers working outside the established studio system. The largest association of independent filmmaker in the United States, more than 10,000 filmmakers and industry professionals use the organization regularly for assistance and guidance.

For those looking for distribution (and financing) the IFP sponsors the IFP Market, which attracts buyers from around the world to view feature and short films, documentaries, works-in-progress, and scripts seeking financing. Some of the leading independent films that have been discovered at the IFP Market include: *Blood Simple* (Joel and Ethan Coen, 1984), *Clerks* (Kevin Smith, 1994), *The Brothers McMullen* (Edward Burns, 1995), *El Norte* (Gregory Nava, 1983), *Metropolitan* (Wilt Stillman, 1990), *Reservoir Dogs* (Quentin Tarantino, 1992), *Slacker* (Richard Linklater, 1991), *Stand and Deliver* (Ramon Menendez, 1987), *Welcome to the Dollhouse* (Todd Solondz, 1995), and the 1999 Academy Award documentary nominee, *The Farm: Angola* (Jonathan Stack and Elizabeth Garbus), among many others.

Cutaway

The Southern California chapter of IFP, which has over 5,200 members, offers educational programs that help members master the art and craft of filmmaking, including seminars on such topics as digital filmmaking and film financing. The chapter also provides filmmakers with professional advice, access to industry leaders, networking opportunities, camera and equipment rentals, discounts to over 200 industry-related vendors, editing facilities, access to a free screening facility, and a fully-stocked Resource Library. IFP/West also promotes independent films to a wider audience through the Los Angeles Independent Film Festival (see the following section) and the nationally televised IFP/West Independent Spirit Awards, the independent world's irreverent version of the Oscars.

The IFP has chapters in Los Angeles, New York, Chicago, Minneapolis, and Miami. You can get more information about this organization that can be a very valuable resource for you from its website at www.ifp.org.

Going Where the Buyers Are: Film Festivals

The oldest film festival still in existence is the Venice Film Festival, which was founded in the 1930s by the fascist Italian dictator, Benito Mussolini. Although its founder and his government did not survive, the Venice Film Festival did and continues to be an important international festival today.

The next oldest film festival is the famous Cannes Film Festival that takes place on the French Riviera in the south of France. It was originally set to debut on September 1, 1939. A number of Hollywood stars were there for the opening and, in what was to become a Cannes tradition, grand and elaborate festivities were planned. The festival, however, was cancelled after presenting only one film because Hitler invaded Poland on the same day, beginning World War II. After Hitler was defeated, the Cannes Film Festival tried again and, since 1946, has been one of the world's most successful film festivals.

From those two early festivals, there are today over a thousand film festivals around the world. There are film festivals that specialize in documentaries, animated films, gay and lesbian films, student films, short films, African-American films, women's films, videos, underground films, weird films, and more. I'll present the most prestigious festivals, cover what you should know about entering your film in a festival and marketing your film if it is accepted at a festival.

How to Submit Entries

Before you submit any applications and pay a fee to have your film considered for inclusion in a film festival, be sure to thoroughly research the possible film festivals and come up with a targeted list of festivals that are right for your film. Following are descriptions of the festivals that are considered the top festivals, but many of them may not be right for your film. You can research other festivals by contacting the Independent Feature Project chapter closest to you, by going online to film websites such as Filmfestivals.com (www.filmfestivalspro.com), or you can buy *The Ultimate Film Festival Survival Guide*, by Chris Gore (Lone Eagle Publishing, Los Angeles, 1999), which contains a list of most of the film festivals out there.

There are several factors that should be considered when deciding what festivals to enter. Festival applications generally require an entrance fee—most are at least $50 or more for a feature-length film—so you should look at your budget and decide how many festivals you can afford to apply to.

Second, decide what your main goal is and enter based on that. If your goal is to get a feature distributor, you must apply to the top festivals that are attended by lots of acquisition executives from companies that distribute films. Those include Sundance, Toronto, and Cannes, as well as a few others that I'll cover in this chapter.

You may not be able to get into one of those very competitive and sought-after festivals, so you should also submit applications to the next level of festivals, which includes Slamdance, Telluride, and others. Also, you should pinpoint festivals that specialize in your film genre or festivals in parts of the country or world that might be especially receptive to your film.

Once your film has been submitted to a number of festivals, sit back and wait—and perhaps do some polite, non-annoying lobbying for your film. As with everything, a squeaky reel (or filmmaker) might get the slot rather than the filmmaker too shy to pick up the phone.

You may be rejected everywhere you have submitted an application but then will mysteriously get a letter from another festival inviting you to enter your film. That's because film festival directors are in touch with each other, and although a film might not make the cut in one festival, the director may recommend it to the director of another festival.

CAUTION **Counterpoint**

Some filmmakers submit rough cuts with their festival applications. It's generally not a good idea if the film is too "rough." If it will help you get your application in early, however, you might consider it. The earlier you apply, the better your chance of getting accepted. Festivals will also accept entries on video, and some screen on video. For those that don't screen on video, you can wait until your video is accepted to blow it up to film.

Sundance

According to most people in the independent film world, Sundance reigns supreme among all the film festivals in the United States and possibly in the world. It is the place to be if you can possibly get your film accepted. The location may lack the sunshine and glitter of its European counterparts like Cannes and Venice, but it compensates with innovation and excitement. Every year, hundreds of filmmakers, film buffs, independent distributors, and Hollywood executives bundle up and trudge through the Park City, Utah, snow to see films made by unknown directors.

Sundance was founded by Robert Redford as a celebration of independent filmmaking, and has grown to attract almost as many Hollywood players as independents. Still, it previews films that wouldn't have a chance in the studio system—for example, it was Sundance that launched the strange phenomenon *The Blair Witch Project* (Daniel Myrick and Eduardo Sanchez, 1999), and many other films too numerous to mention.

Slamdance

Although it does not have the prestige of its older cousin, Sundance, Slamdance is an important film festival. Billed as "by filmmakers, for filmmakers," it started in 1995 and continues to be organized and programmed by active filmmakers. Slamdance runs simultaneously with the Sundance Film Festival in Park City, taking advantage of the crowds that gather for that event. It has a reputation for premiering independent films by first-time directors working with limited budgets. (In order to be eligible, a film must be by a first-time director, shot on a limited budget, over 40 minutes, and without a distributor.)

In 2001, several Slamdance films were picked up for distribution, and almost every film went on to play at other international film festivals. In addition to the festival itself, Slamdance also has an annual screenplay competition, a very active website (www. slamdance.com), and a short film-production wing. Slamdance also plans to establish a new festival in Germany designed to extend the Slamdance label internationally.

Cannes

This renowned Riviera festival is without a doubt the festival with the most Hollywood glitter, big-budgets, premieres, hot parties, cell phones, schmoozing, and films that will turn up on the festival circuit the rest of the year or be in theaters if they are lucky enough to get snapped up during the festival. Held in May, Cannes has both a festival with a prestigious competition and limited entries and a film market, which is open to any film for a fee.

Berlin

Since its opening in 1951, the Berlin Film Festival has had a reputation for bucking the trends and setting its own agenda. Unlike most European festivals, including Cannes, which look askance at the Hollywood blockbuster, Berlin embraces mainstream Hollywood but still maintains an international *ésprit*. During the two weeks of the festival, Berlin features a competition section and several sidebars, including Retrospectives, Kinderfilmfest (a children's film festival), and a New German Films section.

Toronto

From its humble beginning in 1976 as simply a collection of films from other festivals—kind of a "festival of festivals"—the Toronto International Film Festival has become one of the most successful festivals in the world, universally regarded as an ideal platform to premiere films. In 1998, *Variety* said of Toronto that "the Festival is second only to Cannes in terms of high-profile pictures, stars and market activity."

The Toronto International Film Festival has undergone countless changes since 1976 but has remained committed to its principal objectives—to celebrate and promote films and to highlight and place Canadian achievements in an international context. Held in September, Toronto is a well-organized, prestigious festival that attracts both the international media and lots of acquisition executives.

Telluride

Telluride is the film-lovers film festival, rather than the "biz" lover's festival. It is prestigious not because of the number of distribution deals that follow the screenings at Telluride, but because of the number of remarkably good films that you can expect to see there.

Telluride was the first to show ground-breaking films like Louis Malle's *My Dinner with André* (1981), David Lynch's *Blue Velvet* (1986), and Billy Bob Thornton's *Sling Blade* (1996). It hosted the World or North American premieres of such films as *Crouching Tiger, Hidden Dragon* (Ang Lee, 2000), *Secrets and Lies* (Mike Leigh, 1996), *Cinema Paradiso* (Giuseppe Tornatore, 1988), *The Piano* (Jane Campion, 1993), *My Left Foot* (Jim Sheridan, 1989), and *The Crying Game* (Neil Jordan, 1992).

Entry in the Telluride Film Festival is open to professional and non-professional filmmakers working in all film genres—documentary, narrative, animation, and experimental. Features and shorts of all styles and lengths are eligible for consideration provided that they are new works.

Script Notes

Telluride has a wonderful focus on works by young, emerging filmmakers. The "Student Prints" and "Calling Cards" programs screen short films that highlight the work of students currently in film school or those with "resume" short films. Its "Great Expectations" program presents two to four short feature-length films notable for their quality and the potential of their creators. Other selected short films are included in the festival and screened with a feature.

New York Film Festival

The New York Film Festival, held in October, screens only about 30 films out of the 1,300 films that are entered each year, so it's not easy to get into. If you are accepted, however, you are in good company. Over the years, the Manhattan festival has premiered films by many well-known and esteemed filmmakers, including Martin Scorsese, Francois Truffant, Jane Campion, Jonathan Demme, James Ivory, Robert Altman, Barbara Kopple, and Quentin Tarantino.

The New York Film Festival is dedicated to finding new filmmakers, to helping those who are on the verge of mainstream success, and to showcasing the work of distinguished film-makers whose work deserves wider public recognition.

Los Angeles Independent Film Festival

This relatively new festival began in 1993 and has evolved into a world-class event. The festival is for American independent films only and it attracts all of the major acquisition executives, as well as others in the film business, given its location in the heart of Holly-wood. If you get your film screened here, you very well might get a distribution deal. Even if you don't, you are likely to get meetings with studios, media attention, and offers of representation from talent agencies.

Other Festivals

The Seattle Film Festival is a month-long event that screens over three hundred films, so your chances of getting accepted at this May-June festival is greater than at some of the shorter festivals. Still, the odds of acceptance are only about one out of five or six. Don't bother to submit to this festival unless the production values on your film are quite good. (That is true of most of the major festivals, but Seattle specifically mentions it in their materials.)

Austin, Texas, hosts the South By Southwest Film Festival, which gives special attention to Texas and regional filmmakers. This festival, which began in 1994, has also become a good place to debut a film and meet distributors.

Finally, the Taos Talking Pictures Festival in Taos, New Mexico, was called "one of the country's leading festivals" by *MovieMaker Magazine*. It is held in April and has a unique award to its winning filmmaker—five acres of land near Taos. It is a four-day event that screens 70 films, including features, documentaries, and shorts. If your film has a South-western bent, this is definitely a great festival to enter.

Working the Festival

For many filmmakers, acceptance to a top festival is perceived as the ticket to getting a distribution deal, but although an invitation to premiere at a well-known festival is certainly a great accomplishment, it is no guarantee that your film will get a distributor. Entrance into the festival is not a victory, but rather an opportunity to compete with dozens (possibly hundreds) of other films for the attention of the festival-goers, media, and distribution executives.

If you have ever been to one of the top film festivals, you know that there is an enormous amount of hype swirling around the various events. Television cameras and newspaper reporters are trying to get "the buzz" on what's hot and what's not. Movie studios, festival sponsors, smaller distributors, and producers are all trying to capture the attention of the media and those attending the festival. In this section, we'll cover some marketing tips for making your film stand out from the crowd and clutter to get the attention you feel it deserves.

Design and Materials

First, it's important that you design and develop marketing materials for your film that are unique and well done. Take enough time to develop tasteful and effective materials, and use the best graphic artist you can afford.

Some tips for evaluating the design of your materials include the following:

- ◆ Does the design create interest and emotion?
- ◆ Does the design use white space effectively?
- ◆ Is the design too cluttered?
- ◆ Does the design have eye-catching photography or graphics?
- ◆ Does the design say something about your film?
- ◆ Does the copy provoke curiosity or laughter?
- ◆ Does the design and copy appeal to the intended audience for your film?
- ◆ Do you have a great logo as part of the design?
- ◆ Is the design strong and simple?
- ◆ Do the various materials you plan to create have a consistent design, theme, and color scheme?
- ◆ Have you used glossy color reproductions in your materials?
- ◆ Have you resisted the urge to highlight the director's or producer's name (unless it is the selling point of the film)?

Once you have the design, what types of materials should you create? Small handbills or postcards are a definite must. A few volunteers in the street pressing them into the hands of passersby is a tried-and-true method of festival marketing. Very few festival-goers will refuse the handbill, which guarantees at least a cursory glance at your title and information. If your material is interesting enough, the recipient will turn it over and read the when and where of the screening. Contact information should also be included.

Counterpoint

Although stickers are a tempting and inexpensive method for marketing your film, this is a risky method that should be avoided. You can't afford taking the risk that pranksters would plaster your stickers in the wrong places—on the festival signs, a police car, wherever—and you could end up with a vandalism charge, or at least be made responsible for clean-up fees. With the atmosphere as hectic and competitive as it is, you don't need this possible trouble or stress.

T-Shirts, Hats, and Other Giveaways

These promotional items or "giveaways" are a bit more expensive than handbills, but well worth the price. Hats may be more popular than T-shirts, depending on the climate and time of year. Although there is more space on a T-shirt for your promotion, hats are also closer to eye level.

Using clothing to market your film works because you are essentially getting strangers to promote your film for you. If you offer a festival participant something that he or she can use instead of a handbill, sticker, or poster, he or she will generally be glad to have it. If in Park City, Utah, in the middle of winter, you offer someone a warm hat, he or she will probably wear it. In doing so, that person becomes an active participant in your marketing drive. A T-shirt or hat is part of a living, breathing human being who is now representing your film. It is really an endorsement and gives the impression that your film has a fan base and a group of supporters behind it. Of course, if only one person is wearing the shirt or hat, it is not effective. However, 12 people wearing the same promotional item, especially at the same place and time, will definitely give your film attention.

Other giveaways such as mugs, key chains, or comic books may not be visible promotion to others like wearable clothing, but they are often effective with the people you give the item to.

Marketing Teams

Many filmmakers dispatch small groups of friends and family into the streets to give away promotional items. This can be extraordinarily effective, especially if everyone on your team is wearing promotional clothing. Food and/or candy are usually welcome items for most people. Also, hot drinks at a winter festival are very inexpensive and easily win the goodwill of festival-goers.

The members of your marketing teams should, of course, know where and when your film is playing. That information should be indelibly imprinted in their minds and repeated mantra-like to everyone they encounter as they hand out food, drinks, or other giveaways.

Creating a Scene

Nothing attracts a crowd and a buzz like creating a scene and giving people something to talk about. What kind of scene can you create? An example is the scene staged by the filmmakers of *A Galaxy Far, Far Away*, a documentary about *Star Wars* fanatics that screened at Slamdance 2000. The filmmakers and some of the subjects of the documentary dressed up as characters from the *Star Wars* films and gathered in the street shortly before the screening of their film. One of the team carried a portable CD player, which was blasting songs from the film's soundtrack. The group of costumed people attracted a lot of attention and got people to go to the screening.

Script Notes _____

Even if you can't mount a really unique guerrilla marketing campaign, you should still have some sort of giveaway, whether it is a button, a key chain, or mittens. If you weren't an original thinker, you wouldn't have made a film, so think of something cool and give it to people. And you'll probably be the main member of the marketing team yourself, so be sure to introduce yourself and let the festival-goers know how excited you are about your film.

A Publicist

Most successful filmmakers at the large festivals hire a PR person or publicist. If you can't afford to pay one, maybe you can convince a friend who works in PR to help you by giving him or her a trip to the festival.

The advantage of having a professional PR person is enormous in terms of getting a distributor. It's unfortunate but true that an average film at a festival with a lot of "buzz" or "heat" behind it is more likely to get a distributor than a better film without that same heat. A PR firm can do more than you can do with a team of guerrilla marketers on the street. He or she will make you look professional, and that helps. Your PR person should create a great press kit, get some well-timed articles in the trades or newspapers about you and your film, and possibly even help get you a positive review through his or her contacts in the media.

Meeting the Independent Buyers

Who are the buyers that you want to be interested in your film? You should become very familiar with the companies that distribute independent films and know who the key executives are. If you pick up the phone and it's Mark Gill calling, don't say "I'm sorry, who's that?" to the secretary. He's the West Coast President of Miramax, stupid. Okay, maybe you expected Harvey or Bob to call, but it's still no excuse for not knowing who the people are that you want to buy your film.

Many distributors are happy to look at your film whether or not it is in a film festival. Just contacting them cold may be risky, however. Once they turn down your film, that's it. Following are a few of the most important independent distributors, but there are others. You need to find out any and all who might be interested in your film.

The Studio Classics Divisions

Many of the companies that might be interested in acquiring your film are the "classics" departments of major studios. These are divisions that distribute and sometimes produce independent films. Most studios have such a division, and some of the bigger "independent" distributors are actually owned by the major studios, even though the studio may not meddle in their affairs.

Sony Pictures Classics, one of the first of the "classics" divisions, is run by the team that was originally Orion Classics, then part of Orion Pictures. It finances, produces, and distributes independent films from America and around the world. SPC releases are evenly divided between co-productions and acquisitions (either pre-bought at the script stage or upon the film's completion).

Recent SPC releases include Ang Lee's *Crouching Tiger, Hidden Dragon* (2000), Ed Harris's *Pollock* (2000), Terence Davies's *The House of Mirth* (2000), and Marleen Gorris's *Luzhin Defense* (2000).

The classic division at Fox is called Fox Searchlight. It has distributed many excellent films, such as the popular *The Full Monty* (Peter Cattaneo, 1997). Paramount Classics is a newer company. It also does a mix of acquisitions and productions. Fine Line is the specialty division of New Line, and New Line is owned by AOL Time-Warner. It is the little distributor in that conglomerate that might be interested in your film.

Miramax

This is the big independent buyer that everyone seems to want because they do a very good job of distributing independent films. Miramax was founded by brothers Robert and Harvey Weinstein in 1979. They formed the company, which is named after their parents, Mira and Max, in order to create a home for films that were good but had trouble getting distribution. For the first few years, they only released acquisitions. In the mid 1980s, the company began to produce films as well as release them.

In the 1990s, the film-going public, evidently bored with the glossy, commercialized pictures that major film studios were releasing, began to turn to the more personal, meaningful independent films that Miramax made or acquired. The company became the leading independent film distributor in the country. In 1993, Miramax was purchased for $75 million by the Walt Disney Company.

The company's biggest break came in 1994, with Quentin Tarantino's *Pulp Fiction*. That film, which cost $8 million, made over $200 million worldwide. Since then, Miramax has had many commercial and artistic successes, including such films as *Il Postino* (Michael Radford, 1994), *Life Is Beautiful* (Roberto Benigni, 1997), and *Shakespeare in Love* (John Madden, 1998), to name a few. Miramax has a subsidiary, Dimension Films, which releases lower-budget, usually horror or teen films.

USA Films

USA Films is a production, marketing, and distribution company that is actually comprised of several companies—Gramercy Pictures, October Films, USA Home Entertainment, and certain domestic PolyGram Filmed Entertainment assets. The company's mandate is to make movies demonstrating the independent spirit and made in partnership with actors and filmmakers—ones of stature and also ones demonstrating promise. USA Films is also an independent film studio and makes co-production alliances to finance films.

In its short history, USA Films has already worked on multiple productions or releases from filmmakers such as Joel and Ethan Coen, Steven Soderbergh, Michael Douglas, and Billy Bob Thornton.

Its first in-house-supervised production was Steven Soderbergh's Academy Award–winning *Traffic* (2000). *Traffic* earned $124 million domestically, becoming USA's highest-grossing release.

Other significant grossers for USA have included Neil LaBute's *Nurse Betty* (2000, $25 million domestically), and Spike Jonze's *Being John Malkovich* (1999, $23 million domestically).

Lion's Gate

Lion's Gate is the new kid on the block. It is filling its production and distribution pipeline with 15 to 18 releases a year, including 5 to 7 in-house productions. Lion's Gate released the award-winning *Gods and Monsters* in 1998 and the critically-acclaimed *Monster's Ball* in 2001.

Lion's Gate is also big in home entertainment releasing. It acquired Trimark, giving its home video business three distinct labels—Trimark, Studio, and Avalanche, which are more outlets for independently produced films.

Artisan

Artisan Entertainment Inc., which was founded in 1997, is also becoming a leading independent producer and distributor of theatrical, television, and home entertainment products. Artisan, like Lion's Gate, is one of the last truly independent entertainment entities, distributing wide-release films as well as specialty programming designed for a niche platform release. Artisan released the wildly successful *The Blair Witch Project* (1999), which became the most profitable film ever made and redefined movie marketing; the critically acclaimed *Requiem for a Dream* (2000); Robert Altman's *Dr. T and the Women* (2000); and Steven Soderbergh's *The Limey* (1999). The company also showcases works from respected documentary filmmakers, including such recent releases as D. A. Pennebaker's *Startup.com* (2001) and Wim Wenders's *The Buena Vista Social Club* (1999).

Artisan's roots are also in the home entertainment marketplace. The company has continued to enhance its status in the independent film world through expansion of its video business and through its early adoption of the DVD format.

The Least You Need to Know

- ◆ Research film festivals before applying to them and create a strategy that is right for your film.
- ◆ Apply to both a number of the top festivals and a few smaller festivals.
- ◆ For maximum results, hire a publicist to help you plan and execute your festival marketing campaign.
- ◆ Know the distributors you want to attract.

Chapter 23

Television Sales

In This Chapter

- Making a television deal
- The top television sales markets
- Selling your film to public television
- Knowing the major broadcast and cable networks

Even though film theaters and television sets both display films and videos made using similar production techniques, the television business is quite a different business from the film business. It is filled with different people and operates somewhat differently than the film business. Some of you may have made your film with the intention of selling it to television rather than the theaters. This is particularly true of documentaries, which are only rarely distributed theatrically. In previous chapters, I have been focusing on distributing a film theatrically either through studio distribution or though an independent distributor. In this chapter, I'll focus on television—which is where many more people may end up seeing your film—and how television distribution works.

Just as the major studios dominate theatrical film distribution, the majority of television programming is either produced by the television networks and the major cable companies themselves or licensed by them. Episodic series, news shows, talk shows, documentaries, sports programming, and made-for-television movies (which I discussed in Chapter 5, "Making a Hollywood Film") are all in this category.

Television outlets, however, will also buy already produced films—both documentaries and features. The market for already produced television product has greatly expanded with the growth of the cable television networks in the last few decades, as well as the addition of several other broadcast networks besides the original three—ABC, NBC, and CBS. Just as you have learned about the major, mini-major, and independent distributors, you also need to know all of the possible television homes for your film.

The Television Deal

Television sales of a feature film include licensing the film to a broadcast network, a basic cable network, a pay-cable network, or other forms of pay television such as pay-per-view and *syndication*—which is selling a film to television stations independently of the network with which they may or may not be affiliated. These domestic television rights are generally granted to a major or mini-major distributor as part of the initial distribution agreement. Many of the smaller independent distributors, however, do not have the skilled staff necessary to handle sales to television, and you might be better off retaining television rights when you negotiate a distribution deal with them.

If you do not grant your theatrical distributor domestic television rights, then the distributor will request a *window* for the theatrical release—or a period of time to give the film a proper theatrical release before you begin to show your film on television. Although a film may be sold much earlier, films are not usually first premiered on television until a year or two after the theatrical release.

 Script Notes _____

If your feature film contains scenes involving nudity, excess violence, or language that won't get past the television network censors, it's important to shoot television "cover" shots during production. When you make your sale to television, you can replace the "offensive" scenes with the milder scenes you've shot to cover them. This is not usually a problem if you plan to sell your film only to a pay-cable channel.

The money for a television sale will vary depending on a number of factors. First, the box-office gross of your film will have a lot to do with how much you can negotiate for the television rights. Second, it depends on who wants the film and when they want to show it. If it's a major broadcast network that wants to run the film in prime time, they will pay more than a tiny cable channel that wants it for non-prime time.

Your deal, like a film distribution deal, will also vary depending on what you or, preferably, your attorney or other representative can negotiate. It may stipulate a fee for each time the film is shown on television over a certain period of time. Or, it may provide for a flat fee for any number of showings of the film over a certain period. At the end of the period, you may be able to license your film to another television network or cable company, particularly if it has done well in the *ratings* (numbers based on statistics from the Nielsen company, which estimates how many viewers see a television show).

Television Sales Agents

If you have retained the television rights to your film and will be selling them yourself, it might be advantageous for you to work with a television sales agent if you can get one to represent your film. Sales agents are indispensable if you are doing foreign television sales (see later in this chapter) but they can also be valuable for domestic television sales and syndication. They know the network and cable executives who acquire films, and they also know the going rates for films like yours. Even if you think you can make the sale yourself, use an experienced entertainment attorney to negotiate the deal.

National Television Markets

A television market, like a film market, is a place where films are bought and sold. The television networks and cable companies are the buyers and producers, or their sales agents are the sellers. In the United States, the National Association of Television Program Executives (NATPE) holds the major market for buying and selling television product.

The NATPE convention is held each year in Las Vegas and runs for four days. Over 300 companies operate booths at the convention. In addition to the main exhibition halls, pavilions are set up to focus on the latest specialty areas such as interactive programming, virtual reality, multimedia, HDTV, finance, advertising, and cable systems.

You can really get lost in the crowd at NATPE without a sales representative to help you sell your film. Many of the companies will be looking for product that fits into a particular series rather than stand-alone films or documentaries, so your first task, if you attend the market, will be to focus on only those companies that might have a slot for your film.

As with a film festival or film market, make sure you have prepared appropriate marketing materials that you can use to promote your film. The atmosphere at a television market like NATPE (and even the film markets, for that matter) is more professional than at the film festivals, so guerrilla marketing techniques that would work at Sundance might be an annoyance to the buyers at NATPE. These markets are about hard-core selling and the film's potential commercial value, not about the artistic merit of a film.

As with selling theatrical films, it is a good idea to consult with an experienced publicist to plan your marketing campaign, keeping in mind that the audience consists of television executives who have to be convinced that having your film on their network will draw viewers and thus sell advertising.

Foreign Television Markets

MIP-TV is the major market for foreign television sales. It is held in Cannes during April and runs for six days. One of the strongest of the television markets, producers sell completed programs, including television features, television movies and mini-series, children's programs, and general-interest documentaries to major buyers. Most documentaries are actually sold at MIP-DOC, which is held just before the general market. Feature film producers who go to MIP-TV also sell television rights before a film is finished. (See Chapter 4, "Making an Independent Film," where I discussed foreign pre-sales as a way to finance an independent film. Foreign pre-sales include both foreign theatrical distribution and sales to foreign television.)

MIP-TV attracts the most important European and American broadcasters and, for those who are well-prepared, have set up meetings in advance and have researched the appropriate people to approach, this market can be extremely effective, particularly for experienced producers seeking pre-sales so that they have financing to develop and produce their films. For more information about MIP-TV, go to their website at www.miptv.com.

> **CAUTION**
>
> ## Counterpoint
>
> For the documentary producer with a single documentary to sell, MIP-TV can be a very expensive, frustrating, and unproductive experience. The majority of potential buyers are not interested in stand-alone documentaries so the lack of a slate of programs or films will make selling your film difficult. At a market as high-powered as this, the major buyers are looking to develop long-term relationships with regular content suppliers.

The second major television market, MIPCOM, is run by the same company and is also held in Cannes, in September/October for five days. It is really the fall counterpart to MIP-TV. The activities and business handled at MIPCOM are essentially the same as at MIP-TV—producers and buyers make deals for the sale and purchase of films and programs, arrange co-productions and financing, and network. It attracts both programming executives and corporate executives who are concerned about their companies' positioning in the increasingly global television business. It is a well-run market, where large corporations can do multi-million-dollar world sales, and small sales agents can sell films territory by territory.

MIPCOM is preceded by MIPCOM Junior, a series of screenings of children's and youth programs. MIPCOM Junior is held on the Saturday and Sunday before MIPCOM opens.

Public Television

If you are going to try to sell your film yourself, whether directly to a network or cable company or at a television market, you should know something about the kinds of programming each television network or cable company does.

One of the most receptive arenas for new filmmakers is public television. The Public Broadcasting System (PBS), the only non-commercial television network in the United States (supported only by gifts and grants rather than by advertising or paid subscribers), was founded in 1969. It is a non-profit media enterprise owned and operated by the nation's 349 public television stations that, according to its mission statement, seeks quality programs that "inform, inspire, and delight."

Available to 99 percent of American homes with televisions, PBS serves nearly 100 million people each week. Public television gets more viewers than most of the popular basic cable channels. From October to December 2000, 92.7 million viewers in 56 million households watched public TV each week, according to the Nielsen Television Index (NTI). This represents 54.8 percent of America's 102.2 million households with TVs.

During prime time in the same period, public TV was watched each week in 31.1 million households by 44.9 million people. During the October–December 2000 period, public TV's average prime-time rating was 2.0, compared with 1.5 for TBS, 1.3 for USA, 1.3 for Lifetime, 1.2 for Nickelodeon, 1.0 for A&E, 0.9 for Discovery Channel, 0.9 for CNN, and 0.6 for the History Channel.

PBS does not itself produce programs but distributes a comprehensive package of programs to its member stations. Programs include children's, cultural, educational, history, nature, news, public affairs, science, and skills programs. Programs in the package are obtained from PBS stations, independent producers, and sources around the world, like the well-known British Broadcasting Corporation, the BBC.

> **Script Notes** _____
>
> The Corporation for Public Broadcasting (CPB), is a private non-profit corporation created by Congress in 1967. It is the source of partial funding for many PBS programs. When applying for a CPB grant to develop or produce a film, it helps to work through one of the local PBS stations, although it is not a requirement. Other sources of funds for PBS programs include the National Endowment for the Arts, the National Endowment for the Humanities, and many private foundations.

PBS works closely with its member stations to develop programming for its national schedule. Producers may submit projects to PBS directly or through a local public television station. Stations may offer producers advice on matching their project to PBS's mission and content priorities, potential help with development financing, and guidance in the production, marketing, and outreach of an accepted film. In addition, stations broadcast their own local programming, and programs with a local or regional focus often find more acceptance at the local station level. Producers should contact the local station's program director for more information on their programming priorities and proposal submission processes.

If you hope to have your film shown on PBS, there is a set of criteria that are outlined by the network. In general, they require that program topics should be "interesting to a wide audience and be of a high caliber throughout all elements of the production, with a well-crafted story line, strong visuals, and a clear purpose." Of course, if your film isn't all that, it probably won't get distribution anywhere.

PBS also gives the following more specific guidlines for producers to keep in mind when submitting a proposal. All PBS proposals and programs are evaluated according to the following criteria:

- Does the program/proposal match the mission of PBS?
- Does the program/proposal enhance the viewer's understanding of the subject?
- Does the program/proposal educate and inform?
- Is the program/proposal entertaining? Does it engage the viewer?
- Does the program/proposal have obvious opportunities to create programming and promotional links between the national PBS service and the local public television stations through TV, the Internet, and print?
- Can the PBS member stations use the program to benefit their specific communities?
- Does the program/proposal have a plan for interactive platforms?
- Does the program/proposal continue the tradition of high-quality programming that PBS is known for?
- Does the program add to the value of public television?

Of the approximately 846 hours available for national prime-time programming each year, continuing series, such as American Experience, NOVA, and Frontline, make up over 500 hours of the schedule. As a result, PBS has very few slots in each season for new series and specials, so even this most open of networks is very, very competitive. PBS currently receives over 3,000 submissions per year totaling close to 10,000 hours of programming. Programs and proposals that do not adhere to the criteria outlined previously will not be given serious consideration for development, production financing, or broadcast.

Commercial Broadcast Networks

The commercial broadcast networks include the three original broadcast networks—ABC, CBS, and NBC—and a number of newer broadcast networks. Each network both owns some television stations and has other stations that are affiliated with the network. For example, NBC owns 13 stations and has over 200 *affiliates*. The big three networks, plus PBS, also reach approximately 99 percent of American homes.

The other commercial broadcast networks are Fox Broadcasting Company (FBC/Fox), United Paramount Network (UPN), The WB Television Network (WB), PAX TV (PAX Net), Univision, America One Television, FamilyNet, and Trinity Broadcast Network (TBN).

Fox, UPN, and WB are networks that were formed by three major studios—Fox, Paramount, and Warner Brothers (WB)—in the 1990s. Each studio hoped to carve out niches for the programs they produce. The WB network, for example, targets teens and young adults ages 12 to 34. It is available in 88 percent of the country and airs prime-time programming Sunday through Fridays, with children's programming airing weekday afternoons and Saturday mornings.

PAX TV, the nation's seventh broadcast television network, made its debut in August 1998. It is committed to airing "family-friendly" programming. The network promotes itself as featuring shows that embody "strong values," showcase "positive role models," and are "free of excessive violence, explicit sex, or foul language." If you feel that your film is family-oriented, it might be worth contacting this network.

America One and FamilyNet are smaller family-oriented networks. Univision is the Spanish-language network, and TBN is a Christian religious-oriented network.

In deciding whether to approach a commercial network about selling your film, look at the types of movies they broadcast and see if your film appeals to the same audience. A hip/dark thriller, for example, wouldn't work on one of the family-oriented networks, but it might be of interest to Fox, WB, or UPN.

Verbal Action

syndication   Selling television shows or packages of shows to owned and operated local stations rather than distributing through a television network.

window   The period of time a theatrical distributor has to distribute a film before its television debut.

rating   A number that rates how well a television show has done by estimating the number of viewers. Most television ratings are through the Nielsen Television Index.

affiliates   In television, stations that are affiliated with a particular network, such as NBC.

The Major Cable Networks

In the late 1970s and early 1980s, cable networks, such as Home Box Office (HBO), Entertainment and Sports Programming Network (ESPN), Cable News Network (CNN), and Cable Satellite Public Affairs Network (C-SPAN), began to appear that increasingly delivered quality and/or specialized programs to targeted audiences.

Today, there are literally hundreds of networks with programs designed to meet every kind of audience. In addition to the large, well-known networks like Turner Broadcast Systems, which produces news via CNN as well as a variety of entertainment and documentary programs, there are smaller and more specialized networks, such as The Military Channel, The Golf Channel, The Weather Channel, and The Recovery Network, that are going for ever-smaller niche audiences.

Not all networks run in every market. It usually depends on what channels a cable system owner or satellite system decides to carry. Cable systems may range in size from the small-town independent cable operators to large corporations, like Time Warner, Westinghouse, Fox Communications, and TCI. The newer satellite systems include Direct TV, DISH network, and others.

Today, cable and satellite systems attract 80 million viewers nationwide. Cable and/or satellite is available to 80 percent of American households. Cable networks have grown so much that they now have captured more than 30 percent of the prime-time viewing audience, while the major networks have slipped to only 50 percent.

HBO and Cinemax

Launched in November of 1972, the pay-cable station that is the favorite of the Hollywood film community advertises itself as "It's not TV, it's HBO." Home Box Office is certainly the most successful premium television network, whether success is measured by operating performance, number of subscribers, awards, ratings, or critical acclaim. AOL-Time Warner owns both HBO and Cinemax, two 24-hour services, which had grown to 36.7 million U.S. subscribers by 2000. HBO is the highest-rated cable service during the day and in prime time.

HBO shows both original series, including the hits *The Sopranos* and *Sex in the City*, and original movies and mini-series. HBO is also known for its documentaries and major sporting events, such as boxing matches. It also fills its programming slots with Hollywood and independent films, usually those that have done well theatrically. Each month, HBO offers more than 90 theatrical motion pictures—ranging from top box-office hits to award-winning smaller films. HBO and some of the other major cable networks like Cinemax and Showtime also have several subsidiary channels that target specific audiences.

The all-movie service, Cinemax, is the second-highest-rated pay-cable service after HBO. It features more than 1,600 theatrical movie titles a year, more than any other premium service. The two networks are available to subscribers across the United States in the same way other networks are—via cable, C-band satellite, direct broadcast satellite (DBS), and microwave (MMDS). The availability of HBO is also advertised by hotels and motels across the country to lure guests to their facilities.

Showtime

Launched in 1976, Showtime, like HBO, is a major pay-cable network that shows both studio and independent films, original Showtime movies, original series, and documentaries. Considered to be HBO's poor cousin in the Hollywood community because it doesn't pay producers and talent as well as HBO, it still manages to attract major talent for many of its popular and controversial original productions. Showtime also produces more original programming than any other pay-cable network, including HBO.

Like HBO, Showtime buys both studio and independent films to run when it is not showing its own original programming. Also, like HBO, Showtime is owned by a major entertainment company, Viacom, which also owns Paramount. Showtime also operates an all-movie channel, The Movie Channel.

A&E, The History Channel, and The Biography Channel

A&E Television Networks, which owns several cable channels including the Arts and Entertainment Channel (A&E), The History Channel, and The Biography Channel, is a joint venture of the Hearst Corporation, ABC, Inc., and NBC.

A&E, with the advertising tag line "escape the ordinary," offers a range of television programming including original series like the *Biography* series and the critically acclaimed *100 Centre Street*, and original movies and documentaries. Recent A&E original movies have included *The Crossing* with Jeff Daniels as General George Washington (2001) and Oscar-winner Timothy Hutton in *The Golden Spiders* (2000).

A&E reaches over 76 million viewers, according to Nielsen reports. In 1999, A&E received 20 prime-time Emmy nominations, the most of any basic cable network, and won 5, including Best Mini-series for *Horatio Hornblower*.

The History Channel, which reaches over 62 million viewers, bills itself as the only place "Where the Past Comes Alive." The History Channel features documentaries about historical subjects and history series.

The Biography Channel provides viewers episodes of *Biography*, documentaries, and original short features about interesting and famous people 24 hours a day.

Bravo

Bravo features documentary programs, studio and international films, and theater, dance, and music presentations. It is known for showing high-quality independent films and award-winning foreign films. Some recent films on Bravo include *Clockers* (Spike Lee, 1995), *Resurrection* (Daniel Petrie, 1980), and *Run Lola Run* (Tom Tykwer, 1998). Bravo also presents such film-related original series as "Inside the Actors Studio" and is the official U.S. network of Cirque du Soleil. Distributed on basic cable, Bravo is seen in more than 53 million homes nationwide.

The Independent Film Channel

Bravo Networks also manages and operates the Independent Film Channel (IFC), which is an excellent resource for independent filmmakers. Launched in 1994, IFC features award-winning independent films, original series, documentaries and live events. IFC is the first network to show only the best films from the independent film world. Films that have been shown on IFC include *The Opposite of Sex* (Don Roos, 1998), *Breaking the Waves* (Lars Van Trier, 1996), and *Do the Right Thing* (Spike Lee, 1989).

IFC also covers film festivals and events, like the Independent Spirit Awards and the Cannes Film Festival, giving viewers behind-the-scenes looks at the happenings at those events as well as live coverage of the events in progress.

Cutaway

In 1997, Independent Film Channel Entertainment was established to support IFC's goals of creating and showcasing quality independent films to the widest audience possible. With many services available to independent filmmakers, IFC Entertainment might be a valuable resource to contact early in your production process. IFC Entertainment consists of IFC Productions, a feature-film production company; IFC Films, a small theatrical-film distribution company; Next Wave Films, established to provide finishing funds and other vital support to emerging filmmakers; and IFC Originals, which produces original programming for the network. In addition, IFC Productions launched InDigEnt, an entity that aids established filmmakers who want to shoot productions on digital video for the big screen.

The Sundance Channel

The Sundance Channel was launched in the United States in 1996 as a venture between Robert Redford, Showtime Networks, and Universal Studios. Like the Independent Film Channel, it is one of the best resources in television for independent filmmakers. Redford had started the Sundance concept with the establishment of the Sundance Institute in

1981 to support the development of independent film projects. That led to the creation in 1985 of the now world-renowned Sundance Film Festival, held annually in Utah (see Chapter 22, "Independent Feature Distribution"), and finally this television channel.

A premium television service under the creative direction of Redford and the management of Showtime, the Sundance Channel brings to television viewers the film festival experience by presenting a diverse selection of feature films, shorts, documentaries, and international cinema—all uncut and uninterrupted. Since its inception, it has quickly expanded into over 20 million households.

The Sundance Channel believes that "what is possible is more interesting than what is safe." It claims to show more of the world's most innovative films in a day than most people will see in a year. Between screenings, there are original shows that introduce the filmmakers and explore the creative process behind the films.

Turner Network Television

Turner Network Television (TNT), currently available in 75 percent of U.S. television homes, is Turner Broadcasting System (TBS), Inc.'s 24-hour, advertiser-supported service, offering original motion pictures and mini-series, original series, live events, sporting events such as the yearly Wimbledon tennis tournament, reruns of popular television series, and contemporary films from the world's largest film library—the combined Turner and Warner Bros. film libraries.

TBS Superstation and TNT ranked No. 1 and No. 2 among adults in basic cable prime time for the first six months of 2001. In July 2001, TNT unveiled a new look, logo, and tagline, "TNT: We Know Drama." TNT is really more of an outlet for original television movies made by independent producers than a place to sell already produced theatrical films, because most of TNT's non-original television movies will come from those already in the vast Turner and Warner Bros. libraries.

Lifetime

If your film is likely to appeal primarily to women, you might consider approaching the Lifetime Network. Lifetime is dedicated to providing contemporary, innovative entertainment that is of particular interest to women.

Launched in February 1984, Lifetime was created by the merger of Daytime and Cable Health Network (CHN). Daytime, operated by Hearst/ABC Video Services, began in March 1982 as a four-hour-per-day weekday service featuring alternative programming for women. CHN, operated by Viacom, debuted in June 1982 as a 24-hour service offering programs on personal and family health, fitness, science, and medicine. Beginning in 1994, Lifetime began advertising itself as "Television for Women" and also began an ambitious expansion of original programming and public service initiatives targeted to women. The network has subsequently experienced its best ratings ever, with prime-time audiences increasing by over 121 percent since 1993.

In July 1998, Lifetime launched its first sister channel, the Lifetime Movie Network, a 24-hour movie service that shows films that have appealed or are likely to appeal to women.

USA and the SCI FI Channel

The USA Network, owned and operated by USA Cable, a division of USA Networks, Inc.'s entertainment unit, is a basic cable leading provider of original series and feature movies, sports events, off-network television shows, and Hollywood and independent theatrical films. USA Network is available in 80 percent of all U.S. homes—that is, more than 82 million homes.

The SCI FI Channel is also owned and operated by USA Cable. Launched in 1992, SCI FI features a continuous stream of science fiction-oriented films, new and original series, and special events, as well as classic sci-fi series such as *The Twilight Zone*, and fantasy and horror programming. It reaches 75 million homes.

The Family Channel

Available in 97 percent of all households that get basic cable, The Family Channel is one of America's Top 10 basic cable channels, reaching over 63 million households nationwide. Each week, more than 40 million households tune in to original and exclusive series, original movies, and family theatrical features that the network shows. As one of only four basic cable networks the top 30 advertisers buy, The Family Channel is a good outlet for films that appeal to children and family-oriented audiences.

MTV and VH1

MTV Networks owns and operates several popular basic cable television programming services, including MTV: Music Television. MTV is actually the world's most widely distributed television network, reaching 384 million households in 140 territories. VH1, also operated by the MTV Networks, reaches over 103 million households around the world.

Both of these networks air movies, including original television films and already-released films that have as their subject matter music and musicians.

Black Entertainment Television

Black Entertainment Television (BET) is the largest national cable network established to appeal to African Americans, reaching 66 million U.S. households. Owned by Viacom, BET also runs The Jazz Channel, the country's only 24-hour network devoted to jazz music, and BET International, which reaches 30 countries in Europe and 36 countries in Africa. In addition, BET has a production entity, BET Pictures, which produces made-for-TV movies and documentaries. BET also airs already produced films that are of interest to African Americans.

It is clear from this overview, which covers only some of the possible television outlets, that television offers many opportunities to distribute well-produced, entertaining films. But not every film will fit into the slots available or will work with the programming desires of the various television networks, however. In the next chapter, I'll look at what you can do if you haven't found a domestic distributor and haven't been able to sell your film to television.

The Least You Need to Know

- ◆ The amount of money you can negotiate for a television sale of a film will depend, among other things, on the success of your prior theatrical release.
- ◆ Television markets are high-powered sales events, and most producers will do better when working with a sales representative or agent.
- ◆ Although receptive to new filmmakers, public television is very competitive and films must fit into its guidelines.
- ◆ You should be familiar with the audiences targeted by the different commercial broadcast and cable networks if you are interested in selling your film to any one of them.

Alternative and New Media Distribution

In This Chapter

◆ Summarizing the conventional film distribution route

◆ Alternative ways of getting theatrical distribution

◆ Knowing the important non-theatrical film market

◆ Distributing films on the Internet

If you are a new filmmaker with a finished film in your hands, your primary goals now are to get your work seen by audiences, introduce yourself and your work to the people and companies in the film and television businesses, get your investors paid back, and get enough money to develop your next movie. Of course, if you were able to sell your movie to a theatrical distributor, you are already on your way.

If not, then you are among the many filmmakers who still have the above goals, and you have to find a way to distribute your film. Your film is not part of the conventional distribution channels because you didn't make a film that is typically distributed by commercial distributors (such as a short film or an educational film) or because, with all the competition, your film was simply not picked up for distribution by a theatrical distributor. You must find another way to earn back the money spent on your film and get your film seen by audiences.

What do you do? After presenting a timeline for the typical conventional distribution channels that I have discussed in the previous three chapters, I'll cover both some old and some new alternatives for distribution if your film isn't part of that traditional distribution channel.

The Life of a Conventionally Distributed Film

Before covering alternative methods of distribution, let's look at the life of a film that makes it into the conventional film distribution process. Both Hollywood films and independent films that are distributed domestically in theaters and are then picked up by television will follow this basic pattern.

Features that have been picked up by a theatrical distributor that believes the film will be able to compete in the theatrical marketplace are released in theaters, using the marketing and distribution services of that distributor—either a major, mini-major, or smaller independent motion picture distributor. The initial theatrical release is usually for two to six months. Sometimes distributors may release features in the foreign market first, especially if foreign pre-sales have been obtained.

About three months after the theatrical release begins, a film will start either its home video (and DVD) or pay-per-view distribution and continue to play in that market for at least seven months. About six months after its theatrical release starts, the film will be released to pay-per-view, (if it was previously released to home video) or to home video (if it was previously released to pay-per-view). The film may be simultaneously released in the foreign markets, if the film had started in the domestic theatrical market first. The movie will play in the home video or pay-per-view market for about six months and in the foreign markets for at least thirteen months.

About one year after the start of theatrical release, a typical film will then go to pay-cable for about six months. Very successful features may then premiere on network TV about two years after the initial theatrical release. After a series of runs on network TV for a period of about two years, those films will then usually return to pay-cable for another year and a half.

Low-budget movies or films that were not as successful at the box office will most likely skip network TV and go directly into syndication, where they are sold to the thousands of independently owned television stations nationally and internationally. Syndication will generally start about three and a half years after the film's initial theatrical release and continue for at least two and a half years—possibly for as long as ten years.

That's not even it for the life of a film. By the time it's that old, it may even then be sold to one of the cable networks that play film classics! So it's great to get your film into this long distribution channel, with opportunities for it to be seen and revenue coming from different sources at different times. Unfortunately, very few films each year make it into this conventional track, particularly given the number of films that are produced. For those that don't, there are some alternatives.

Four Walling and Distributors for Hire

Television sales and home video distribution are virtually impossible without a theatrical release first. If you have been unable to get a theatrical distributor, you might want to consider *four walling* your film to get that all-important theatrical release.

This process involves contacting theater owners directly and making a deal with them, usually to rent a theater for a weekly flat fee. In order to rent a theater, you must be able to provide the theaters with one-sheets and also have all the materials for an advertising campaign, including newspaper ads and possibly radio blurbs (see Chapter 21, "The Hollywood Distribution System"). It may be easier to make a deal with one of the rapidly disappearing independent theaters than with a theater that is part of a large national theater chain, but either is possible.

You will generally be able to keep all the box-office receipts when you four wall your film. You may not be able to break even or earn a profit, however, after you subtract the cost of renting the theater and paying for the advertising campaign.

There are also small distributors for hire who will basically do the same thing for you in many different markets for a price. In this scenario, however, you will not be able to keep your box-office receipts. For a fee of $100,000 or more, a distributor for hire will take your film around to small, privately owned theaters around the country. The distributor will pay the exhibitor a small fee to show the film and the exhibitor will also be able to keep the box-office income. You will have to supply the distributor with a certain number of release prints, one-sheets, and newspaper ads. This is an expensive alternative but it may ultimately help you to get a television sale and/or a decent home video distributor.

Direct-to-Video

With the increase in the number of films made each year and the ever-increasing costs of marketing theatrical films, it makes economic sense for many feature films to go directly to the home video market without a theatrical release. Unfortunately, only certain genres of films tend to go directly to video. If your film doesn't fit into one of those categories, it may be difficult to get a distributor for home videos without a theatrical release.

Typical direct-to-video films are those in the horror, erotic thriller, and martial arts genres, what are also called "B" movies or "exploitation" films of the *Killer Klowns from Outer Space* variety. The budgets for these films are rarely over a million. They are often shot on

16mm or on video and the stories are usually recycled versions of movies from the same genre. Many companies and producers make their livings making these direct-to-video films.

Hollywood studios also occasionally make direct-to-video films. Usually, they are inexpensively made sequels to well-known films. Or a studio may decide after making a film that it is too weak to be successfully marketed theatrically, so the studio will send it directly to the video market through its home entertainment division.

Independent films that are released and distributed outside the studio system unfortunately have a difficult time getting home video distribution because they are often not stocked in the big video chains like Blockbuster. They usually end up being sold in video stores that specialize in independent films, or through outlets such as Alwaysi.com or IndieDVD (see the following section).

Short Film Distribution: Your Calling Card

Short films are often shown in festivals, and some may get distribution on the Independent Film Channel or the Sundance Channel or may be packaged as part of a collection by companies like IndieDVD or Matrixx Internet Distribution (discussed later in the chapter).

Most short films, however, are used as a sample of a filmmaker's work—a calling card. Your film can be the way you introduce yourself and your work to people in the Hollywood community that you want to represent you or develop your next film with you. A film is an expensive resumé, but then film is an expensive art form.

Script Notes _____

Many Hollywood film executives don't want to view short films, although some will. A better strategy than sending your film around might be to find a script that you are passionate about, try to get a meeting to pitch that project and leave behind both the script and a copy of your film. The combination of an exciting new project and the proof of your abilities that your calling-card film provides may convince the company to work with you.

Non-Theatrical Distribution

There are many forms of non-theatrical film distribution, including educational (schools and universities), institutional (such as libraries, clubs, and community groups), ships, airlines, trains, hotel movies, and corporate distribution.

Some films are made specifically for the non-theatrical market only. These include educational films designed as curriculum aids, training how-to films and industrial films. Non-theatrical distribution, however, can also be a significant aftermarket for movies that have already appeared in theaters or on television. Many producers lose potential revenue by ignoring the non-theatrical market for their films.

If you have retained non-theatrical rights to your film or have made a film for the non-theatrical market, you should either contact a non-theatrical distributor or, depending on the kind of film, consider self-distribution non-theatrically.

Non-theatrical distribution is a specialized business, and some companies do this exclusively. Some theatrical home video distributors have a non-theatrical division, and others may contract with a subdistributor to handle this market.

Most non-theatrical distributors sell their films through a catalogue that lists all the video or multimedia products that they handle. They have extensive mailing lists of people and institutions that have rented or bought similar movies in the past. They may also have a sales force with key personnel in school systems, libraries, and corporations. For some distributors, however, mailing out the catalogue once a year is the extent of their marketing effort.

Theatrical distributors generally deduct marketing expenses from the producer's share of the income, but many non-theatrical distributors do not. Instead, they pay the producer a flat percentage or royalty for each video sale or rental. The producer might get anywhere from 10 to 30 percent of the gross, depending on the deal.

If you decide to self-distribute, you may be able to make more money because you will be able to do marketing that is targeted to your movie, as opposed to being part of a catalog with many other films. Self-distributors generally print up a flyer or brochure and may do a mass mailing using computerized mailing lists. There are lists available for almost every category of buyer or field of study. Your flyer should list awards, reviews, and endorsements by people in the field you are targeting. The response rate to a mailing is often only a few percent, but this may be enough to generate a profit. You should also have a poster made that can be distributed with the film for individual screenings. Many non-theatrical movies are also accompanied by study guides or training materials.

If you decide to self-distribute in the non-theatrical market, you will need to invest at least several thousand dollars. A campaign requires expenses for videos, publicity, business forms, shipping, and costs such as festival entrance fees. There are also the continuing expenses of telephone and promotional mailings. It can be a full-time job, especially in the first few months of the movie's release, unless you use a *fulfillment house* that takes the orders, ships the videos, and does the billing for a fee.

Certain costs, such as advertising, do not increase much for two films to share, so it can be cheaper to work with someone who is distributing a similar film. Distribution cooperatives, like New Day Films (www.newday.com), help keep costs down by pooling resources.

Cutaway
Begun in the early 1970s by filmmakers who had produced feminist films that most distribution companies considered too controversial to distribute, New Day is a unique cooperative. The organization distributes films about social issues to educational organizations nationwide, including high schools, colleges, universities, and libraries, among others. Its central office books and ships films, bills customers, issues monthly accounting and royalty statements, and provides mailing lists of market-tested customers. New Day's collection is small and specialized to maximize its effectiveness in the educational film market. New Day members screen and select new titles from among those submitted by filmmakers seeking admission to the co-op. On the average, filmmakers who distribute through New Day keep 67 percent of their gross revenues after paying their share of New Day costs. Most commercial distributors, on the other hand, take 80 percent of gross, leaving the filmmaker with only 20 percent.

Certain non-theatrical videos that fall within popular categories such as exercise, health, or inspirational films, may be handled by specialized distributors. Other videos may accompany a book about the same topic and be sold in bookstores. Still others may feature a lecturer and be sold at his or her lectures or seminars. The important thing in finding a distributor is to see what other videos that distributor has handled and how successful the distribution has been. Don't hesitate to call another filmmaker to ask about his or her experience with a potential non-theatrical distributor.

The Internet

The rapid development of digital technology may bring some radical changes to the distribution of films. It is a little too early to tell exactly what may happen in the future, but already the Internet has become a viable new tool for both promoting and distributing films, giving independent filmmakers audiences they have never had access to before.

Distributing your film via the Internet is possible in several ways today. This form of distribution is evolving so rapidly that many things may have changed by the time this book is printed, but what follows is an overview of some of the opportunities that are available to filmmakers at the time of writing.

There are two warnings as you look over the companies and the services listed here. First, the fact that a company is included here is not an endorsement of that particular company over any other company that is doing Internet distribution. The companies were selected only because they seem to cover the range of film distribution activities available on the Internet and because links to these companies came up on various independent film sites. You should do a thorough investigation and consult an entertainment attorney who is experienced in Internet or new media deals before signing a contract with any company.

Second, it may not be wise to give away the Internet distribution rights to your film until you have exhausted all other avenues of distributing it. If you do, you may not be able to get a good (if any) theatrical distribution deal because you will have prematurely sold off those rights to your film.

Some of the companies that distribute films on the Internet are backed by studios and some are independent. CinemaNow, for example, is a two-year-old online feature distributor backed by Lion's Gate. Another site, which is backed by five major studios, will be opening in 2002. By getting involved in Internet distribution themselves, the major studios may be hoping to avoid a movie version of the music downloading site Napster.

Script Notes

Five major studios will launch together an Internet distribution site in 2002. The infusion of Hollywood dollars into Internet distribution could create better delivery systems and bring online film to more mainstream viewers. It might enable the opening of movies with limited theatrical releases to anyone with a broadband connection. Non-studio filmmakers will be allowed to submit their features to the yet-to-be-named site and filmmakers will be able to release their films online through other companies in a non-exclusive agreement.

To use online film distribution, Internet users must usually have DSL or at least a high-speed modem on their computer and must download software that is compatible with the distribution method used by the particular site. Most sites charge per-film or per-month fees for viewing films and also draw revenues from advertising and corporate partnerships brought in by their user demographics.

Some of the companies that are doing Internet distribution now include the following.

BijouFlix

Founded in April, 1998, BijouFlix is one of the longest-running indie videostream sites on the web. It has received media coverage in *Newsweek* (Best of the Web), *WIRED* (Top 10), *Fade In* (Top 100 of the Web), and many others, along with television coverage on ABC's *World News Tonight* and the same network's *WebShow*.

BijouFlix was founded by movie-makers to create what movie-makers desperately need—distribution to new worldwide audiences. The company started as a distribution cooperative but has grown into much more. BijouFlix does not buy movies from their creators and then take most of the profits as do most distributors. Instead, the co-op helps filmmakers find distribution in both new and traditional media outlets. BijouFlix shares gross (not net) royalties with all movie-makers.

An important difference between BijouFlix and other Internet distributors is that it is non-exclusive for the net, which lets a filmmaker maintain control over his or her work and still receive royalties.

BijouFlix is looking for "movies" shot in any format, rather than the kind of "films" that dominate art festivals. They want movies that entertain, whether they are deconstructed, experimental, non-narrative, animated, or a classic story.

CinemaNow

CinemaNow (www.cinemanow.com) is a leading distributor of feature films on-demand over the Internet and is currently delivering movies to over 550,000 users per month. CinemaNow is owned by Lion's Gate Entertainment, Microsoft, and Blockbuster. The company holds the exclusive Internet distribution rights to the most extensive and comprehensive library of feature films available on-demand via the Internet and through private broadband networks.

The CinemaNow film library of approximately 1,000 feature-length films includes titles from Lion's Gate Entertainment, Trimark Pictures, Tai Seng Video, Allied Artists, and Salvation Films. In addition, CinemaNow continually acquires both libraries and individual films by means of its own acquisition department and as part of its relationship with Lion's Gate.

CinemaNow provides films on an ad-supported as well as a pay-per-view and subscription basis. Ad-supported films feature video ads that are targeted to viewers through user profiles. The pay-per-view system offers films at a variety of prices while the subscription service provides users with an unlimited number of viewings of select titles for a single monthly fee. The user experience on CinemaNow is best described as "online DVD," where the viewer can watch the film and also access a database of images, information, and interactivity related to that particular film.

The films on CinemaNow are shown using a customized version of Microsoft's Windows Media Player with a bookmarking function called "CinemaLater" that allows users to save their places at any time during a film and resume watching at that exact point whenever they return to the site. The CinemaNow player also provides the ability to change *streaming* speeds while the film is playing. CinemaNow seeks to provide the best video-on-demand experience available via the Internet. CinemaNow also licenses its films to a wide range of third-party websites.

Verbal Action _____

four walling   In film distribution, when a filmmaker independently contracts with a theater to show his or her film for a flat fee for a period of time, usually a week.

fulfillment houses   Companies that handle taking orders, billing, and mailing items that are for sale, such as self-distributed videos.

streaming   In Internet jargon, a term for information flowing across a channel, such as a film viewable on a computer via the Internet.

IndieDVD

Founded in 1999, IndieDVD is an alliance of independent filmmakers and promoters that distributes films that have only been in film festivals to the home retail market through creating and marketing quality DVDs. An independent entertainment DVD label, IndieDVD representatives travel to film festivals, such as Cannes and Sundance, to acquire high-quality feature films that will appeal to a wide variety of audience tastes. The company also distributes a regular series of short film compilations called "The Fusion Series," giving short films a distribution outlet besides festivals.

IndieDVD offers profit-sharing deals with filmmakers and works through several channels of distribution—Internet sites, self-fulfillment at maximum retail (where the order is forwarded to the filmmaker who is responsible for shipping the DVD or video), Tapeworm, Amazon.com, Django's, Rentrak, Barnes & Noble, and other video distributors, specialty video sales outlets, and by subscription. The company is working to expand its distribution base to obtain a larger audience for independent filmmakers, and is joining with new retailers and distributors all the time. IndieDVD can be reached online at www.indidvd.com.

IFILM

IFILM (www.IFILM.com) claims to be the largest Internet portal celebrating the world of film. Through a number of online and offline distribution deals, it provides filmmakers with options for getting films onto other websites, as well as onto DVDs, television, and even into movie theaters. With over 80,000 films, IFILM has the most comprehensive listing of feature and short films online, providing consumers with the largest online video-on-demand library in the world, programmed in genre-specific movie channels by film experts. IFILM also offers news, reviews, trailers, and movie showcases, as well as robust user communities and a comparison DVD and video shopping guide. IFILM has partnerships with AMC Theatres, TiVo, Yahoo!, and the Independent Film Channel.

The Bit Screen

The Bit Screen delivers first-run Internet films and web series directly to your desktop. The company adds new programs every week on its main site and on The Best of The Bit Screen on Broadcast.com (www.broadcast.com/video). It also e-mails a weekly newsletter to let viewers know what's coming up next on the screen. The company advertises, "If you want reruns, go watch cable. If you want something new, keep watching the screen—The Bit Screen."

The Bit Screen looks for Internet-based films, animations, and episodics, 1 to 10 minutes long. The Bit Screen considers itself a lab for exploring how an interactive Internet medium impacts storytelling. It is looking for shorts that are created to work in and with the Internet environment—programs that will define and expand the concept of film in the future.

The Sync

The Sync is an Internet film production company that also distributes independent films. The mission of the company is to create compelling, interactive content that is specifically tailored for the "Net Generation," the highly online 16–34 year-old demographic. The Sync aims to create "a totally new medium," aimed at the needs and expectations of the Net Generation audience. The Sync's shows have won acclaim from publications such as *Entertainment Weekly*, *Rolling Stone*, and *USA Today*. And The Sync was the first webcaster to have its work displayed at the New York Museum of Modern Art. Besides all-original productions, The Sync also works with content partners and independent filmmakers to bring a wide mix of entertainment and tech-entertainment shows to its viewers.

ALWAYSi

ALWAYSi seeks to deliver motion picture and television-type entertainment to a potential audience of millions worldwide. The company wants to work with creators of independent entertainment and develop with them new revenue and distribution opportunities. They also provide independent filmmakers with an exhibition platform to showcase their material to entertainment talent representatives, acquisitions executives, and other industry professionals. And their website is a place where working professionals can keep current on industry news. ALWAYSi has a library of over 2,000 feature-length films, short films, animation, and TV-like series that is available to view in streaming formats.

AtomShockwave

AtomShockwave distributes entertainment properties across the Internet, broadband services, and mobile devices, as well as traditional outlets such as television, theaters, and airlines. AtomShockwave has an extensive catalog of games, film, and animation content. It has two Internet destinations that reach a mass audience of more than 15 million unique users every month—AtomFilms.com and shockwave.com. It is seeking quality films and animations for worldwide commercial distribution, and accepts live-action and animation submissions with running times under 30 minutes.

> **CAUTION**
>
> **Counterpoint**
>
> Some Internet distribution companies may ask for the copyright to your film, but you shouldn't give them the copyright to your film. You also shouldn't allow any Internet company to charge you more than 30 percent of the revenues generated from the Internet release of your film, even if the company is affiliated with a major studio. That high of a fee is excessive, since it takes much less effort to distribute movies over the Internet than through conventional channels.

eDigiFilm Entertainment

eDigiFilm Entertainment claims to be looking for "a few good films from independent filmmakers and producers." They distribute not just through the Internet but also do limited theatrical distribution, video/DVD, and television—pay-per-view, cable, and broadcast. If eDigiFilm Entertainment makes an offer for your project, the company promises to work with you to develop an individual strategy specifically tailored for selling and marketing your film.

Matrixx Internet Distribution

Established in February of 1996, Matrixx Internet Distribution (MID) is probably the first Internet distribution company for video-on-demand or VOD. MID offers filmmakers and their investors a way to recoup the cost of the film by distributing it over the Internet by broadband fiber optics, DSL, and last-mile and laser/wireless technologies. MID calls its service "Movies-on-Demand" and has both a Home Video Network website—the world's first online video store—and a pay-per-view website.

Other companies use a "streaming" paradigm instead of a "downloading" paradigm for distributing films on the Internet. MID believes that streaming will ultimately be possible over the Internet but feels it is easier to use the download model now.

At this time, MID is interested in distributing the following types of films or videos over the Internet: 5- to 20-minute shorts, 30-minute shows or documentaries, 85- to 120-minute features, public domain features, sports shows, and music videos.

Conventional distributors typically charge between 30 and 40 percent to distribute feature films. MID charges 25 percent to distribute a film over the Internet and delivers income from gross proceeds of distribution within 24 hours of credit card clearance. MID also offers help to independent filmmakers who are producers interested in constructing their own distribution websites through its BackBone Enterprises consulting division.

As most of the these companies believe, in the not-so-distant future, more and more people will get their movies not from the video store, not from cable TV or from pay-per-view, but directly from their computers. Some companies estimate that by 2003 over 150 million moviegoers may have high-speed access to the Internet as well as computers that can easily display full-color, full-motion video on their monitors or their NTSC and digital TV screens. Increasing bandwidth will provide new high-speed access to films over the Internet making hundreds, if not thousands, of downloads possible each day. Filmmakers and independent producers will benefit from the ability to deliver motion picture product in almost unlimited amounts to new worldwide audiences. Within the next five to ten years, filmmakers could be selling and renting many more copies of their films online than are now possible in home video stores.

Whatever the channel of distribution, however, someone still has to make the films and videos. Films still have to be written, directed, produced, and edited, and still require the collaboration of all of the talented people who are part of the filmmaking process—both behind and in front of the camera. Hopefully, you will be among the makers of quality films for new and growing audiences worldwide. Good luck.

The Least You Need to Know

- A film that is accepted into the conventional distribution channels may be distributed in one venue or another for 6 to 10 years or more.

- A theatrical distribution can be obtained by four walling a film or using a distributor for hire.

- The non-theatrical film market is a specialized market for certain kinds of film, but it should also not be ignored as an aftermarket for films that have already been distributed through conventional channels.

- The Internet is now a viable method for distributing a film, but filmmakers need to carefully investigate the possible options available.

Who's Where?

It's not always easy to find information about companies and organizations involved in the vast entertainment industry. The following list of networks, studios, guilds, and organizations should help.

Broadcast Networks

ABC Entertainment
500 S. Buena Vista Street
Burbank, CA 91521
818-460-7777

America One Television
100 E. Royal Lane
Irving, TX 75039
214-868-1000
214-868-1662 (fax)

American Broadcasting
Company (ABC)
77 W. 66th St.
New York, NY 10023
212-456-7777

CBS Entertainment (LA)
7800 Beverly Blvd.
Los Angeles, CA 90036-2188
323-575-2345

CBS Entertainment (NY)
51 W. 52nd St.
New York, NY 10019
212-975-4321
212-975-7452 (fax)

Familynet
6350 West Freeway
Fort Worth, TX 76150

FOX Broadcasting Co.
10201 W. Pico Blvd.
Los Angeles, CA 90035
310-369-1000

National Broadcasting Company
(NBC)
30 Rockefeller Plaza
New York, NY 10112
212-664-2074
212-664-7541 (fax)

NBC Entertainment
3000 W. Alameda Avenue
Burbank, CA 91523-0001
818-840-4444

Pax Resources/Stations
Paxson Communications Group
601 Clearwater Park Road
West Palm Beach, FL 33401
561-659-4122
561-659-4252 (fax)

PBS
1320 Braddock Place
Alexandria, VA 22314-1698
703-739-5000

Trinity Broadcast Network (TBN)
P.O. Box A
Santa Ana, CA 92711
714-731-1000

United Paramount Network (UPN)
11800 Wilshire Blvd.
Los Angeles, CA 90025
310-575-7000

Univision (Miami)
9405 NW 41st St.
Miami, FL 33178-2301
305-471-3900

Univision (NY)
605 Third Ave.
New York, NY 10158-0180
212-455-5200

W.B. Television Network
4000 Warner Blvd., Bldg. 34-R
Burbank, CA 91522-0001
818-977-5000

Cable Networks

American Independent Network (AIN)
6125 Airport Freeway
Suite 200
Halton City, TX 76117
817-222-1234
817-222-9809 (fax)

Arts & Entertainment (A&E)
The History Channel
235 E. 45th St.
New York, NY 10017
212-661-4500
212-210-9755 (fax)

Bravo
150 Crossways Park West
Woodbury, NY 11797
516-364-2222

Cinemax
1100 Avenue of the Americas
New York, NY 10036
212-512-1000

Comedy Central
1775 Broadway
New York, NY 10019
212-767-8600

Encore
5445 DTC Parkway
Suite 600
Englewood, CO 80111
303-267-4000

FOX Family Channel
10960 Wilshire Blvd.
Los Angeles, CA 90024
310-235-5100

FX Networks
10000 Santa Monica Blvd.
Los Angeles, CA 90067
310-286-3800

HBO (LA)
2049 Century Park East #4100
Los Angeles, CA 90067-3215
310-201-9300

HBO (NY)
1100 Avenue of the Americas
New York, NY 10036
212-512-1000

Lifetime Television (LA)
2049 Century Park East, Suite 840
Los Angeles, CA 90067
310-556-7500

Lifetime Television (NY)
Worldwide Plaza
309 W. 49th St.
New York, NY 10019
212-424-7000

MTV Networks (LA)
2600 Colorado Ave.
Santa Monica, CA 90404
310-752-8000

MTV Networks (NY)
1515 Broadway
New York, NY 10036
212-258-8000

Nickelodeon/Nick At Nite
1515 Broadway, 37th Floor
New York, NY 10036
212-258-7500

Showtime Networks Inc. (NY)
1633 Broadway
New York, NY 10019
212-708-1600

Showtime Networks Inc. (LA)
10880 Wilshire Blvd., Suite 1500
Los Angeles, CA 90024
310-234-5200

The Crime Channel
42335 Washington St. F371
Palm Desert, CA 92211
760-360-6151
760-360-3258 (fax)

The Discovery Channel
7700 Wisconsin Ave.
Bethesda, MD 20814-3522
301-986-0444 ext. 294

The Disney Channel
3800 W. Alameda Ave.
Burbank, CA 91505
818-569-7897

The Family Channel
2877 Guardian Lane
Virginia Beach, VA 23450
Mailing Address:
P.O. Box 64549
Virginia Beach, VA 23467-4549
804-459-6000

The Independent Film Channel
150 Crossways Park West
Woodbury, NY 11797
516-364-2222
516-364-7638 (fax)

Turner Entertainment Group (Atlanta)
1050 Techwood Drive, NW
Atlanta, GA 30318-5604
404-827-1500

Turner Network Television (TNT) (LA)
1888 Century Park East, 14th Floor
Los Angeles, CA, 90067
310-551-6300

USA Network
1230 Avenue of the Americas
New York, NY 10020
212-408-9100

Video Hits One (VH1)
1515 Broadway
New York, NY 10036
212-258-7800

Motion Picture Studios/Distributors

Artisan Entertainment
2700 Colorado Avenue, 2nd Floor
Santa Monica, CA 90404
310-449-9200
www.artisanent.com/

Castle Rock Entertainment
335 N. Maple Drive, #135
Beverly Hills, CA 90210-3867
310-285-2300
www.castle-rock.warnerbros.com/

Dreamworks SKG
100 Universal City Plaza, Bldg. 10
Universal City, CA 91608-1085
818-733-7000
www.dreamworks.com

Fine Line (LA)
116 N. Robertson, Suite 200
Los Angeles, CA 90048
310-854-5811
www.flf.com/

Fine Line (NY)
888 7th Avenue
New York, NY 10106
212-649-4800

Fox Searchlight Pictures
10201 W. Pico Blvd.
Los Angeles, CA 90035
310-369-3226
www.fox.com

Lion's Gate (LA)
4553 Glencoe Avenue, Suite 200
Marina del Rey, CA 90292
310-314-2000
www.lionsgate-ent.com/

Lion's Gate (NY)
561 Broadway, Suite 12B
New York, NY 10012
212-966-4670

Metro Goldwyn Mayer/U.A.
2500 Broadway St.
Santa Monica, CA 90404-3061
310-449-3000
www.mgm.com/

Miramax Films (LA)
7966 Beverly Blvd.
Los Angeles, CA 90048
323-951-4200
www.miramax.com

Miramax Films (NY)
375 Greenwich St.
New York, NY 10013-2338
212-941-3800

New Line Cinema (LA)
116 N. Robertson, Suite 200
Los Angeles, CA 90048
310-854-5811
www.newline.com

New Line Cinema (NY)
888 7th Ave.
New York, NY 10106
212-649-4900

Overseas Film Group/First Look Media
8800 Sunset Blvd.
Los Angeles, CA 90069
310-855-1199
www.firstlookmedia.com

Paramount Classics
5555 Melrose Ave.
Los Angeles, CA 90038
www.paramountclassics.com

Paramount Studios
5555 Melrose Ave.
Los Angeles, CA 90038
323-956-5000
www.paramount.com

Samuel Goldwyn Films
9570 West Pico Blvd., Suite 400
Los Angeles, CA 90035
310-860-3100

Seventh Art Releasing
7551 Sunset Blvd., Suite 104
Los Angeles, CA 90046
323-845-1455
www.7thart.com

Shooting Gallery
609 Greenwich St.
New York, NY 10014
212-905-2000
www.shootinggallery.com

Sony Pictures Entertainment
10202 W. Washington Blvd.
Culver City, CA 90232-3195
310-244-4000
www.spe.sony.com

Sony Pictures Classics
550 Madison Ave., 8th Floor
New York, NY 10022
212-833-8833
www.spe.sony.com/classics/

Strand Releasing
1460 Fourth St., Suite 302
Santa Monica, CA 90401
310-395-5002
www.strandrel.com

Stratosphere Entertainment
767 Fifth Ave.
New York, NY 10153
212-605-1010
www.stratospherefilm.com

Twentieth Century Fox
10201 W. Pico Blvd.
Los Angeles, CA 90035
310-369-1000
www.fox.com

Universal
100 Universal Plaza
Universal City, CA 91608-1085
818-777-1000
www.mca.com

USA Films (NY)
65 Bleeker St., 2nd Floor
New York, NY 10012
www.octoberfilms.com/

USA Films (West Coast)
100 N. Crescent Drive
Beverly Hills, CA 90210
310-385-4400

Viacom Entertainment
5555 Melrose Ave.
Los Angeles, CA 90038
323-956-5000
www.viacom.com

The Walt Disney Company
500 South Buena Vista St.
Burbank, CA 91521-0001
818-560-1000
www.disney.com

Warner Bros. Studios
4000 Warner Blvd.
Burbank, CA 91522-0001
818-954-6000
www.warnerbros.com

Guilds/Unions/Associations

Academy of Motion Picture Arts and
Sciences (AMPAS)
8949 Wilshire Blvd.
Beverly Hills, CA 90211-1972
310-247-3000
310-859-9351 (fax)
www.oscars.org

Academy of Television Arts &
Sciences (ATAS)
5220 Lankershim Blvd.
N. Hollywood, CA 91601
818-754-2800
818-761-2827 (fax)
www.emmys.org

Actors Equity Association (LA)
5757 Wilshire Blvd, Suite 1
Los Angeles, CA 90036
323-634-1750
323-634-1777 (fax)

Actors Equity Association (NY)
165 West 46th St.
New York, NY 10036
212-869-8530
212-719-9815 (fax)

Alliance of Motion Picture &
Television Producers
15503 Ventura Blvd.
Encino, CA 91436
818-995-3600
818-382-1793 (fax)

American Association of Producers (AAP)
10850 Wilshire Blvd., 9th Floor
Los Angeles, CA 90024
310-446-1000
310-446-1600 (fax)
www.tvproducers.com

American Federation of Television and Radio
Artists (AFTRA) (LA)
5757 Wilshire Blvd., Suite 900
Los Angeles, CA 90036
323-634-8100
323-634-8246 (fax)

American Federation of Television and Radio
Artists (AFTRA) (NY)
260 Madison Avenue, 7th Floor
New York, NY 10016
212-532-0800
212-545-1238 (fax)

American Film Institute (AFI)
2021 N. Western Ave.
Los Angeles, CA 90027
323-856-7600
323-467-4578 (fax)
www.afionline.org

American Film Marketing Association
10850 Wilshire Blvd., 9th Floor
Los Angeles, CA 90024
310-446-1000
310-446-1600 (fax)
www.afma.com

American Society of Composers, Authors &
Publishers (ASCAP) (LA)
7920 Sunset Blvd., 3rd Floor
Los Angeles, CA 90046
323-883-1000
323-883-1049 (fax)

American Society of Composers, Authors &
Publishers (ASCAP) (NY)
1 Lincoln Plaza
New York, NY 10023
212-621-6000
www.ascap.com

American Women in Radio &
Television, Inc. (AWRT)
1650 Tysons Blvd., Suite 200
McLean, VA 22102
703-506-3290
703-506-3266 (fax)
www.awrt.org

Association of Film Commissioners
International (AFCI)
7060 Hollywood Blvd.
Los Angeles, CA 90028
213-462-6092
213-462-6091 (fax)
www.afciweb.org

Broadcast Music Incorporated
(BMI) (LA)
8730 Sunset Blvd., 3rd Floor W.
Los Angeles, CA 90069
310-659-9109
310-657-6947 (fax)

Broadcast Music Incorporated (BMI) (NY)
320 W. 57th St.
New York, NY 10019
212-586-2000
212-489-2368 (fax)
www.bmi.com

California Arts Council
1300 I St., #930
Sacramento, CA 95814
916-322-6555
916-322-6575 (fax)
www.cac.ca.gov

Casting Society of America
606 No. Larchmont Blvd., Suite 4B
Los Angeles, CA 90004-1309
323-463-1925

Directors Guild of America (DGA) (LA)
7920 Sunset Blvd.
Los Angeles, CA 90046
310-289-2000
310-289-2029 (fax)

Directors Guild of America (DGA) (NY)
110 W. 57th St.
New York, NY 10019
www.dga.org

Filmmakers Alliance
4120 Franklin Ave.
Los Angeles, CA 90027
310-281-6093 (Hotline)

Independent Feature Project/
West (IFP)
1964 Westwood Blvd., #205
Los Angeles, CA 90025
310-475-4379
310-441-5676 (fax)
www.ifpwest.org

Motion Picture Association of America
15503 Ventura Blvd.
Encino, CA 91436
818-995-6600
818-382-1799 (fax)
www.mpaa.org

Multicultural Association of Television
Program Executives
9244 Wilshire Blvd.
Beverly Hills, CA 90212
310-285-9743
310-285-9770 (fax)

National Association of Television
Program Executives
2425 Olympic Blvd., Suite 550E
Santa Monica, CA 90404
310-453-4440
310-453-5258 (fax)
www.natpe.org

Producers Guild of America (PGA)
400 S. Beverly Drive, Suite 211
Beverly Hills, CA 90212
310-557-0807
310-557-0436 (fax)

Recording Musicians Association (RMA)
817 Vine Street, Suite 209
Hollywood, CA 90038
323-462-4762
323-462-2406 (fax)

Screen Actors Guild (SAG) (LA)
5757 Wilshire Blvd.
Los Angeles, CA 90036-3600
323-954-1600
323-954-6603 (fax)

Screen Actors Guild (SAG) (NY)
1515 Broadway, 44th Floor
New York, NY 10036
212-944-1030
212-944-6774 (fax)
www.sag.com

Scriptwriters Network
11684 Ventura Blvd., #508
Studio City, CA 91604
323-848-9477
www.scriptwritersnetwork.com
scriptwritersnetwork@artnet.net

Society of Composers and Lyricists
400 S. Beverly Drive, Suite 214
Beverly Hills, CA 90212
310-281-2812
310-990-0601 (fax)
www.filmscore.org

The Actors Fund of America (LA)
4727 Wilshire Blvd., Suite 310
Los Angeles, CA 90010
323-933-9244
323-933-7615 (fax)

The Actors Fund of America (NY)
1501 Broadway, Suite 518
New York, NY 10036-5697
212-221-7300
212-764-0238 (fax)

The American Society of
Young Musicians
9244 Wilshire Blvd., Suite 201
Beverly Hills, CA 90212
310-285-9744
310-285-9770 (fax)

The Organization of Black
Screenwriters, Inc.
P.O. Box 70160
Los Angeles, CA 90070-0160
213-882-4166

Women in Film
6464 Sunset Blvd., #1018
Los Angeles, CA 90028
323-463-6040
323-463-0963 (fax)
www.wif.org

Writers Guild of America East (WGAE)
555 West 57th St., Suite 1230
New York, NY 10019
212-767-7800
212-582-1909 (fax)
www.wgaeast.org

Writers Guild of America West (WGAW)
7000 W. 3rd St.
Los Angeles, CA 90048
323-951-4000
323-782-4800 (fax)
Agency Listing: 323-782-4502
www.wga.org

Online Resources

The Internet is filled with useful information on films and filmmaking. The following list contains many but not all of the sites you might find interesting or helpful. However, keep in mind that things change rapidly on the Internet, so some of the following websites may no longer be operating or may have different addresses by the time you're reading these pages.

Top General Sites

AIVF (Association of Independent Video and Filmmakers)

www.aivf.org

The official site for AIVF, a non-profit organization established by a group of independent filmmakers to offer support and resources to independent artists.

American Film Institute

www.afionline.org

The official site for the American Film Institute, an independent, non-profit organization dedicated to preserving the heritage of film and television, identifying and training new talent, and increasing recognition and understanding of the moving image as an art form.

Cinemedia

www.cinemedia.org

Lists over 25,000 websites in the following categories: TV, Cinema, New Media, Radio, Shows, Actors, Films, Directors, Networks, Video, Studios, Theaters, Organizations, Magazines, Schools, Festivals, Production, and Research.

Documentary Net

www.documentaryfilms.net/

Provides news of, information about, and reviews of documentary films.

Hollywood Creative Directory

www.hcdonline.com

This is the site for buying or subscribing to industry directories, which give up-to-date listings of production companies, agents, distributors, and so on.

Hollywood Reporter

www.hollywoodreporter.com

Keep up on the biz at the trade magazine's website.

Independent Feature Project

www.ifp.org

The official site for the Independent Feature Project, a not-for-profit service organization dedicated to providing resources, information, and avenues of communication for its members: independent filmmakers, industry professionals, and independent film enthusiasts.

Independent Film Channel

www.ifctv.com

The official site of the Independent Film Channel, which features independent films, original series, documentaries, live events, and new media programming.

The Internet Movie Database

www.imdb.com

A great site to find information about movies and their cast and crew.

Public Broadcasting Services

www.cpb.org/services.html

The official site for the Corporation for Public Broadcasting, which provides funds for public broadcasting programs.

showbizdata.com

www.showbizdata.com

Similar to the Internet Movie Database.

Sundance Channel

www.sundancechannel.com

Features independent films and programs of interest to independent filmmakers.

Variety

www.variety.com

The other trade magazine's website.

Screenwriting

CineStory

www.cinestory.com

Works with emerging screenwriters to hone their craft.

James Russell Publishing

www.powernet.net/~scrnplay

Provides writer resource links, sample author query letters, and advice for authors and screenwriters.

Pitch Factory

www.pitchfactory.com

Lists techniques for pitching a story.

Pro Screenwriter

http://members.aol.com/linkwrite/profwrt.html

Has links for professional screenwriters and people looking for screenwriters and plays.

Qwertyiop.net

http://qwertyuiop.net

A site written by two screenwriters featuring news of interest to screenwriters.

The Screenwriters' Room

www.screenwritersrm.com/

Helps with inexpensive and professional screenplay consultations.

Screenwriters Utopia

www.screenwritersutopia.com/

A site developed by screenwriter Chris Wehner that features articles, news, and interviews of interest to screenwriters.

ScriptShark

http://scriptshark.com/

Provides the first step to selling your screenplay or manuscript.

The Mad Screenwriter

http://fade.to/madscreenwriter

Has a screenwriting and filmmaking directory.

The Spec Script Library

www.thesource.com.au/scripts/

Connects those who write scripts with those who source original scripts for TV and film.

Storybay

www.storybay.com

Storybay was founded to help writers efficiently and affordably market their work by giving them access to executives in film and publishing.

Writers' Script Network

www.WritersScriptNetwork.com

Helps you get the right script into the right hands.

Professional Resources

ACTING UP

www.acting-up.net/

Provides job information services for professional actors.

Action/Cut Directed By
www.actioncut.com
Offers film and TV industry seminars.

Artistwebsite
www.artistwebsite.com/
The film casting website.

Business Strategies
www.moviemoney.com/
Offers information for filmmakers and financing.

Cinematography World
http://cinematographyworld.com
Provides cinematography resources.

CineWeb
www.cineweb.com/
Serves as a gateway to the entertainment industry: locations, equipment, and so on.

CoProductions
www.coproductions.com/cine.htm
Provides international film industry and audio-visual resource info, exchanges, ads, projects.

Europa Cinemas
www.europa-cinemas.org
Has established a network for a better circulation of European films.

Film & TV Connection
www.film-connection.com
Provides on-the-job training in major film/video studios and television stations.

Film Intelligence Agency
www.filmintelligenceagency.com/
Has production resources and more.

Film Sound Design
www.filmsound.com
Lists the complete terminology and theory behind film sounds.

FIPRESCI
www.fipresci.org
Links to the worldwide organization of film critics.

Hollywood Home Page
http://beverlyhills.freeyellow.com/./index.html
Helps actors and writers to exchange information, ideas, and help.

How to Start and Operate Film and Video Festivals
www.filmdependent.com/festbook/
Helps those who are operating a film festival.

Indigenous Pictures

www.indigipix.com

Helps with quality pre-production, production, and post-production services for beginning film-makers.

Ireland Film and Television Net

www.iftn.ie/

Has global information services about the audiovisual industry in Ireland.

Kodak Professional Motion Imaging

www.kodak.com/US/en/motion/index.shtml

Provides lots of interesting information for cinematographers.

LicenseMusic

www.licensemusic.com/

Lists an online music catalog of pre-cleared original recordings available for sourcing and licensing use on the web, broadcast media, and audiovisual productions.

Lone Eagle

www.loneeagle.com/catalog.html

Has professional reference directories.

Making Film

www.makingfilm.com/

Positions itself as an online resource for the production process.

Mandy's International Film and TV Production Directory

www.mandy.com

Serves as a web resource of film/TV professionals.

Media-match

www.media-match.com

Provides a production crew search engine for the United States.

Movie Market

www.movie-market.com

Lists producers, distributors, and news in the making.

My Entertainment World

www.myentertainmentworld.com

Provides global Australian resources.

nextPix.com

www.nextpix.com

Offers production services and software; also is a production company.

Netribution

www.netribution.co.uk

Provides resources for U.K. filmmakers.

Producer's Masterguide
www.producers.masterguide.com/
Publishes directories.

ProductionLink.com
www.ProductionLink.com
Offers directories, classifieds, production news, web resources, free e-mail boxes, and more.

rUa Struggling Artist?
www.rUaStrugglingArtist.com
Helps with ideas for artists, from make-up to photographers.

SACD
www.sacd.fr/index2.asp
An organization managing authors' rights for the audiovisual and performing arts (in French and English).

Salmac
www.salmac.com/acting up
Has acting, writing, and producing resources for the film industry.

Screen West
www.screenwest.com.au
Helps with studios and post-production information.

T2M
www.todsmurray.com/industry/film.html
Provides legal advice to the screen industries.

The Knowledge Online
www.theknowledgeonline.com
Has web resources for film, TV, and new media industries.

The Power Broker
www.thepowerbroker.com
Sells and rents professional video equipment.

UniqueFilms.com
www.uniquefilms.com/
Offers post-production services, extensive links, classifieds, forums.

Independent Filmmaking

Caipirinha Productions
www.caipirinha.com
Independent film company and electronic music record label.

Cashiersducinemart
www.cashiersducinemart.com
A provoking look into the world of underground film.

Digital Idiots
http://Digitalidiots.com
A guide to digital filmmaking.

Film Forum
www.filmforum.com/
New York movie house for independent premieres.

FILMMAG
www.filmmag.com
Another online resource for the independent filmmaker.

Filmmaking.net
www.filmmaking.net
A resource for new and professional filmmakers covering a wide variety of frequently asked film-making questions and other film- and movie-making issues.

Film Threat
www.filmthreat.com/
Hollywood's indie voice.

Film Underground
www.filmunderground.com
Filmmaking resource for professional independent filmmakers.

Hedtec Moving Pictures, Ltd.
www.hedtec.com/
Online network of independent filmmakers.

Indic
www.indic.co.il
A site by independent filmmakers for independent filmmakers.

IndieDVD
www.indiedvd.com
An independent DVD label and Internet film distributor.

Indie Network
http://indienetwork.com/indexmain.html
A great site for information about the film business. It includes news from the trade papers and links of interest to independent filmmakers.

indieWIRE
www.indiewire.com/
Film news, discussions, classifieds—a leading voice for independent film online.

Indigenous Pictures
www.indigipix.com
Production company specializing in Native American films.

International Independent Film Online
http://indiekino.com/
Covers indie filmmaking in the international market.

nextPix
www.nextpix.com
Provides information on how to become a guerrilla filmmaker.

Reelmind
www.reelmind.com
An online community for filmmakers, animators, and musicians.

Surfview Entertainment
www.surfview.com
Provides a place where producers and active investors can meet and subsequently finance, produce, distribute, and exhibit independent productions

Film Festivals

Filmfestivals.com
www.filmfestivalspro.com
Dedicated to showcasing film festivals around the world and fostering new film and filmmaking talent.

Cannes Film Festival
www.festival-cannes.fr

Film Festivals-Non Stop Festivals
www.filmfestivals.com

Los Angeles Film Festival
www.laiff.com

New York Film Festival
www.filmlinc.com/nyff/nyff.htm

San Francisco International Film Festival
www.sffs.org

Seattle International Film Festival
www.seattlefilm.com

Sundance Film Festival
www.sundancechannel.com/festival00

Sundance Online Resource Center
www.sundanceonlineresourcecenter.org
Designed to help filmmakers selected to show their films at Sundance promote and display their films and the process for making them.

Telluride Film Festival
www.telluridefilmfestival.com

Toronto International Film Festival
www.e.bell.ca/filmfest

Venice Film Festival
www.labiennaledivenezia.net/gb/cinema.html

Motion Picture Studios

Artisan Entertainment
www.artisanent.com/

Castle Rock Entertainment
http://castle-rock.warnerbros.com/

Columbia/TriStar/Triumph Films
www.spe.sony.com/Pictures/index.html

Dimension Films
www.dimensionfilms.com

Disney
www.disney.com

Fine Line Films
www.flf.com/

First Look Media
www.firstlookmedia.com

Hollywood Picture and Touchstone Pictures
www.movies.com

Lion's Gate
www.lionsgate-ent.com/

MGM/UA
www.mgm.com/

Miramax Films
www.miramax.com

New Line Cinema
www.newline.com

Paramount
www.paramount.com

Paramount Classics
www.paramountclassics.com/

Sony Classics
www.spe.sony.com/classics/

Sony Pictures Entertainment
www.spe.sony.com

Trimark Pictures
www.trimarkpictures.com

Twentieth Century Fox
www.fox.com

Universal Studios
www.mca.com

USA Films (formerly October Films)
www.octoberfilms.com/

Warner Bros. Animation
www.wbanimation.com

Warner Bros.
www.warnerbros.com

Theatrical and Non-Theatrical Distributors

Artistic License
www.artlic.com
Film distribution company seeking films with strong potential in the competitive marketplace.

Atomshockwave.com
www.atomshockwave.com
Licenses content to online companies, as well as domestic and international TV, airlines, VHS/DVD, major Internet sites, and some theatrical outlets.

Canadian Filmmaker Resource Centre
www.cfmdc.org
Canada's oldest artist-run organization is a prime disseminator of experimental, gay, and lesbian titles from around the world.

Canyon
www.canyoncinema.com
One of the world's leading distributors of experimental and independent film, Canyon is an artist-run organization dedicated to the support, promotion, distribution and preservation of motion picture film as an art form.

Electronic Arts Intermix
www.eai.org
A resource for art videos and alternative media.

Films for the Humanities and Sciences
www.films.com
The largest distributor of videos and CD-ROMs to schools, colleges, and libraries in North America. Primary focus is documentaries.

First Run/Icarus Films, Inc.
www.frif.com
Distributors of documentary film and video in the United States and Canada, with a primary focus on non-theatrical markets.

Fox Lorber
www.foxlorber.com
A leading distributor of specialty programming to the worldwide home video, theatrical, and television marketplaces.

Lot 47
www.lot47.com
Independent distribution company interested in North American rights of diverse independent American features, documentaries, and foreign-language films.

Mediarights.org
www.mediarights.org
Nonprofit community website designed to make social-issue documentaries and advocacy videos easy to find.

New Day Films
www.newday.com
Distribution cooperative of independent filmmakers making social-issue films. Primarily works with colleges and universities, libraries, high schools, and community groups.

Noodlehead Network
www.Noodlehead.com
Distributors and producers of videos made with kids. Specialize in videos on geography, video production, health, and guidance issues for K-12 schools.

PBS Home Video
www.PBS.org
The home video arm of PBS promotes PBD programming via direct-to-consumer distribution services that include: shopPBS, the PBS Home Video catalog, on-air direct response sales, and third-party catalog and special market outlets.

Porchlight Entertainment
www.PorchLight.com
An independent distributor of films and TV focusing on programs that promote positive values and/or are family-friendly.

Seventh Art Releasing
www.7thart.com
Theatrical distributor with a video label and a full-time world sales unit, working mostly in documentaries.

Shadow Entertainment
www.mint.net/movies/shadow
Small distribution company based in Maine that specializes in 35mm features, especially with political or ethnographic content.

Shooting Gallery

www.shootinggallery.com

A film, TV, music development/production/distribution company that produces and acquire pictures, and has co-produced productions such as the award-winning *You Can Count on Me*.

Strand Releasing

www.strandrel.com

Independent distribution company that handles shorts and feature films, especially those with lesbian and gay themes.

Stratosphere Entertainment

www.stratospherefilm.com

Theatrical motion picture distribution company based in New York, interested in quality independent work at any stage of production.

Third World Newsreel

www.twn.org

A non-profit media arts organization that fosters the creation and dissemination of independent film and video made by and about people of diverse racial, ethnic, and cultural backgrounds.

University of California Extension

www-cmil.unex.berkeley.edu/media/

Distributes high-quality documentaries and educational media of all kinds to colleges and universities, primary and secondary schools, libraries, health organizations, museums, and other institutions worldwide.

V Tape

www.vtape.org

A distribution system for media works by artists and independents, strongly committed to the medium of video and media artworks.

Video Data Bank

www.vdb.org

A non-profit organization that has assembled and distributes one of the largest collections of videos by and about artists to museums, galleries, alternative spaces, festivals, and in curricular programming.

Women Make Movies

www.wmm.com

A national non-profit media arts organization that facilitates the production, promotion, distribution, and exhibition of independent film and video by and about women.

Online Distribution

Atom Films

www.atomfilms.com

Distributes all genres of short independent films.

The Bit Screen

www.thebitscreen.com

Features original short films made specifically for the Internet.

Destiny Media Technologies, Inc.

www.dsny.com

Provides information about a company developing technologies to distribute digital media through the Internet.

Eveo

www.eveo.com

The site for a web video-publishing application.

FilmUnlimited

www.filmunlimited.co.uk/

The film website of the Guardian newspaper.

IFILM

www.ifilm.com

Provides a comprehensive guide for finding and watching feature and short films.

Indie Film Web

www.indiefilmweb.net/

Seeks to match independent films with buyers and distributors.

Internet Film Community

www.inetfilm.com

Distributes films online.

Key East Entertainment
edigifilm.com/

www.edigifilm.com/

Handles film acquisition, development, and consulting.

MediaTrip

www.mediatrip.com

Produces original entertainment and displays it on this site.

Microcinema

www.microcinema.com

Distributes films online.

New Venue

www.newvenue.com

Features short indie films which break aesthetic and technical barriers, bringing story and style to the Internet, and also empowers digital filmmakers with "FlickTips," a complete guide to making web movies.

The Sync

www.thesync.com

Provides streaming audio and video services to businesses, as well as original content on its site for Internet viewership.

Underground Film

www.undergroundfilm.com

Showcases the work of independent filmmakers who have little or no access to the traditional tools of distribution.

Movie Fan Sites

Ain't It Cool News

www.aint-it-cool-news.com

News and reviews.

Animation World Network

www.awn.com

Publisher of animation information.

asSeenonScreen.com

www.asSeenonScreen.com

Buy the stuff you've seen in the movies and on TV.

CineMatter

www.shreck.com

Movie releases and reviews.

Coming Attractions

http://corona.bc.ca/films/mainFramed.html

Movie reviews and "coming attractions."

Eonline

eonline.com/

Entertainment news, gossip, movies, star attractions, reviews, games, and more.

Film Scouts

www.filmscouts.com

News, reviews, festivals.

Film.com

www.film.com

Reviews, coming soon, screening room.

Filme von Greta Garbo

http://gretagarbo.esmartweb.com

Site dedicated to Greta Garbo and her films.

FilmZone

www.filmzone.com/

One-step source to the movies.

FlixUSA.com

www.FlixUsa.com/

Discussion and networking forums for entertainment professionals.

ForeignFilms.com

www.foreignfilms.com

For information related to foreign films.

Gist TV Listings

www.gist.com/

Everything TV: features, prime time, movies, gossip, and more.

Gouvenel Studio, Movie Stars Pictures

www.gouvenelstudio.com

Pictures of hundreds of French and American movie stars.

Internet Ten

www.iten.net/ or www.watchingmovies.com

Internet Talk and Entertainment Network.

Kino On-line

www.kino.com

Reviews, synopses, new releases.

MovieNet

www.landmarktheatres.com

Provides news about movies coming to the Landmark art house theater chain.

MovieWeb

www.movieweb.com

Features information on movies coming to theaters.

MrShowbiz

mrshowbiz.go.com/

Movie guide, headlines, celebrities, music, and more.

Now Network

www.film.now.com/

Now Network of the world, film and art, global cinema.

One World

www.1worldfilms.com/

Film list by country.

Reel.com

www.reel.com

Offers a variety of film-related information designed to help consumers select and view movies in theaters, at the video store, or for purchase.

The Hollywood Network

www.hollywood.com

Provides information about the movies, show times, reviews, and celebrity gossip.

The Picture Palace
www.picpal.com
A site to buy old movies and other items on video or DVD.

The Silent Era
www.silentera.com/
A website about the silent era of filmmaking.

The Silents are Golden
www.silentsaregolden.com/
Reviews and information about silent films.

The Silents Majority
www.silentsmajority.com/indexold.htm
A fan club and online journal about silent films.

The Trailer Park
www.movie-trailers.com/
Provides information about movie trailers.

The Junkie.com
http://thejunkie.com
An arts and entertainment portal.

TicketWeb
www.ticketweb.com
A full-service ticket distribution company.

TV Guide Online
www.tvguide.com/
TV Guide's website.

Films and Reviews

The Z Review
www.thezreview.co.uk
Provides information to take "a stand against Hollywood's never-ending barrage of dire movies."

Zentertainment
www.zentertainment.com
Lists movie, video, DVD, and television reviews.

Web Magazines and TV

24 Frames Per Second
http://24framespersecond.com/
A journal of original writing and in-depth review of film and filmmaking.

Art Deadlines
http://artdeadlineslist.com
A monthly newsletter: competitions, call for entries, contests, jobs, casting calls, auditions.

Filmmaker Magazine
www.filmmakermagazine.com
The official website of the magazine dedicated to independent filmmaking.

Guerrilla Filmmaker Magazine
www.7dazemedia.com
Quarterly publication for the indie scene.

Insidefilm
www.insidefilm.com/calendar.html
Online magazine about films.

Kinematrix
www.kinematrix.net
Keeping an eye on movie-making in Italian.

Megasitio Cine Independiente
www.cineindependiente.com.ar
Spanish-language site specializing in independent film.

Movie Maker Hands On Pages
www.moviemaker.com/hop/
The art and business of making movies.

OffbeatTV
www.offbeattv.com/
Provides streaming films and videos and links to sell videos and DVDs.

Classic TV and Movies

Premiere
www.premiere.com
An interactive movie magazine.

Screensaver
www.fromusalive.com/screensaver
Features top screenwriters and producers.

The Wild Wild Web
www.wildweb.com/theshow
Lists digital celluloid news and TV show.

Appendix C

Further Reading

There are books available on all aspects of filmmaking if you want more in-depth information on the various topics covered in this book. The following list of books, guides, and directories is a start.

Budgets and Deals

Litwak, Mark. *Contracts in the Film and Television Industry*. Los Angeles: Silman-James Press, 1995.

———. *Deal Making in the Film and Television Industry*. Los Angeles: Silman-James Press, 1994.

Singleton, Ralph S. *Film Budgeting: How Much It Will Cost to Shoot Your Movie*. Los Angeles: Lone Eagle Press, 1996.

Wharton, Brooke A. *The Writer Got Screwed (But Didn't Have To): A Guide to the Legal and Business Practices of Writing for the Entertainment Industry*. New York: Harper Collins, 1997.

Wiese, Michael and Deke, Simon, ed. *Film & Video Budgets*. 2nd Ed. Studio City, CA: Michael Wiese Productions, 1995.

Directing

Crisp, Mike. *The Practical Director*. Boston: The Focal Press, 1998.

Gelmis, Joseph. *The Film Director as Superstar*. New York: Doubleday, 1970.

Harmon, Renee. *Film Directing: Killer Style & Cutting Edge Technique.* Los Angeles: Lone Eagle Press, 1998.

Katz, Steven D. *Film Directing Cinematic Motion: A Workshop for Staging Scenes.* Studio City, CA: Michael Wiese Productions, 1992.

———. *Film Directing Shot by Shot: Visualizing from Concept to Screen.* Studio City, CA: Michael Wiese Productions, 1991.

Lumet, Sidney. *Making Movies.* New York: Alfred A. Knopf, 1995.

Rabiger Michael. *Directing: Film Techniques and Aesthetics*, 2nd ed. Boston: The Focal Press, 1997.

———. *Directing the Documentary.* 2nd ed. Boston: The Focal Press, 1992.

Sherman, Eric. *Directing the Film: Film Directors on Their Art.* Boston: Little, Brown and Company, 1988.

Travis, Mark W. *The Director's Journey: The Creative Collaboration Between Directors, Writers and Actors.* Studio City, CA: Michael Wiese Productions, 1997.

Weston, Judith. *Directing Actors: Creating Memorable Performances for Film and Television.* Studio City, CA: Michael Wiese Productions, 1996.

Editing

Murch, Walter. *In the Blink of an Eye.* Los Angeles: Silman-James Press, 1996.

Rosenblum, Ralph and Robert Karen. *When The Shooting Stops…The Cutting Begins.* New York: Penguin Books, 1979.

Film Financing

Cones, John. *Film Financing.* Los Angeles: Silman-James Press, 1995.

Levinson, Louise. *Filmmakers and Financing: Business Plans for Independents.* Boston: The Focal Press, 1994.

Wiese, Michael. *Film and Video Financing.* Studio City, CA: Michael Wiese Productions, 1991.

Marketing and Distribution

Harmon, Renee. *The Beginning Filmmakers Business Guide: Financial, Legal, Marketing, and Distribution Basics of Making Movies.* New York: Walker and Company, 1994.

Lukk, Tiiu. *Movie Marketing: Opening the Picture and Giving It Legs.* Los Angeles: Silman-James Press, 1997.

Pierson, John. *Spike, Mike, Slackers and Dykes.* New York: Miramax Books, Hyperion, 1996.

Squire, Jason E., ed., *The Movie Business Book.* 2nd ed. New York: Fireside/Simon & Schuster, 1992.

Trent, Barbara, W. B. Peale, and Joanne Doroshow. *Taking It to the Theaters: The Empowerment Projects Guide to Theatrical and Video Self-Distribution of Issue-Oriented Films and Videos.* Chapel Hill, NC: 1993. (Order from The Empowerment Project, 2007 Jo Mack Road, Chapel Hill, NC 27516 919-967-1963.)

Warshawski, Morrie, ed., *The Next Step: Distributing Independent Films and Video.* New York: 1995. (Available from AIVF, 304 Hudson Street, 6th Floor, New York, NY 10013 212-807-1400.)

Wiese, Michael. *Film & Video Marketing.* Studio City, CA: Michael Wiese Productions, 1988.

PBS-Related Publications

National Endowment for the Arts Guide to Programs, Media Arts Program Guidelines, and Annual Report. Information Office, NEA, Washington, D.C. 20506.

National Endowment for the Humanities Program Announcement and Media Program Guidelines, and Media Log (listing of 800 film, TV, and radio programs supported by NEH), NEH Public Information Office, Washington, D.C. 20506.

PBS Program Producers Handbook, PBS, National Programming and Promotion Services, 1320 Braddock Place, Alexandria, VA 22314-1698; or call 703-739-5450.

Producers Guide to Public Television Funding (free), CPB, 901 E St., NW; Washington, D.C. 20004-2006.

Producing

Baumgarten, Paul A., Donald C. Farber, and Mark Fleischer. *Producing, Financing and Distributing Film.* New York: Limelight Editions, 1992.

Broughton, Irv. *Producers on Producing: The Making of Film & Television*. Jefferson, NC: MacFarland Publishing, 1986.

Buzzell, Linda. *How to Make It in Hollywood*. New York: HarperPerennial, 1992.

Corman, Roger with Jim Jerome. *How I Made a Hundred Movies in Hollywood and Never Lost a Dime*. New York: Random House, 1990.

Gaines, Philip and David J. Rhodes. *Hollywood on $5,000, $10,000, or $25,000 a Day: A Survival Guide for Low-Budget Filmmakers*. Los Angeles: Silman-James Press, 1994.

———. *Micro-Budget Hollywood: Budgeting (and Making Feature Films for $50,000 to $500,000)*. Los Angeles: Silman-James Press, 1995.

Gates, Richard. *Production Management for Film and Video*. Boston: The Focal Press, 1995.

Glimcher, Sumner and Warren Johnson. *Movie Making: A Guide to Film Production*. New York: Pocket Books/Simon & Schuster, 1975.

Gold, Donald L., Don Gold, and Paul Mason. *Producing for Hollywood: A Guide for the Independent Producer*. New York: Allworth Press, 2000.

Goodell, Gregory. *Independent Feature Film Production*. New York: St. Martin's Press, 1982.

Gregory, Mollie. *Making Films Your Business*. New York: Schocken Books, 1979.

Hamilton, Peter and David Rosen. *Off-Hollywood: The Making and Marketing of Independent Films*. New York: Grove Weidenfeld, 1990.

Hamsher, Jane. *Killer Instinct: How Two Young Producers Took on Hollywood and Made the Most Controversial Film of the Decade*. New York: Broadway, 1997.

Harmon, Renee. *Film Producing: Low Budget Films That Sell*. Los Angeles: Samuel French, 1998.

Honthaner, Eve Light. *The Complete Film Production Handbook*. Los Angeles: Lone Eagle Press, 1996.

Hourcourt, Amanda, Neil Howlett, Sally Davies, and Naomi Moskovic. *The Independent Producer: Film & Television*. London: Faber & Faber, 1986.

Jacobs, Bob M. and Robert M. Jacobs. *The Independent Video Producer: Establishing a Profitable Video Business*. Woburn, MA: Butterworth-Heinemann, 1999.

Lindenmuth, Kevin J. *The Independent Film Experience: Interviews with Directors and Producers*. Jefferson, NC: McFarland and Company, Inc., 2001.

Linson, Art. *A Pound of Flesh*. New York: Grove Press, 1993.

McAlevey, Peter. *Succeeding as an Independent Film Producer: Based on the Acclaimed UCLA Course*. New York: Overlook Press, 1998.

Merritt, Greg. *Film Production: The Complete Uncensored Guide to Filmmaking*. Los Angeles: Lone Eagle, 1998.

Puttnam, David and Neil Watson. *Movies and Money*. New York: Alfred A. Knopf, 1998.

Rosenthal, Alan. *Writing, Directing and Producing Documentary Films*. Carbondale, IL: Southern Illinois University Press, 1990.

Schmidt, Rick. *Feature Filmmaking at Used-Car Prices*. New York: Penguin Books, 1995.

Vachon, Christine and David Edelstein. *Shooting to Kill: How an Independent Producer Blasts through the Barriers to Make Movies That Matter*. New York: William Morrow, 1998.

Wiese, Michael. *Producer to Producer: Insider Tips for Entertainment Media*. Studio City, CA: Michael Wiese Productions, 1997.

Screenwriting

Atchity, Kenneth and Chi-Li Wong. *Writing Treatments That Sell: How to Create and Market Your Story Ideas to the Motion Picture and TV Industry*. New York: Henry Holt, 1997.

Bayer, William. *Breaking Through, Selling Out, Dropping Dead and Other Notes on Filmmaking*. New York: Limelight Editions, 1989.

Berman, Robert A. *Fade In: The Screenwriting Process*. 2nd ed. Studio City, CA: Michael Wiese Productions, 1997.

Blacker, Irwin R. *The Elements of Screenwriting: A Guide for Film and Television Writers*. New York: Collier Books, 1988.

Blum, Richard A. *Television and Screen Writing: From Concept to Contract*. New York: Hastings House, 1995.

Brady, John. *The Craft of the Screenwriter*. New York: Simon and Schuster, 1981.

Callan, K. *Script Is Finished, Now What Do I Do? The Scriptwriter's Resource Book & Agent Guide*. Studio City, CA: Sweden Press, 1997.

Cole, Hollis R. and Judith H. Haag. *The Complete Guide to Standard Script Formats*. North Hollywood, CA: CMC Publishing, 1994.

Cowgill, Linda J. *Secrets of Screenplay Structure*. Los Angeles: Lone Eagle, 1999.

———. *Writing Short Films: Structure and Content for Screenwriters*. Los Angeles: Lone Eagle, 1997.

Dancyger, Ken. *Alternative Scriptwriting: Writing Beyond the Rules*. Boston: The Focal Press, 1991.

Engel, Joel. *Screenwriters on Screenwriting: The Best in the Business Discuss Their Craft*. New York: Hyperion, 1995.

Field, Syd. *Screenplay: The Foundations of Screenwriting*. New York: Dell, 1982.

———. *The Screenwriter's Problem Solver: How to Recognize, Identify, and Define Screenwriting*. New York: Dell, 1998.

———. *The Screenwriter's Workbook*. New York: Dell, 1984.

Froug, William. *The New Screenwriter Looks at the New Screenwriter*. Los Angeles: Silman-James Press, 1992.

———. *Screen-Writing Tricks of the Trade*. Los Angeles: Silman-James Press, 1992.

———. *Zen and the Art of Screenwriting: Insights and Interviews*. Los Angeles: Silman-James Press, 1996.

Goldman, William. *Adventures in the Screen Trade*. New York: Warner Books, 1983

Hauge, Michael. *Writing Screenplays That Sell*. New York: HarperPerennial, 1991.

Horton, Andrew. *Writing the Character-Centered Screenplay*. Berkeley, CA: University of California Press, 1999.

Hunter, Lew. *Lew Hunter's Screenwriting 434*. New York: Perigee Books/Putnam Publishing Group, 1993.

Keane, Christopher. *How to Write a Selling Screenplay: A Step-By-Step Approach to Developing Your Story Writing Your Screenplay by One of Today's Most Successful Screenwriters*. New York: Broadway Books, 1998.

McKee, Robert. *Story: Substance, Structure, Style, and the Principles of Screenwriting*. New York: Regan Books, 1997.

Sautter, Carl. *How to Sell Your Screenplay: The Real Rules of Film and Television*. New York: New Chapter Press, 1992.

Schanzer, Karl and Thomas Lee Wright. *American Screenwriters: The Insiders' Look at the Art, the Craft, and the Business of Writing Movies.* New York: Avon Books, 1993.

Seger, Linda. *The Art of Adaptation: Turning Fact and Fiction into Film.* New York: Henry Holt, 1992.

———. *Creating Unforgettable Characters.* New York: Henry Holt, 1990.

———. *Making a Good Script Great.* New York: Dodd, Mead & Company, 1994.

Seger, Linda and Edward Jay Whetmore. *From Script to Screen, The Collaborative Art of Filmmaking.* New York: Henry Holt, 1994.

Swain, Joye R. and Dwight V. Swain. *Film Scriptwriting: A Practical Manual.* Boston: The Focal Press, 1988.

Taylor, Thom. *The Big Deal: Hollywood's Million-Dollar Spec Script Market.* New York: William Morrow, 1999.

Trottier, David. *The Screenwriter's Bible: A Complete Guide to Writing, Formatting, and Selling Your Script,* Los Angeles: Silman-James Press, 1995.

Vogler, Christopher. *The Writer's Journey: Mythic Structure for Writers.* 2nd ed. Studio City, CA: Michael Wiese Productions, 1998.

Walter, Richard. *Screenwriting: the Art, Craft and Business of Film and Television Writing.* New York: Penguin, 1988.

———. *The Whole Picture: Strategies for Screenwriting Success in the New Hollywood.* New York: Plume, 1997.

Wolff, Jurgen and Kerry Cox. *Top Secrets: Screenwriting.* Los Angeles: Lone Eagle Press, 1993.

Zaza, Tony. *Script Planning: Positioning and Developing Scripts for TV and Film.* Boston: Focal Press, 1993.

Resources and Directories

Baseline.Hollywood.Com, an entertainment industry database, provides access to up-to-date entertainment information. To subscribe go to http://www.pkbaseline.com/ or write to 30 Irving Place, Fifth Floor, New York, NY 10003, 212-254-8235 or 115 West California Blvd., #401, Pasadena, CA, 91105, 626-943-8075.

Bowser, Kathryn. *AIVF (Association of Independent Video and Filmmakers) Guide to Film and Video Distributors* and *AIVF Guide to International Film and Video Festivals*. New York: 1996. Order from the Association for Independent Video & Filmmakers, 304 Hudson Street, 6th Floor, New York, NY 10013, 212-807-1400 or www.aivf.org.

Detmers, Fred, ed., *American Cinematographers Manual*, The ASC Press, Hermosa Beach, CA, 1986.

Hollywood Creative Directory, calling itself the "insider's guide to the insiders," this directory of producers and companies and other directories are published several times a year. Order from: IFILM Publishing, 1024 N. Orange Drive, Hollywood, CA 90038, 323-308-3490 or 800-815-0503. Order online at www.hcdonline.com.

Writer's Guide to Hollywood Producers, Directors, and Screenwriter's Agents. Rocklin, CA: Skip Press, 1997.

Appendix D

Glossary

3:2 pulldown (a.k.a. 2:3 pulldown) The method for telecining 24-frames-per-second film to 30-frames-per-second videotape.

above-the-line In film budgeting, costs associated with writing, directing, producing, and performing, listed in the top section of a budget.

adaptation A film that is based on a novel or a play and is transformed into the medium of film by the film's screenwriter; also, the right to change or "adapt" a musical composition.

aerial shot *See* overhead shot.

affiliates In television, stations that are affiliated with a particular network, such as NBC.

agent A person who represents the interests of others. A "talent agent" represents actors and actresses, and a "literary agent" represents writers and directors.

analog A device or signal that is continuously varying in strength or quantity, such as voltage, audio, or video.

answer print The first color-timed print from the cut negative of a film.

antagonist The character in a screenplay, play, or other literary work who opposes the main character.

aspect ratio The ratio of the width to the height of the projected film. In television the aspect ratio is 1.33:1, in U.S. films it is 1.85:1, and in most European films it is 1.66:1.

backstory Facts and background information about a character that makes the character who he or she is. The details in a character's backstory may or may not come out in the story.

barn doors   Hinged, solid black doors that fit on lights and are used to control light during filming.

below-the-line   In film budgeting, labor and other costs associated with physical production and post-production, listed in the lower section of a budget.

billboard   To visually or verbally name the title of a film from which a clip originated when it is shown in a film.

broadcast quality   A term that originally meant the quality of the signal that broadcasts television shows to television sets. It has now come to mean the image quality of a show made for television.

casting   The act of finding actors and actresses for roles in a film, usually done by a casting director or, in film financing, actors or actresses whose names don't help get financing for the film.

character arc   A term used to describe the growth and development of a character throughout the course of a story.

cinéma verité   Literally, "cinema truth"; originally a term to describe filmmaking that utilized lightweight equipment, small crews, and direct interviews. The term is now used to refer to any documentary technique.

clearance   In film, getting the rights to use copyrighted material.

climax   A moment of great or culminating intensity in a narrative film or play, especially the conclusion of a crisis, when the tension created by the problem set up in act one is resolved.

close-up (CU)   Also called close shot, it normally indicates a shot of the head and shoulders of a person. Close-ups can also be focused on some small part of the scene—a hand or an object like a phone ringing, for example. The purpose of the shot is to draw the audience's attention to that element to create a dramatic effect.

cold reading   A reading of a scene or part of a scene by an actor who has not had a chance to memorize the dialogue or otherwise prepare for the performance.

composition   The arrangement of various objects in a picture so that the whole shot will be balanced and pleasing to the viewer, and will direct the viewer to the main subject of the picture.

conform   To cut the original camera negative (OCN) to match the final cut of a film.

continuity   The necessity for the details of a scene to match the order of the scenes in a final edited film.

cover set   A set that is available on a flexible timetable so that it can be used for filming on a day when weather or other problems prevent filming at the scheduled location.

coverage   In film script development, a written synopsis, critique, and recommendation prepared by a script reader employed by a studio or production company.

coverage   In film production, getting enough shots to cover transitions or cuts within scenes and from scene to scene, or simply enough different shots in a scene to pick up the pace of the movie and make it visually interesting.

crane shots   Mounting the camera on a crane and moving the crane during the shot.

credit   Acknowledgement of work on a produced film in one's capacity as a writer, director, producer, in an acting role, or as another member of the crew.

cross-cutting   Often used interchangeably with parallel cutting, it is the inter-cutting of shots from two or more scenes so the fragments of each scene will be presented to the viewer's attention alternately; also cutting between different points of view of one subject.

cutaway   A brief shot that takes the viewer out of a scene for a moment. Cutaways are often used to bridge cuts within a scene or between scenes.

dailies   Prints of takes that are made immediately after a day's shoot ends so that they can be examined before the next day begins.

deficit financing   The production financing of a television movie or series episode by a production company, which will be repaid in full or in part by a license fee from a network.

depth of field   The varying range of distances from the camera at which an object remains in sharp focus.

development   In the film industry, the term used for the process of getting a script ready for production.

digital   The conversion of an analog signal into a binary form with regular strength as opposed to varying strength.

dissolve   A transitional device that superimposes a fade-out over a fade-in.

dolly or tracking shots   Mounting the camera on a dolly and moving the dolly on tracks during a shot.

dupe negative   (a.k.a. inter-negative) A negative printed from a positive print (an inter-positive) from which release prints are printed.

edge code   (a.k.a. edge number) A number printed on the edge of the film to keep the film and sound track in sync.

edited master   The final edited videotape created at the online editing session.

elements   The people who will play a major part in the production of the film, including the director, producer, and cast for the leading roles.

establishing shot   (a.k.a. master shot or cover shot) This is a type of long shot that orients the viewer by showing the general location of the scene that follows.

expendables   Small items needed for a film shoot, such as gaffer's tape or plastic gels, which must be purchased rather than rented from equipment houses.

extreme close-ups (ECU)   Shots in which the camera is very close to the subject.

f-stop   The measure of the camera diaphragm's opening. A high f-stop number indicates a small opening and little light entering the camera lens.

fades   A technique for gradually bringing an image up from black or another color to the full image (a fade-in) or gradually making the image disappear to a black or another color screen (a fade-out).

fair use   A provision of the copyright law that authorizes limited use of copyrighted material.

fast motion   Action filmed at slower than normal speed, which when projected at normal speed, appears faster; also an optical that increases the apparent speed of the action by printing every other frame to double the speed or every third frame to triple the speed.

femme fatales   In film or in literature, a mysterious woman of great seductive charm who leads men into compromising or dangerous situations.

field   One half of a video frame, with each field containing either the odd scan lines or the even scan lines.

film genres   Categories, classifications, or groups of films that have similar, familiar, or instantly recognizable patterns, techniques, or conventions, such as comedies or thrillers. In a film genre, one or more of the following—setting, content, themes, plot, purpose, motifs, styles, structure, situations, characters (or characterizations), and stars—are consistently the same.

filter   A plate of glass, plastic, or gelatin which alters the quality of light entering a lens.

flags   Devices placed in front of lights to cast shadows.

focal length   The length of a lens, measured from the outside surface of the lens to the film plane.

focus   The clarity and sharpness of an image, limited to a certain range of distance from the camera.

foley   The creation of sound effects that are synced to the picture on a sound stage by a foley artist.

four walling   In film distribution, when a filmmaker independently contracts with a theater to show his or her film for a flat fee for a period of time, usually a week.

freeze frame   A shot that replaces a still photograph, achieved by printing a single frame many times in succession.

fulfillment houses   Companies that handle taking orders, billing, and mailing items that are for sale, such as self-distributed videos.

gaffer   A film's lighting director and electrician, who sets up lights and makes sure there is adequate power for the lights and equipment.

generation   In film or video when there is a loss of quality of an image as a result of transferring from one format to another or copying.

ghost image   A type of double exposure in which one or more preceding frames are printed together with the main frame to give a multiple exposure.

greenlight   The term for when a movie studio puts a film it has been developing into production.

hiatus   A gap in television series production—the time of year when a series is not in production, usually sometime between May and July, giving the actors in the series time to work on other projects.

imaginary line   In film production, an imaginary line parallel to the camera that is drawn through the actors. With rare exceptions, the camera should always be on the same side of that line in filming a particular scene.

impact dissolve   A dissolve using a series of flash cuts (very short cuts) of two different shots in which the images will appear to be simultaneously present.

inter-positive print (IP)   A fine-grain print made from the conformed original negative which is used to produce subsequent dupe negatives.

iris   A progressively circular narrowing or expanding out of the image, like the iris of an eye, usually against a black background.

jump cut   A cut which breaks the continuity of time by jumping forward from one part of an action to another.

Kinetograph   The first viable motion picture camera, invented by William Dickson in 1889.

Kinetoscope   A projection machine invented by William Dickson to display images filmed on a Kinetograph. It was essentially a peep-show device used by individual viewers to view short, unsophisticated film strips.

legal effects   The lengths for fades and dissolves which can be executed by most printers (16, 24, 32, 48, 64, and 96 frames).

lens   The optical devices used in cameras and projectors that focus light rays by the process of refraction.

license   The proof of legal permission to use copyrighted material in a film or video, usually in the form of a contract.

limited liability company   A business structure that is often used in raising money for films that combines the tax benefits of limited partnerships with the limited liability benefits provided by a corporation.

limited partnership   A business agreement that includes at least one general partner (such as the film producer) and one or more limited partners.

logline   A pithy, one-sentence description of a script or story, often using other movies as a reference, such as: "Rambo" meets "Gone With the Wind": the epic story of a hard-driving confederate commando in love with a high-strung Southern belle.

long shot (LS)   A shot which gives the viewer the context of the setting by showing it from a greater distance and including at least the full figure of a subject. Long shots are also sometimes called wide shots or full shots.

looping   When an actor attempts to match dialogue to his or her performance while watching a short piece of film formed into a loop. Looping is usually required because of faulty dialogue recorded under noisy conditions.

low- or high-angle shot   A shot that is taken at an angle below (low) or above (high) eye level.

mag stock   Magnetic sound recording stock which has edge perforations that match those perforations on the picture stock, thereby allowing it to be pulled along with the picture at the same speed and relative position.

magazine   A container that fits into a motion picture camera that does not admit light and feeds and takes up the film.

manager   A person who manages the careers of actors, writers, or directors.

mark   The place on the floor of a set which the actor must move to or stay at during a scene in order to stay within the frame of the shot.

mask   A covering of some type placed in front of the camera lens to block off part of the photographed image. Also, the shield inserted behind a projector lens in order to obtain a desired aspect ratio. Also an optical like an iris that doesn't expand or narrow and may have the shape of a keyhole or other viewing device.

matching cut   (a.k.a. match cut) A cut in which the two shots cut together are linked logically and visually, often by action or movement within the shots.

mechanical rights   The right to include a musical composition in a film's soundtrack album or CD.

medium shot (MS)   A shot that provides approximately a knee to head view of a subject. Medium shots are further broken down into medium long shots or medium close-ups. Two shots or three shots are usually medium shots in which two or three subjects appear in the frame.

method acting   A style of acting that focuses on reaching the emotional truth of a character through using internal methods such as relaxation and sense memory exercises.

montage   A stylized form of editing short, expressive shots together to provide a lot of information in a short period of time.

most favored nations   In film deals, when everyone in a category accepts the same fee as the "most favored" person.

narration   In either a dramatic or non-fiction film, the telling of a story, either spoken by an on-camera narrator or by voice-over, to provide information not already evident in the story.

negative pick-up   A financial deal made with a film distributor, usually before the start of production, to distribute the film when it is completed.

non-linear editing   Editing a film or video out of sequence. The term is often used to refer to computer-based digital editing systems.

offer   A proposal for work on a film in exchange for money, credit, and a share of profits. At minimum, an offer includes the actor's fee and the start date of the production.

on-line editing   The process of editing the original videotapes into the final broadcast quality viewing tape, including adding opticals.

one-sheet   A poster-sized advertisement for a film that is graphically eye-catching and usually displayed outside of or on the inside walls of theaters.

optical   An operation done in the film laboratory that creates an effect, such as a fade or dissolve.

optical printer   A camera that re-photographs images to make optical effects.

optical sound master   The mixed soundtrack of a film that is printed on a piece of film and used for striking release prints of films.

option   The exclusive right, obtained for an option fee against a purchase price, to sell a script, book, or life story rights within a specified period of time.

original camera negative (OCN)   The negative film that originally passed through the camera.

overhead or aerial shot   A shot from above, usually made from a plane, helicopter, or crane.

pacing   The rhythm, tempo, or rate of movement of the shots in a film.

package   A presentation, including a script and the elements attached to the script, such as the producer, director, and cast for the leading roles.

pan   Any pivotal movement of a camera around an imaginary vertical axis running through the camera. The pan is the most common camera movement.

paper edit   A list of shots in their selected order, usually prepared prior to editing non-fiction films.

parallel action   (a.k.a. parallel cutting) A device of story construction in which the development of two pieces of action are presented simultaneously.

per diem   The amount of spending money given to a crew member for daily living expenses.

persistence of vision   The physiological reason for the illusion of motion in films: the fact that an image remains on the retina of the eye for a short period of time after it disappears from the field of vision.

phonograph   A machine invented by Thomas Edison that reproduces sound by means of a stylus in contact with a grooved rotating disk.

pick-up shot   A continuation shot of a scene that is picked up before a point where there is a problem.

platform release   To open a film in a few major cities and gradually expand the release to other markets if the movie is successful.

plot point   An event or turning point in a story that spins the action in another direction. In three-act structure, there should be a plot point at the end of act one and act two.

point-of-view (POV) shot   A shot which shows a scene from the point of view of a character.

pre-dub   Mixing several sound tracks together prior to the final mix.

premise   The theme, thesis, central idea, or motivating force of a film or play. A premise is also a thumbnail synopsis of the story.

private placement   The sale of securities or limited partnerships through private contacts to a limited number of investors.

production board   A board with moveable colored strips that show the schedule for every day of a shoot and list the actors, locations, and elements needed for each day. Traditionally put together manually, production boards can also be created and assembled through computer programs.

prop   In filmmaking or in a play, any physical object that is needed in a scene, such as chairs, books, and paintings.

protagonist   The main hero or heroine in a screenplay, play, or other literary work, whose actions drive the plot.

public domain   Material that was never copyrighted or for which the copyright has lapsed.

public offering   The sale of securities to the public, usually with the services of an underwriter, in a transaction that must be registered with the Securities and Exchange Commission.

public performance rights   The right to perform a musical composition in public.

rating   A number that rates how well a television show has done by estimating the number of viewers. Most television ratings are through the Nielsen Television Index.

reenactments   Scenes acted out by actors that re-create either factual or hypothetical situations in a non-fiction film.

Regulation A offering   A small public offering that allows a corporation or limited partnership to raise up to $5 million.

Regulation S-B and S-1 offerings   Types of complicated public offerings used for raising large amounts of money from the public.

resolution   The final pages of a story in which the complications of the plot are resolved and the character's growth or change is evident.

reverse action   Printing the last frame first to show the movement in a shot in reverse.

reverse-angle shot   A shot from the opposite side of a subject. Two-party dialogue scenes are often constructed using alternating reverse-angle shots.

ripple dissolve   A wavy blending of the adjacent images as if oil were pouring over the screen.

roll   The movement of a camera around an imaginary axis that runs between the lens and the subject.

room tone   The ambient sound on a location site, which is generally recorded during production and is used to replace any silences on dialogue or effects tracks.

rough cut   First assembly of a film that the editor prepares from selected takes, in script order, leaving the finer points of timing and editing to a later stage.

S corporation   A corporation that is taxed differently than a regular corporation. It is limited to 35 individual shareholders and is often used for the purpose of raising money for a single film, because the profits will not be reinvested in the business but will be distributed to the shareholders.

saturation   A major studio film distribution strategy that involves opening a movie in thousands of theaters nationwide on the same date.

scene   A series of shots in a movie constituting a unit of continuous related action in the story or narration.

set-up   The position of the camera, lights, sound equipment, actors, and so on for any given shot.

short-ends   Ends of a can of film that are too short to be used for the next scene to be shot.

shot   The basic unit of film; a continuously exposed, unedited piece of film of any length or a single cinematic view or take.

shot list   A director's list of every shot that will be needed in the film.

sides   In casting, the pages containing a scene or parts of scenes from a script that actors must read or act out in an audition.

signatory   A production company, studio, or network that has signed the negotiated Minimum Basic Agreement (MBA) of the Writers Guild (or of other entertainment guilds).

silks   White cloths used for modifying the amount and quality of light during filming, often used to "bounce" light in a particular direction.

slow motion   Action filmed at a speed faster than normal, which when projected at normal speed, appears slower on the screen than in reality; also an optical that slows down the action by printing every frame more than once. (Slow motion produced by an optical effect will appear jerkier than slow motion achieved by running the camera at a high frame rate.)

small corporate offering registration   A form of public offering designed to reduce the costs and paperwork involved in public offerings. This offering requires the completion of Form U-7, which sometimes can be done without the assistance of an attorney. The form can only be used, however, when the amount of money being raised does not exceed $1 million.

special effects   In filmmaking, a broad term for a range of shots and processes, including model shots, matte shots, rear projection, or other effects that are artificially created for the camera.

split-screen image   Two or more separate images within the frame, not overlapping.

spotting   The process of going through the final picture edit of a film and deciding where to place sound effects and music.

staging area   An area near a set where crew members can set up and store equipment and supplies.

stock footage   Archive material from film libraries, such as World War II shots or sequences, that are recycled from other films and are available for a fee.

streaming   In Internet jargon, a term for information flowing across a channel, such as a film viewable on a computer via the Internet.

stunt   In filmmaking, an action that appears different and more incredible than the actual action filmed.

superimposition   (a.k.a. multiple exposure) An image printed over another one or several images printed over each other.

sweetening   In videotape and digital editing, the process of building up tracks and mixing sound and all audio post-production sound work.

synchronization rights   (a.k.a. sync rights) The right to include a musical composition in a film.

syndication   Selling television shows or packages of shows to owned and operated local stations rather than distributing through a television network.

take   An individual piece of film with no cuts, or one shot of a scene. A shot may be filmed several times until a satisfactory take is achieved.

technical acting   A style of acting that uses external acting techniques to create the character.

telecine   A device that takes a film image and converts it into a video image.

tilt   Any movement of a camera up and down so that it rotates on an imaginary horizontal axis running through the camera.

timing   (a.k.a. grading) The process of correcting color values in various film shots and scenes shot at different times of the day, in different places or under different lighting conditions once the negative has been conformed.

tracking shots   *See* dolly shots.

trades   The film and television industry trade papers, *Daily Variety* and *The Hollywood Reporter*.

transitional shot   A shot such as a cutaway that bridges two scenes, shots, or camera angles within a scene.

treatment   An initial written narrative telling of a story, which a writer or production company wishes to develop into a script.

turnaround   In the film industry, when a script that was optioned by a studio or production company is no longer being developed by said company and is available for purchase by other companies.

turnaround or flip wipe   A flipping of the on-screen image to reveal the incoming image on its reverse side.

voice-over   The voice of the narrator or of another character when he or she is not seen on film. The device is used in both fiction and non-fiction films.

wild track   A sound recording of a line of dialogue or other sound made independently of the camera.

wild walls   Walls in a theater or on a sound stage that can be moved to create a set.

window   The period of time a theatrical distributor has to distribute a film before its television debut.

wipes   An optical process whereby one image appears to wipe the preceding image off the screen. This technique was a common transitional device in 1930s films but is used much less frequently now.

workprint   Also called a cutting print, is the positive print used in editing that is printed directly from the original camera negative.

Index

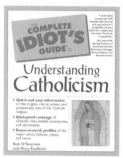

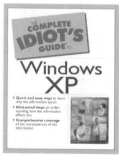